Designing Groupwork
Strategies for the Heterogeneous Classroom

Third Edition

A New Edition by

Elizabeth G. Cohen
& Rachel A. Lotan

Forewords by Linda Darling-Hammond and John I. Goodlad

TEACHERS COLLEGE PRESS
TEACHERS COLLEGE | COLUMBIA UNIVERSITY
NEW YORK AND LONDON

Published by Teachers College Press, 1234 Amsterdam Avenue, New York, NY 10027

Library of Congress Cataloging-in-Publication Data

Cohen, Elizabeth G., 1931–2005
    Designing groupwork : strategies for the heterogeneous classroom / Elizabeth G.
    Cohen & Rachel A. Lotan ; foreword by Linda Darling-Hammond.—Third edition.
      pages cm
    Includes bibliographical references and index.
    ISBN 978-0-8077-5566-2 (pbk. : alk. paper)
    ISBN 978-0-8077-7320-8 (ebook)
      1. Group work in education. 2. Interaction analysis in education. I. Title.
    LB1032.C56 2014
    371.3'95—dc23   2014009977

ISBN 978-0-8077-5566-2 (paper)
ISBN 978-0-8077-7320-8 (ebook)

Printed on acid-free paper
Manufactured in the United States of America

21   20   19   18   17   16   8   7   6   5   4   3

To the Stanford School of Education graduate students,
who taught me about schools

—Elizabeth G. Cohen

To the memory of Elizabeth G. Cohen,
who taught us about research in service of meaningful practice

—Rachel A. Lotan

Contents

Foreword to the Third Edition

There are few practices in education that are better grounded, more lasting, and more widely successful than complex instruction, the subject of this fascinating and useful volume. Initially conceived from the theoretical work of sociologist Elizabeth Cohen, and developed and refined with the pedagogical expertise offered by Rachel A. Lotan, Complex Instruction has transformed many thousands—perhaps millions—of classrooms in the United States and throughout the world. As a fortunate colleague of both Cohen and Lotan at Stanford University, I have had the privilege of experiencing this work up close and personal, as it plays out in the hundreds of diverse classrooms staffed by graduates of the Stanford Teacher Education Program (STEP) and alumni of the Complex Instruction program throughout the Bay Area.

When Rachel and I redesigned STEP in the late 1990s, we agreed that the heterogeneous classrooms course that she had taught as an elective would become part of the core curriculum of STEP, as it provides an essential body of knowledge and a set of valuable tools for all teachers. It has continued to be one of the most popular courses in the program, and its precepts are now infused in many of the other courses as well. The value of collaborative learning is well known, but so are the practical challenges. Every one of us has no doubt had bad experiences with groupwork, in which some members of the group are excluded or have difficulty focusing on the task, while one or two others end up taking responsibility for getting an assignment done, often resenting the others. Many a classroom debacle has resulted from a teacher assigning groupwork without knowing how to organize the task and the students' learning process so that it is productive for all.

In contrast, here is what you will see if you go into a Complex Instruction classroom: A productive buzz of conversation permeates the room. Students in heterogeneous groups are leaning into intense conversations with three or four of their peers about a meaty problem that they are jointly trying to solve—one that requires the attention and efforts of all of them (i.e., a groupworthy task). Some of them are explaining their ideas, others are writing down their thoughts or procedures, while still others are working with physical materials to further their task. These will have been secured by a materials manager, while a timekeeper helps everyone keep track of the progress they are making within the time allotted for the task, after which the group will share what they have found and learned. Students have learned processes and norms for how to work together, so the groups are able to function independently without continually asking the teacher to come over and resolve questions or problems. They know they should ask one another first—as their own best resources—before they seek outside assistance. Most of the time students problem-solve successfully to advance their work. The teacher observes the work carefully, intervening only to ask a helpful question, to provide feedback on the group process, or to provide a "status treatment" that raises the group's (or class's) attention to a useful contribution from an under-used or under-appreciated member of the group, so that reinforcement for the value of each member heightens inclusion and participation.

You are also likely to see student work produced by these groups, and by students individually, all around the room, offering evidence of what counts in this classroom where student learning is at the center. And if you were to watch this classroom over the course of a semester or a school year, you would see increased achievement for all of the students, and a narrowing achievement gap as students grow increasingly proficient together in a respectful and equitable setting for learning.

More than an effective process for engaging students with one another, Complex Instruction works to produce large gains in learning—and to reduce the inequity we have grown too used to accepting in American education. This new, third edition of *Designing Groupwork*—Rachel A. Lotan's tribute to her long-time colleague Liz Cohen, who passed away in 2005—includes much of what has been learned by educators, teachers, and scholars over the past 20 years since the second edition of this book. This includes both classroom strategies that have been developed to refine the pedagogical approach, as well as research that has documented successes of the approach in a wide range of settings, including those serving large numbers of English learners.

This version of the book expands previous chapters and adds new ones based on these learnings. It offers more insights about how to create groupworthy tasks that set the stage for deep learning and equitable participation, and it expands understanding of how to use

Complex Instruction to develop students' understanding of "academic language"—that is, the language of the discipline and of the classroom—not only for students who are new English language learners, but for all students who are perennial learners of academic discourse.

As someone who has worked for many years with experienced teachers as well as teacher candidates, Rachel A. Lotan has gained enormous experience in making these ideas relevant and practical. This new version includes teachers' voices about their use of Complex Instruction, drawn from the many teachers with whom Rachel has worked. These voices add to the authenticity and practicality of the book, while unpacking the complexity of this pedagogy in vivid and useful ways for practitioners.

The goal of building equitable classrooms and schools is particularly important today, as schools are introducing new curricular frameworks, standards, curriculum, and assessments that require more ambitious and complex pedagogy. I have no doubt that this important book will be of enormous practical value, while it offers solid theoretical insights and well-documented empirical evidence as well. There is nothing as practical as a good theory, experts often say. Complex Instruction is surely one terrific theory, and *Designing Groupwork* is certainly one terrific book.

—*Linda Darling-Hammond, Stanford University, April 19, 2014*

Foreword to the Second Edition

Goals for schools—whether at local, state, or national levels—suggest to the reader an active learning process in classrooms. One conjures up visions of students exchanging viewpoints on issues, checking the validity of diverse views through reading, sharing their findings, and preparing individual and group reports. Research shows that teachers generally perceive as desirable such practices as student involvement in setting goals, student interaction in small groups, and student involvement in ongoing classroom dialogue.

Alas, research reveals teaching practices and learning opportunities that fall far short of these expectations and ideals. Teachers lecture, explain to, and question the total class and monitor seatwork most of the time, especially in secondary schools. It has been found, for example, that teachers far outtalk *all* of their students together during 150 minutes of daily talk recorded in hundreds of classrooms. During these 150 minutes, students initiated talk through unsolicited comments or questions very rarely, such initiations consuming some 7 or 8 minutes on the whole.

Teachers rarely question the validity of such findings. Usually, they recognize themselves in the data and become uncomfortable; some become defensive. But most teachers quickly move beyond defensiveness into questions of how to proceed differently. They know there are other ways. Indeed, many have engaged in an internal struggle brought about by the shortfall between their own perceptions of what good teaching is and daily circumstances that seem to frustrate methods other than those they most often observed when they were students. And some wince over the memories of brief forays into alternatives: total class discussions dominated by a few aggressive students, small group sessions that got out of hand, and so-called cooperative learning endeavors that exacerbated incipient racism. They have no desire to repeat those disasters.

For a long time, I have been looking for something useful to put in the heads and hands of teachers who recognize the need to go beyond the conventional ways of teaching described above and especially those whose brief experiments with alternatives has been less than satisfying. Principles alone will not suffice. Prescriptions, devoid of understanding, undoubtedly will lead to more disasters.

Elizabeth Cohen's book, *Designing Groupwork: Strategies for the Heterogeneous Classroom,* comes closer to what I have been seeking than any sources known to me. First, it is an almost ideal blend of theory and practice, with principle bridging the two and specific examples clarifying the application of these principles. Second, in addition to providing ample research support for the general concepts of groupwork introduced early on, specific research studies are then used to document the usefulness of practices derived from these concepts. Third, the illustrations range widely over ages and grades, subjects, special problems likely to be encountered, and processes to be used. Fourth, there is surprising sensitivity to the step-by-step training needs of teachers venturing into using groupwork as a way to maximize students' learning. My surprise stems not from Cohen's background (her research interests often have been guided by precisely this sensitivity), but from firsthand experiences with the difficulty of being this practical while remaining true to basic principles. One is reminded once again of the practicality of good theory.

Overall, what Elizabeth Cohen succeeds in doing is to provide a technology in the very best sense of rigorously linking a practical human endeavor with knowledge bearing on that endeavor in a pedagogical domain that has tended to defy such rigor. Although Cohen illustrates many different uses for this technology, she makes clear at the outset that groupwork is only one way to provide students with meaningful encounters with knowledge. She views groupwork as particularly relevant to the higher-order cognitive processes and to goals stressing democratic values. One is brought back to the writings of John Dewey and the enormous impact of his works on the thinking of educators. But efforts to translate this thinking into a technology have suffered either in not going beyond principles or in rigidity and prescription. As I stated earlier, Cohen manages to provide technology without falling victim to either of these two shortcomings—a rare and valuable contribution, indeed.

There is no point in my summarizing what the author has to say about each of the many themes and topics in her book. This is best left for the reader to peruse and reflect upon. For the reader interested in knowing why group approaches to student learning are useful, what is encompassed by the term "groupwork," and how to proceed with a class, not much is missing. The book has something for a wide range of readers, but clearly is intended for and will be most useful to teachers.

One theme of schooling is emerging with such importance, however, that I am impelled to say something about Cohen's treatment of it. Even though most schools are structured for purposes of reducing the heterogeneity of the student populations with which teachers must deal through tracking and the separation of "special" students into segregated groups, the problems experienced by teachers in dealing with individual differences appear to be increasing. Part of the difficulty arises out of the fact that organizational arrangements seeking group homogeneity are crude mechanisms that create more problems than they solve. The inequities produced are such that corrective actions soon will be taken through the courts if schools and communities fail to redress them. The difficulties also grow out of the changing pupil populations in which it appears that increasing numbers of students are at the margins and at risk. We are running out of organizational and special grouping types of solutions.

Cohen effectively argues the case for groupwork in heterogeneous classes and provides useful examples of how students are drawn naturally into learning from one another, regardless of their differing levels of attainment. Indeed, these differences become assets rather than liabilities. The principles underlying groupwork presented in the early chapters come into play most effectively as she points clear directions through issues complicated by special interests and often charged with emotion and bias. Teachers who have become increasingly uncomfortable with tracking, for example, will be both encouraged and helped in learning to proceed with an appealing, defensible alternative.

Prior to receiving the manuscript of *Designing Groupwork,* I had resolved to write no more forewords or introductions to books (except for those of former students). But I knew that Elizabeth Cohen's book would reflect a lifetime of serious study and reflection on schools and classrooms, and so I accepted her invitation (albeit rather reluctantly) to read the manuscript and write the Foreword. It was a good decision because the time spent was negligible when compared with what I learned.

—*John I. Goodlad, May, 1986*

Acknowledgments

ACKNOWLEDGMENTS FOR THE THIRD EDITION

My appreciation and gratitude go to the many teachers who shared with me their knowledge and expertise, their tenacity, and their commitment to make the world a better place for all youngsters. Among them, graduates of the Stanford Teacher Education Program have had a special place in my heart as I learned with and from them.

I am grateful to my colleagues and to the many affiliates of the Program for Complex Instruction. Thank you for your friendship and for your trust in me. Together, we are in it for the long haul. Special thanks to Dr. Nicole Holthuis, whose support, feedback, and good spirits kept me organized and on track.

FROM ACKNOWLEDGMENTS FOR THE SECOND EDITION

The early work on this book was supported by the National Institute of Education, Grant No. OB-NIE-G-78-0212 (P-4).

I am grateful for the careful reading and constructive criticism of Annike Bredo, Susan Rosenholtz, Theresa Perez, Rachel A. Lotan, Joan Benton, and my sister and favorite editor, Miriam Finkelstein.

Professor Amado Padilla provided invaluable advice on the revision of the chapter on the bilingual classroom. I would also like to acknowledge the assistance and influence of Cecilia Navarrete, who brought to me so much understanding of the exigencies of classroom life as well as insights concerning the education of the language-minority student.

Finally, I am grateful to the many classroom teachers who have worked with me in using these techniques, helping a sociologist develop useful knowledge for the practitioner.

Preface to the Third Edition

It has been with mixed emotions that I undertook the third edition of this book. I wish Elizabeth Cohen and I could have done it together. Elizabeth's distinctive and courageous voice as she advised, supported, and admonished teachers was deeply respected and cherished. Her scholarly and activist legacy lives on in those of us who work unrelentingly to make classrooms equitable places for all students.

At present, many teachers in the United States are working in challenging contexts. While we seem to be moving beyond and away from scripted curricula, constrained instruction, and narrow tests, responses to the pedagogical and curricular challenges from the professional ranks and from policymakers range from highly supportive to decidedly suspicious.

We are setting ambitious goals for ourselves. We are beginning to realize the promise of the newly introduced curricular frameworks and standards. We are crafting assessments that capture students' varied domains of knowledge and skills, and reflect more authentically what they have accomplished. We are planning, implementing, and analyzing pedagogical practices that support and enhance student learning. We are asking students to perform at a high intellectual and academic level and to read, write, and speak adeptly in the various content areas.

To accomplish some of these goals, groupwork remains an effective pedagogical approach. Since the publication of the second edition of this book, we have expanded and refined our knowledge about how to structure groupwork to produce the anticipated results. In this, the third edition, I included related research and findings published since 1994 from doctoral dissertations, journal articles, books, and book chapters based on work at the Program for Complex Instruction and the School of Education at Stanford University, as well as that of many scholars at other institutions. Scholarship about various models of groupwork, implemented from early elementary grades to graduate seminars, has proliferated. Many high-quality studies of small- and large-scale interventions based on instructional strategies in which cooperative learning is a main component have been published. We continue to explore the social-psychological processes involved in small-group interactions, as well as the societal impact of our increasingly diverse student population. I made connections to many of these new developments throughout the book.

And yet, the perennial dilemma of groupwork persists. How do we make sure that we build an environment where students benefit from equal-status interactions with peers and have equal access to the learning tasks, to material resources, and to the teacher? How do we provide opportunities for students to demonstrate what they have learned, and how do we recognize and value their intellectual growth and contributions? This book provides practical responses, based on well-established theoretical frameworks and solid empirical evidence.

For almost three decades, I worked to support teachers who want to use groupwork more consistently in different school subjects, at different grade levels, and in classrooms with significant proportions of students who are learners of the language of instruction. Together we crafted learning tasks that provided opportunities for students to engage in intense interactions as they talked and worked together, to collaborate in producing group products, and to hone their academic and social skills. Using backwards design, we specified the assessment criteria for group and individual products and thus deepened the process of assessment for learning. In describing the features of groupworthy tasks and providing examples in Chapter 6, I lay out a roadmap, best realized when colleagues collaborate. Developing groupworthy tasks is a groupworthy task in itself.

Working together in small groups provides an optimal setting for language development. Depending on the requirements of the task, students use different varieties, modes, and genres of communication, from single words to elaborate sentences. They express their ideas, their feelings, their wonderings, their triumphs, their hesitations. Through talking and working together, they develop their proficiency in the discourse of the various disciplines, as well as their comfort level with the language demands of academic settings. In Chapter 7, new to this edition, I describe in more detail the opportunities afforded by groupwork for such language development. All students, not only students who have been formally designated as English language learners, benefit from using language actively and persistently.

In the third edition, I emphasize the benefits of formative assessment, including specific feedback on the process in which students engage during groupwork. I reiterate the importance of summative assessments of individual student's work that is the product of groupwork. Assessment is seen as a lever for designing the learning tasks and for deepening learning. Furthermore, planning for systematic evaluation of the implementation of groupwork in the classroom is proposed as a valuable tool for recognizing the academic and social benefits of groupwork, for reflecting on its outcomes, and for deepening the quality of instruction and therefore students' learning.

The primary intent of this book has remained unchanged. The basic principles for designing equitable, intellectually rigorous groupwork for heterogeneous classrooms have proven themselves to be practical and generative for many teachers who yearn to provide quality instruction for their students. The current edition includes the lessons learned and descriptions of experiences of teachers and students from the previous editions, as well as new ones collected over the years through my work with experienced and beginning teachers in the United States and in other countries. I hope this book will be of use to teachers who delight in seeing their students talking and working together productively and equitably.

—*Rachel A. Lotan*

Groupwork as a Pedagogical Strategy

"Children learn by talking and working together? I wish someone had shown me how to actually accomplish that in my classroom," said a 3rd-grade teacher who tried to engage children at learning stations with limited success. Have you noticed that you learn more about concepts and ideas when you talk about them, explain them, and argue about them with others than when you listen to a lecture or read a textbook? Although many of us as adults realize that this is so, often not enough class time is spent allowing students to talk and work together. This is a book for teachers who want to know how to make this principle of learning work for students of all ages. If a teacher wants to produce active learning, then groupwork, properly designed, is a powerful tool for providing simultaneous opportunities for all class members.

Small groups are not a panacea for all instructional problems. They are only one tool, useful for specific kinds of teaching goals and especially relevant for classrooms where students have a wide mix of previous academic achievement and proficiency in the language of instruction. The choice of groupwork as a strategy depends on what the teacher is trying to achieve. Most teachers will want to use groups in combination with a variety of other classroom formats for different tasks.

WHAT IS GROUPWORK?

This book defines *groupwork* as students working together in a group small enough so that everyone can participate on a clearly assigned learning task. Moreover, students are expected to carry out their task without direct and immediate supervision of the teacher. Groupwork is not the same as ability grouping, in which the teachers divide up the class by academic criteria so that they can instruct a more homogeneous group. It should also be distinguished from small groups that teachers compose for intensive instruction, such as the flexible and temporary grouping procedures often used in individualized reading instruction or differentiated instruction.

When the teacher gives students a group task and allows them to struggle on their own and make mistakes, she has delegated authority. This is the first key feature of groupwork. Delegating authority in an instructional task is making students responsible for specific parts of their work; students are free to accomplish their task in the way they decide is best, but are still accountable to the teacher for the final product. Delegating authority does not mean that the learning process is uncontrolled; the teacher maintains control through evaluation of the final group product and of the process by which the students arrived at the final product. The teacher also holds group members accountable through a short written report completed individually after the work in groups.

In contrast to delegation of authority is the more common practice of direct supervision. The teacher exercising direct supervision tells students what their task is and how to do it. She monitors the students closely to prevent them from making mistakes and to correct any errors right away.

The question of who is in charge of the group is critical; if a teacher is in charge, regardless of the age and maturity of the students, he will do more talking than the students. The teacher's evaluation of each member's performance will have far more weight than that of any group member. If the teacher plays the role of a direct supervisor of group activity, members will talk, not to one another, but to the teacher as the authority figure who is overseeing performance. Group members will want to know what the teacher expects them to say and will be mostly interested in finding out what she thinks of their performance. Even if the teacher assigns a task to the group but hovers nearby waiting to intervene at the first misstep or sign of confusion, she is not delegating authority; she is using direct supervision.

A second key feature of groupwork is that members need one another to some degree to complete the task; they cannot do it all by themselves. Students take over some of the teaching function by suggesting what other people should do, by listening to what other people are saying, and by deciding how to get the job done within the time and resource limitations set by the instructor.

Students in a group communicate about their task with one another. They ask questions, explain, make suggestions, criticize, listen, agree, disagree, and make joint decisions. Interaction may also be nonverbal, such as pointing, showing how, nodding, frowning, or smiling.

This process of group interaction can be enormously interesting to students. Some students who usually do anything but what they are asked to do become actively involved with their work and are held there by the action of the group. There are several reasons why this is so. Face-to-face interaction with other group members demands a response or, at least, attentive behavior. In addition, students care about evaluations by classmates; often, they do not want to let the group down by refusing to participate. Last, peers provide assistance so a student does not become hopelessly confused about what he is supposed to do. Students who are disengaged from their work in the classroom are often students who do not understand the assignments.

A third key feature of groupwork is the nature of the task. If the teacher wants students to communicate in the ways just described, they need something to communicate about. If the teacher wants students to engage in substantive, high-quality talk, the task needs to pose complex problems or dilemmas, have different potential solutions, and rely on students' creativity and insights.

Although groupwork has potential for supporting learning, talking and working together with peers is the source of a whole series of problems. Neither children nor adults necessarily know how to work successfully in a group setting, so learning *how* to work in groups becomes necessary. These problems can be overcome with proper preparation of the task and of the students. This volume presents some of the problems and suggests solutions.

THE POWER OF PRINCIPLES

Contrary to what many practitioners believe, there is nothing as practical as a good theory. Sociologists and social psychologists have generated useful theories and relevant research on small groups in laboratory and classroom settings. From these theories and research have come some general principles applicable to the instructor's situation. Using these principles, you can analyze your class and your goals in order to design a suitable small-group format. These same general principles suggest ways to evaluate the success of the approach so that you can decide whether it works for your class, and in what way it can be improved for next time.

The advantage of providing general principles is that they can be used in any classroom from elementary to college level. The particulars can be adapted or engineered for differences in age of the students and in the nature of the setting. The general principles continue to guide the design, even while the context varies. For example, the simplicity of the instructions will vary with the age of the students, as will the analysis of what skills group members already have in comparison to what they will need for the group task. Classroom management issues are different for younger groups than for older ones. Such differences may mean that the teacher will need to spend more or less time preparing students, or that the groups will move differently in completing their task. However, principles such as delegating authority to support students teaching one another remain the same.

USE OF RESEARCH

Most relevant for this book is the research that has applied useful theories to classrooms. In some cases, the theory and research are sufficiently strong to say with some confidence that there are specific desirable effects of groupwork on student behavior. As a professor of education who was also a research sociologist, Elizabeth Cohen directed classroom research for many years. Her research centered on team teaching, treatment of interracial status problems in the classroom, and managing groupwork in academically and linguistically heterogeneous classrooms. Many of the techniques for groupwork come from these research situations, where they have proven to be highly effective. The two kinds of elementary school settings where much of this groupwork research took place were the desegregated classroom and the bilingual classroom.

With Rachel A. Lotan's experience teaching at the secondary level, the Program for Complex Instruction at Stanford University expanded the work to apply the same theories that have proven so useful at the elementary level to middle school and high school. The experience of secondary school teachers who used the results of the elementary school research suggests that the basic principles are indeed applicable to older students (Cohen & Lotan, 1997a). These teachers reported the same level of success as those who have used the research results presented in the first edition of this book.

During their years of classroom research, Cohen and Lotan worked closely with teachers who have left the classroom for graduate work. Many of the doctoral dissertations of these teachers are the sources of evidence in this book. It is these graduate students who made the research relevant and practical for the classroom instructor. Going from the laboratory to the infinitely more complex and challenging world of the classroom, we have worked together to help teachers use pedagogical practices that support the learning of all students in their classrooms.

As a teacher of beginning secondary school teachers, Cohen used the first and second editions of this book to help them design groupwork for their own classrooms. Some of the examples in the text are taken from their projects. As a teacher of beginning and veteran teachers and as director of the Stanford Teacher Education Program, Lotan has used this book to introduce beginning and experienced teachers nationally and internationally to the academic and social benefits of well-executed groupwork. Some examples in the text are taken from their projects implemented and evaluated in secondary classrooms.

HOW TRUE ARE THE PRINCIPLES?

Experienced practitioners obviously want to know how true our assertions are for their own classrooms. Will these ideas work in all settings? What are the dangers of things going wrong? Are the risks worth the gains and the extra work?

Let us be perfectly frank: We do not know for sure whether the principles hold under all conditions. But we do know of a variety of classroom conditions where the data support the propositions we have set out. What the practitioner will do is think about what is likely to happen when these principles are applied. No set of recipes in a book will relieve the instructor of this responsibility. If it appears that nothing untoward is likely to happen, then it may well be worth the risk and the extra effort to try to accomplish certain teaching goals that cannot be reached in any other way.

2 Why Groupwork?

Groupwork is an effective technique for achieving certain kinds of intellectual and social learning goals. It is a superior technique for conceptual learning, for creative problem solving, and for developing academic language proficiency. Socially, it will improve intergroup relations by increasing trust and friendliness. It will teach skills for working in groups that can be transferred to many student and adult work situations. Groupwork is also a strategy for addressing common classroom management problems such as keeping students involved with their work. Most important, groupwork provides greater access to the learning tasks to more students in classrooms with a wide range of academic skills and linguistic proficiency. Productive groupwork increases and deepens opportunities to learn content and develop language and thus has the potential to build equitable classrooms.

INTELLECTUAL GOALS

Groupwork can help students grow academically, as in this example of Geraldo learning about magnification:

Geraldo watches the other children as they complete their task of making a water drop lens. "What do you see?" Geraldo asks another child, as he tries to peer into the finished lens. The other child looks up and lets Geraldo look more carefully at it. Geraldo very eagerly goes back to his own lens-making task. He appears to be having trouble taping a piece of clear plastic on a white index card with a hole in the middle; he keeps getting the plastic bunched up on the tape instead of getting the tape to hold the plastic on top of the card. "Oh shoot!" Geraldo says and gets up to see what another child is doing in constructing her lens. He returns to his task only to be distracted by the child next to him. "Oooh, it gets bigger!" she exclaims. Geraldo gets up and looks at her water drop lens. He raises his eyebrows and very quickly goes back and finishes his lens. Geraldo appears to have understood what the problem was in completing the lens because he rapidly tapes it together without any further trouble. He now reaches over and takes the eye dropper from a glass filled with water. He very carefully fills it with water, centers it over his lens card and squirts one drop over the plastic where the hole is cut. Apparently satisfied with what he did, he puts the excess water in the eye dropper back in the jar. He gets a piece of cloth to examine under his lens. The water slides around the plastic covering the paper and he cries out, "Oh, no!" He puts his lens down, straightens out the cloth and then carefully slides the lens on top of the cloth. He very slowly looks into his lens and shouts out, "Oooh-bad-oooh!" "What did you see?" asks one of the girls. "Look how big mine got," says Geraldo. "What are you going to write?" she asks. Geraldo looks into the lens again and says, "It gets bigger." He then takes other flat objects and places his water drop lens on top of each one. As he looks at each object with his lens, he nods his head and says, "Yep!" Talking to himself he says, "They all get bigger." He looks at the girl he has been talking with and finally asks her "Did yours get bigger too?" (Navarrete, 1980, pp. 13–14)

Geraldo has "discovered" the principle of magnification. The process has not been an easy one, and he would probably not have been successful without the assistance of a classmate working on the same task. Just being able to watch others at work gave him some important information. And being able to talk things over seemed to help even further. Notice that Geraldo understands the idea in such a way that he can apply it to a new setting—when he is able to understand a concept in a new setting, we know that he has a true grasp of the abstract idea.

How else could Geraldo have learned about magnification? Could he have understood it through a teacher's explanation? By reading about it? By completing some paper-and-pencil exercises on the subject? In order for him to understand much at all, the materials and talk would have to be in English and Spanish, but Geraldo struggles with reading in both languages. It is unlikely that he would grasp the idea in such a way that he could transfer it to new settings. In the setting where this interaction was recorded, Geraldo had access to instructions in English, Spanish, and pictographs; he also had access to Spanish-speaking as well as

English-speaking classmates, and to teachers who spoke both languages. A major advantage of combining a manipulative task with a group setting is that Geraldo has a number of helpful resources, including concrete materials to represent abstract ideas and other people engaged in the same task. He can watch them; he can ask them questions; he can discuss and argue with them; he can try to explain things; and he can demonstrate ideas nonverbally with the materials. Most important, Geraldo is allowed to struggle on his own, to make his own mistakes. No adult rushes in to tell him what to do and to give him a verbal explanation—such assistance might well have short-circuited his discovery.

Conceptual Learning

Often, after an instructor has introduced new concepts and has illustrated how they apply, students engage in some active practice using these new ideas and applying them in various ways. This is as true for students in graduate seminars as it was for Geraldo, a 4th-grader. Traditional methods of accomplishing these goals include writing essays, completing individual assignments during class time (seatwork), practicing on computers, or listening to a lecture in large-group instruction. Sometimes during question-and-answer activities, teachers ask questions and one student at a time tries to answer while the rest of the class listens.

There are obvious limitations to these techniques. Clearly, when recitation is used, only one student at a time gets the active practice. There is no evidence that listening to other people assimilate new concepts is the same experience as doing it for oneself. Nor can language be acquired and developed when there are few or no opportunities to use it. Exercises and essays are the time-honored methods of many teachers everywhere. Yet low achievers and less-motivated and less-engaged students are often reluctant to do these prescribed exercises and may complete them partially, if at all. If the teacher assigns the work during class, these students are very likely to be disengaged from their task (Berliner et al., 1978). If the teacher assigns homework, many students will be unwilling or unable to do it, especially in schools with a poor climate for learning or lower-level tracks.

Even among the more highly motivated high school students, essay assignments or written reports have their limitations. Understanding and assimilating new concepts and writing about them demand cognitive processes, writing skills, and well-developed language proficiency. Problems with writing are compounded with problems of thinking. Take, for example, the high school biology student who writes: "In the case of chlorophyll, photosynthesis will take place." Does the student understand that photosynthesis cannot take place without chlorophyll? The teacher can only guess about the student's understanding of the process. Furthermore, until the student gets back the corrected essay or exercise, there is no chance to discover confusion and error. As every busy instructor knows, the lag between students turning in a paper and receiving it back with adequate comments may be embarrassingly long. Although new technologies are providing teachers with novel ways of assessing student learning, the accomplishments and learning challenges of individual students are still not readily available. For example, when clickers are used to get a snapshot of how many students choose the correct response to a prompt or respond appropriately to a true/false statement, such responses are still not enough for gauging individual understanding of complex problems or applications of theoretical concepts.

Groupwork can be more effective than these traditional methods (as well as other newer ones) for gaining a proper understanding of abstract concepts. This is not to say that groupwork under all conditions will be more effective. Two basic conditions to be met for groupwork to facilitate conceptual learning are:

- The learning task requires conceptual thinking rather than mere application of an algorithm or memorizing factual information.
- The group has the necessary resources to complete the assignment successfully. These include appropriate cognitive and linguistic skills, relevant information, and properly prepared instructions to the task.

Too many classroom tasks simply require students to memorize information or rules. After memorizing the rule, they must learn to recognize a problem as a place to apply the rule. Examples of such routine tasks in the early elementary years are memorizing number facts or learning to apply a spelling convention, such as dropping the final *e* before adding *–ing* to a word. In contrast, tasks like reading and interpreting complex texts or understanding the principles underlying calculations with fractions call for more conceptual thinking. Many tasks at the secondary level require memorization or rule application as well. Students memorize a lot of vocabulary words, definitions, and science facts, or learn to solve a set of math problems that all have the same format by using an algorithm. In contrast, designing an experiment, drawing evidence from literary or informational texts to support an argument, analysis and reflection, and writing a research paper are conceptual tasks.

There is no particular advantage in giving groups a set of routine computational examples to complete. They will respond by doing the most sensible and expedient thing—copying the answers of the student who is perceived as best and probably fastest at computation. The same thing might happen if the teacher gives the group a quiz on facts of science or history. Contrast these examples with assigning a group the task of solving a challenging math problem, discovering how a flashlight works, contextualizing a historical document, understanding the phototropic behavior of plants, deciding how to resolve an ethical dilemma, planning on how to reduce carbon emissions, or learning how to represent data collected through precise observations. These are all examples of conceptual tasks that can be highly effective in a group setting.

In tasks that are conceptual, students interact in ways that assist them in understanding, applying, and communicating ideas. Researchers have been able to show that group interaction has a favorable effect on communicating mathematical understandings (Cossey, 1997), constructing scientific understandings (Bianchini, 1997), and engaging in scientific principles (Holthuis, 1998). In bilingual classrooms where children were talking and working together on tasks using math and science concepts that demanded thinking skills, the more students were talking and working together, the higher were the average classroom gains on tests with word problems (Cohen, Lotan, & Leechor, 1989).

How does talking and working together assist conceptual learning? To answer this question, researchers listen to what students are saying to one another in the groups, code the interactions, and relate the types of interaction to gains in measured achievement. For example, Webb (1991) reviewed 17 studies of junior and senior high school groups where students were assigned math problems and told to work together. One of the most consistent findings was that the student who took the time to explain, step-by-step, how to solve a problem, was the student who gained the most from the small-group experience. Putting concepts into words in the context of explaining to a peer is particularly helpful for concept attainment (Durling & Shick, 1976).

The student who does not initially understand the concept also stands to gain from the peer process. Learning with and from a more knowledgeable other is crucial for cognitive growth: "learning awakens a variety of internal developmental processes that are able to operate only when a child is interacting with people in his environment and in cooperation with his peers" (Vygotzky, 1978, p. 90). Even kindergarten children have been shown to learn very abstract concepts when placed in a group with peers who already understand the idea (Murray, 1972). Tudge (1990) found that students who tested at a lower level of cognitive development on a pretest with a very challenging mathematical balance beam task were able to make significant gains on a posttest after working with another student who exhibited higher levels of cognitive development. Groups can help the formerly low-achieving student in still a different way. Although the student may be perfectly capable of discussing and coming to understand the conceptual goals of the task, he may not be able to read and understand the instructions. When groups worked with activity cards on learning tasks that included inquiry, those students who were reading below grade level particularly benefitted from group interaction and showed significant gains in understanding of mathematical concepts (Leechor, 1988).

Interaction, talking and working together, provides students with opportunities to participate and act as members of a learning community. This point has been made persuasively by science educators and researchers in science education. They argue that when students interact, they become members of a scientific community for whom the process is less about the acquisition of specific facts and procedures, but rather about acquiring a culturally produced way of thinking, knowing, and valuing (Rosebery, 1992). Students working in small groups on tasks that allow for inquiry, data collection, and argumentation get a chance to learn how to "talk science."

In an experimental design study, Schultz (1999) randomly assigned students to groups and individual conditions and compared what students learned from the activities in an environmental science unit. She administered three kinds of assessments: a multiple-choice test, a concept-mapping exercise, and a performance assessment in which students designed and conducted an experiment. All assessments were done independently by students in both conditions. Schultz found better performance on all three measures by students working in groups versus students working independently. Furthermore, in the group condition, the previously lowest-scoring third of students made the greatest gains and reading ability was not predictive of performance tasks.

When the groupwork assignment demands thinking and discussion and when there is no clear right answer, everyone in the group benefits from that interaction. People of any age deal with the uncertainty of a challenging task better if they consult fellow workers or students than if they try to work by themselves. This is why the frequency of interaction on the task consistently predicts individual and group learning when groups are working on inquiry tasks (Cohen, 1991). Scarloss (2001) found that interaction in small groups contributes to students' sensemaking in social studies. Disagreement and intellectual conflict can also be a source of conceptual learning for groups. As a result of extended arguments in small groups, 6th-graders showed much better results on an achievement test and a deeper understanding of opposing perspectives than groups of students who were instructed not to argue, but to come to agreement on a controversial topic (Smith, Johnson, & Johnson, 1981). The students who engaged in conceptual conflict in this study, however, were carefully instructed as to how to conduct a productive argument. In addition, students prepared pro and con arguments from their materials and then switched sides to argue the opposite point of view before coming to a synthesis. Johnson and Johnson (1992), who have worked extensively with cooperative learning groups in classrooms, see conceptual conflict resulting from controversy in the group as forcing individuals to consider new information and to gain cognitive understanding in a way that will transfer to new settings. Exposure to different points of view in interaction helps children to examine their environment more objectively and to use perspectives other than their own. Johnson and Johnson (2009a) reviewed the theory underlying constructive controversy as an important instructional tool and summarized the positive outcomes it can have on student learning and well-being.

In review, if a teacher's goal is conceptual learning, properly structured groupwork can be particularly useful when the task is thoughtfully and deliberately crafted, and the students have access to the necessary linguistic and academic resources to achieve a required level of intellectual discourse. There is no point to a discussion that reflects collective ignorance and leads to confusion and frustration for both the students and the teacher. Furthermore, teachers need to ensure that students listen attentively and explain carefully to one another, ask questions, and provide some constructive (and, when necessary, corrective) feedback. Students also need to participate in the group conversations equally and have equitable access to the materials needed to work on the task. In her analysis of well-functioning groups, Barron (2003) found that "groups that did well engaged the ideas of participants, had low rates of ignoring or rejecting, paid attention and echoed the ideas of one another" (p. 349).

All of this is unlikely to take place by magic; the teacher has to lay the groundwork through meticulous planning, as discussed in subsequent chapters.

Creative Problem Solving

Ed and Carl (8 and 7 years old, respectively) are trying to figure out how a balance scale works:

> *Ed:* Now [let's start.]
> *Carl:* Why don't you put 4 on this side and I can put 4 on this side? [points to Ed's first peg.]
> *Ed:* I'll put 5 on that side.
> *Carl:* No.
> *Ed:* Ok, but it all should balance; we all know it, cause, see. . . . Now take them [take the blocks out]. See, balance. Now, put them back on. [He is referring to putting blocks back on the scale.] Now you leave it. [He wants Carl to leave his weights alone while he changes his.]
> *Carl:* I'll put one.
> *Ed:* Uh-huh. Hey. [It didn't balance.] I have five—1, 2, 3, 4, 5.
> *Carl:* 1, 2, 3, 4, 5. [Both count their weights on the pegs at the same time.] And let's put the rest [of the weights] on the end [the last peg].
> [Ed nonverbally complies.]
> *Ed:* I got it. [He removes block to see if it balances; and he is predicting it will balance.]
> *Carl:* Hey [it balances]. (Marquis & Cooper, 1982, Table 2)

This is a creative problem-solving task. At the beginning, neither child has the information or the basic principles required by the task. Through experimentation they gather information and stimulate each other to think about solutions to the problem. The insights and suggestions of both members are part of the success of the pair. In other words, the group is somehow greater than the sum of its parts.

When working on a problem that does not have a clear answer or a standard way to come to a solution, a group can be "smarter" than any single individual member. When members contribute ideas that stimulate the thinking of other members, the group is able to create new understandings and new representations of the problem, leading to excellent solutions and learning on the part of all members (Schwartz, Black, & Strange, 1991).

One of the serious criticisms of traditional curricula is the failure to provide experiences with creative problem solving—experiences such as Ed and Carl had. The tasks faced by adults in work and social settings clearly require creative problem solving, yet too few adults have many of the necessary skills in this area. At present, there is a growing understanding that creative problem solving, multidisciplinary engineering, and design thinking are often better done by groups than by individuals working alone. For many years business consultants and educators have used the demonstrations developed by Jay Hall (1971) to teach the simple lesson that groups are superior to individuals in creative problem solving. Hall uses tasks involving problems of survival for a hypothetical group. One activity, for example, is called Lost on the Moon. The group must pull together the creative insights and knowledge of individual members to rank objects in the order of their importance for the group's survival. In these demonstrations it usually turns out that the group score on the task is superior to that of any individual in the group.

Students have much to gain from participating in creative group problem solving. They learn from one another, they are stimulated to carry out higher-order thinking, and they experience an authentic intellectual pride of craft when the product is more than what any single member could create.

Developing Skills and Practices in the Subject Areas

Closely connected with the understanding of abstract concepts and with creative problem solving is the development of skills and practices associated with the disciplines taught in schools. Recent curricular reform initiatives led by educators, subject-matter experts, and policymakers, with support from state and federal leaders as well as some of the business community, seek to raise academic standards, increase graduation rates, and improve assessments. In widely distributed documents, they provide clear and consistent frameworks that define the knowledge and skills students should have to be prepared for college and career. The Common Core State Standards (CCSS) for Mathematics and for English Language Arts & Literacy in History/Social Studies, Science and Technical Subjects (National Governors Association Center for Best Practices & Council of Chief State School Officers, 2010a, 2010b, 2010c), adopted in 2010 by 45 states, and the Next Generation Science Standards (NGSS Lead States, 2013) place renewed emphasis on developing students' abilities to think analytically, critically, and creatively in each of the subjects of study in schools. Following the mathematical practices put forth by the National Council for Teachers of Mathematics, the CCSS for Mathematics describe mathematically proficient students as students who construct viable arguments, who justify and communicate their conclusions, and who listen and ask useful questions to clarify or improve the reasoning of others. Similarly, as stated in the National Research Council science framework and the Next Generation Science Standards, science students, like scientists, need to be able to examine, review, and evaluate their own knowledge and ideas and critique those of others. Among the essential practices of K–12 science and engineering curricula are asking questions and defining problems, planning and carrying out investigations, building models, constructing explanations and designing solutions, building arguments from evidence, and evaluating and communicating information. The CCSS in English Language Arts & Literacy lay out a vision of what it means to be a literate person. Along with developing proficiency in reading and writing, these standards emphasize the development of students' skills in listening and speaking—the foundations for purposeful expression in language. The National Curriculum Standards for Social Studies released in 2010 echo the message embedded in the previous documents. In addition, they call for students to be able to actively seek to understand other perspectives and cultures through communicating effectively with people of varied backgrounds.

These calls for reform are a response to the judgment that knowledge acquired by rote memory is insufficient for the challenges of modern social problems and modern technology. Future citizens should not only know how to think and how to deal with very uncertain problems, but they should also know how to communicate and share those thinking processes with others.

The group situation is ideal for the development of the thinking skills and practices associated with each discipline. Cooperative groups provide learners with the opportunity to practice generating causes and effects, hypothesizing, categorizing, deciding, inducing, and problem solving (Solomon, Davidson, & Solomon, 1992). In comparing cooperative learning with competitive and individualistic learning, the Johnsons (1992) found that there were more frequent experiences of discovery and use of higher-level reasoning strategies in the group setting. These two experts in cooperative learning summarize their extensive research on why cooperation aids in the development of higher-level cognition and the ability to communicate thinking: Discussion within the group promotes more frequent oral summarizing, explaining, and elaborating what one knows; cooperative learning promotes greater ability to take the perspective of others (an important thinking skill in social studies); in the group setting, one's thinking is monitored by others and has the benefit of both the input of other people's thinking and their critical feedback.

Group interaction is not only the most effective but the most practical way of achieving these goals. Standards such as those of Bassarear and Davidson (1992), renowned math educators, cannot be accomplished by having students work by themselves—there is simply too much for the teachers to "teach." These two math educators feel that students can often address other students' questions more effectively than the teacher. In addition, discussion often captures various students' misconceptions that the teacher may never uncover. Research in mathematics education consistently emphasizes the power of small-group interaction for learning and teaching mathematics (Boaler & Staples, 2008; Yackel, Cobb, & Wood, 1991).

Cooperative learning is also an effective strategy in helping students understand and retain information as well as in improving their basic skills. Many researchers have compared the effectiveness of cooperative groups to traditional methods of instruction in teaching students skills that are measured on multiple-choice tests. In general, there have been some very significant positive effects on achievement as a result of cooperative learning (Johnson, Johnson, & Maruyama, 1983; Johnson, Maruyama, Johnson, Nelson, & Skon, 1981). In some studies, however, cooperative learning was associated with results that were merely as good as those with more traditional forms of instruction and not necessarily superior (Davidson, 1985; Newmann & Thompson, 1987). Up-to-date summaries of the literature on the many benefits of cooperative learning can be found on the website of the International Association for the Study of Cooperation (www.iasce.net/home/newsletters).

The important message that this literature on effectiveness has for the classroom teacher is that there are clearly some conditions under which cooperative learning is more effective than traditional methods of instruction. Whether or not groups are more effective than other methods of instruction depends on factors such as the choice of task, whether or not students are willing to help one another, and what motivations members have to become engaged in the group activity. Simply telling students to get in a group and carry out familiar classroom tasks designed to improve basic skills is not sufficient to ensure learning gains.

Language Development

Cooperative tasks are an excellent tool for still one more cognitive teaching goal: the learning of language and the improvement of oral communication skills. In any language-learning setting, in bilingual classrooms, and for students of any age who need to improve skills in oral and written communication, active practice is essential. Recitation and drill are of limited usefulness, producing much less active practice than a group exercise where students talk with one another to exchange information and ideas, and subsequently document and record their understandings.

Specialists in language learning argue, for example, that there is too much reliance on pattern drills in the English as a Second Language approach. Children acquire language by using it in a more natural, meaningful context. If the instructor of the classroom where children need to increase oral proficiency in English sets up a series of tasks that stimulate children to talk to one another, using language associated with an interesting task, the possibilities for active language learning can be greatly enhanced.

In a review of research on second language acquisition in cooperative learning, Mary McGroarty (1989) finds evidence that students gain both in comprehension and production of the second language. She finds that tasks used in cooperative learning foster many different types of verbal exchange. There are more possibilities for fluent speakers to tailor speech and interactions so that they can be understood by the less-proficient speaker. Even when all the students in a group lack fluency in English, the students will correct one another and attempt to fill in the gaps of their understanding by repairing and rephrasing what their partners say in order to come to agreement. The challenge for many students to simultaneously acquire the language of instruction and to master disciplinary content will be addressed in more detail in Chapter 7.

The very same proposition applies to the teaching of languages other than English in secondary school and to speech classes where the instructor is trying to increase skills in oral communication. Compare the traditional approach of having one student stand up and make a presentation to the class with setting up small groups where each member is responsible for communicating a key part of the task. If the group needs to understand what each member has to say in order to accomplish the goal, they will ask questions and urge the presenter to communicate clearly. Groupwork will provide far more active and relevant practice than having students take turns in making a speech to the whole class.

SOCIAL GOALS

Social research has gathered impressive evidence to show that when people work together for group goals, there are a number of desirable effects on people's feelings for one another. When groups engage in cooperative tasks, they are more likely to form friendly ties, to trust one another, and to influence one another than when the task stimulates competition among members (Deutsch, 1968, 1992). More recently, Johnson and Johnson (2009b) theorized about the positive outcomes of social interdependence not only on achievement and productivity but also on the lasting positive quality of social interactions and on the psychological health of individuals. Sharan and colleagues (1984) found that when students were taken out of class and given a group task, those who came from classes using cooperative learning showed far more helpful and cooperative behavior and much reduced negative or competitive behavior than those coming from classrooms where only whole-class instruction was in use. Training students in productive interpersonal behaviors seems to have lasting effects. Gillies (2002) compared the interactions among 5th-grade students, half of whom had received training in cooperative learning 2 years prior to the study and half of whom who had not. Even after 2 years, the students who experienced the training displayed more helpful and cooperative behaviors than the students who had not.

Positive Intergroup Relations

Cooperative groups and teams are particularly beneficial in developing harmonious interracial relations in desegregated classrooms. Slavin (1983) reviewed 14 cooperative classroom experiments whose groups were ethnically and/or racially mixed. In 11 of these studies, there were significantly more friendship choices across racial and ethnic lines among those students who had worked in cooperative, interracial groups than among students who had not had this opportunity. Particularly striking are the results of Slavin's team method (1983, p. 13), where interracial groups are given an overall score achieved by combining the test scores of individual members of the team. In his book on cooperative learning, Slavin concludes that it is high-quality positive interpersonal interaction that leads to interpersonal attraction; through interaction individuals perceive underlying similarities across racial lines (Slavin, 1983). Cooperative goals or group rewards help to produce this deeper level of interaction, interaction that is not usually available in desegregated classrooms.

Sharan and his colleagues have examined how members of different ethnic groups treat one another while working together on a cooperative goal. Their comparison of techniques of cooperative learning such as Group Investigation with traditional whole-class instruction shows that cooperative learning produces more cross-ethnic cooperation and less negative and competitive behavior between members of different ethnic groups (Sharan et al., 1984, pp. 73–103; Sharan & Shachar, 1988).

An instructor is more likely to establish and maintain positive intergroup relations with cooperative groups than with a competitive or individualized reward system. Yet even under cooperative conditions, groups can fail to "mesh" and to achieve a unified "we" feeling. Interpersonal relations can at times be the opposite of harmonious; certain individuals can completely dominate the interaction of the group. To obtain the benefits of cooperation, it is necessary to prepare the students for the cooperative experience. As we discuss more fully in Chapter 4, researchers and educators who work with cooperative classroom groups have developed ways to prepare students for working productively in small groups.

Socializing Students for Adult Roles

Sharan and Sharan (1976) pointed out that when the teacher delegates authority to a student group and allows that group to make decisions as to how it will proceed on its task, there is a special socializing effect. The authors argued that having students experience making decisions on their own rather than telling them exactly what to do will have a desirable political socializing effect on them. They will have more of a sense of control of their own environment, and they will learn how to be active citizens (in a collective rather than in an individualistic sense). This constitutes an antidote to methods of classroom organization where the teacher does all the directing and tells others what to do while the student plays a passive role.

Another way in which groups socialize students for adult roles is by teaching them how to carry on a rational, organized discussion and how to plan and carry out a task as a result of that discussion. This is a set of skills that many adults frequently lack. Often they do not know how to listen to others or how to work with other people's ideas; they are more concerned with dominating the discourse than with listening to others. In many aspects of adult work and organizational life, working in groups becomes critical. Thus, it behooves us to teach children how to do so successfully.

The Sharans attribute both the idea of an active decision-making role for students and the importance of being able to think for oneself and being able to exchange ideas and opinions freely with others to Dewey (Sharan & Sharan, 1992, pp. 2–6). Dewey felt that schooling "should embody in its very procedures the process and goals of democratic society" (Sharan & Sharan, 1992, p. 4). In this way, students will prepare for their role as adult citizens in a democracy through public deliberation and critical analysis of social policies and priorities (see also Westheimer & Kahne, 2004).

IMPROVING CLASSROOM MANAGEMENT

From the teacher's point of view, groupwork addresses two common classroom management problems. It helps with the challenge of the low-achieving student who is often found doing anything but what she is supposed to be doing. Moreover, it helps to solve the problem of what the rest of the class should be doing while the teacher works intensively with one group. The most typical strategy is to have the rest of the students working individually at their seats. However, this produces all kinds of discipline problems. If the rest of the class has been trained to work independently in groups, teachers will be free to devote their attention to giving direct instruction to one small group.

Research has led many schools to become concerned with how much time children are actually spending on learning tasks. The issue is important because of the frequently observed relationship between the amount of time children spend in classroom learning activities and their scores on achievement tests. Slavin (2003) defines *time-on-task* or *engaged time* as the time students spend actually engaged in learning.

One of the major ways that children lose time on task is through the use of seatwork techniques. The Beginning Teacher Evaluation Study, a monumental work of classroom observation and achievement testing, revealed that on the average, students observed in grades 2 and 5 spent at least 60% of their time in seatwork (Berliner et al., 1978). For over half the time during reading and mathematics, the students observed worked on their own, with no instructional guidance. The amount of time children were on task in these self-paced settings was markedly lower than in other classroom settings.

This means that students are often doing something other than their assigned work when they are left to their own devices—and the students observed in the Beginning Teacher study were the students who needed to work hard; they were achieving in the 30–60th percentile on standardized tests. Furthermore, regardless of the achievement level of the students in the fall, this study found strong relationships between time on task and achievement test scores in the spring. Martella, Nelson, and Marchand-Martella (2003) report that students spend about 42% of their school day engaged in learning. Researchers continue to find that engaged time is the most important influence on academic achievement (Greenwood, Horton, & Utley, 2002; Marks, 2000; Slavin, 2003).

Studies of seatwork consistently find this method of instruction has higher rates of disengagement than whole-class instruction. Although seatwork can be supervised effectively, this is frequently not the case. Students often find seatwork assignments meaningless and confusing; they may lack the resources to complete the task properly. In a study of Title I schools (Anderson, 1982), young children were interviewed about what they thought they were doing during seatwork. Many did not understand the purpose of the assignment; "getting it done" was what many students, both high and low achievers, seemed to see as the main reason for doing the task. Of these students, about 30% (all of whom were low achievers) apparently did not expect their assignments to make any sense.

Choosing a method of classroom organization that leaves the student who rarely succeeds in schoolwork quite alone may indeed be the root cause of the observed disengagement on the part of low-achieving students in seatwork settings. These students are receiving very little information on the purpose of their assignment, on how to complete it successfully, on how they are doing, or on how they could be more successful. The tasks themselves are rarely sufficiently interesting to hold the students' attention. Students drift off task simply because there is nothing to compel them to stay with it except the teacher's command to "get the job done."

Groupwork will usually produce more active, engaged, task-oriented behavior than seatwork. The interactive student situation provides more feedback to the struggling student. Interaction provides more opportunities for active rehearsal of new concepts for students of all achievement levels. Students who struggle to read or do not understand the instructions can receive help from their peers (as in the case of Geraldo). If the group is held accountable for its work, there will be strong group forces that will prevent members from drifting off task. Finally, peer interaction, in and of itself, is enormously engaging and interesting to students. All these factors help to account for research findings such as that of Ahmadjian (1980), who studied low-achieving students in 5th- and 6th-grade classrooms. She found dramatically increased rates of time on task for these students doing groupwork as compared to seatwork.

PROMOTING EQUITY IN HETEROGENEOUS CLASSROOMS

Many teachers are in classrooms where students have a wide range of academic skills and oral and written proficiency in the language of instruction. This is particularly prevalent in schools serving students from lower socioeconomic backgrounds. As every teacher knows, this creates tremendous pedagogical challenges. What level of instruction is appropriate? Should students who lack prerequisite academic and English skills be given the same assignment as everyone else, even though they need more support and resources? What should the teacher do with the students who are operating on grade level while giving much-needed attention to students who are struggling with grade-appropriate tasks?

The most commonly attempted methods of solving these dilemmas are ability grouping and individualized seatwork. But there is no evidence that putting low-achieving students into a homogeneous ability group is effective (Slavin, 1987). On the contrary, low-achieving students clearly benefit from heterogeneous groups and classrooms where there are more academic resources available to them (Dar & Resh, 1986; Hallinan & Kubitschek, 1999; Kerckhoff, 1986; Oakes, 2005). The problems with giving seatwork assignments to students who are operating below grade level have already been emphasized.

An alternative strategy is the use of heterogeneous groups and students trained to serve as academic and linguistic resources for one another. If two students in the group can read fluently, they can read the instructions to others. If the group problem requires subtraction, and only one student knows how to do subtraction, then that student may be able to show the others how to do it. If several students speak only Spanish and one student is fully bilingual, then the bilingual student can serve as interpreter between the English- and Spanish-speaking students.

This format allows the teacher to challenge all the students intellectually rather than to teach to "the middle," or to what is often referred to as the "lowest common denominator." If each group member is required to turn out a product demonstrating understanding, yet is allowed to use resources of the group in order to achieve that understanding, the student who might still be lacking the requisite academic skills will not sit back, but rather will go along with the group. If the task is challenging and interesting, he will become actively engaged and will demand assistance and explanation. For students more advanced in academic skills, the act of explaining to others represents one of the first ways to solidify their own learning (Webb, 1983).

In review, if students are properly prepared, heterogeneous groups can represent a solution to one of the most persistent problems of classroom teaching. If students are able to use one another as resources, everyone can be exposed to grade-level curriculum and even more challenging material. Temporary lack of skills in reading, writing, and computation need not bar students from exposure to lessons and tasks requiring conceptualization. At the same time, these students can develop their basic skills with assistance and support from their classmates.

3 | The Dilemma of Groupwork

Teachers and researchers have described some of the common challenges of groupwork in classrooms. Selected authentic narratives written by teachers were collected in a book entitled *Groupwork in Diverse Classrooms: A Casebook for Educators* (Shulman, Lotan, & Whitcomb, 1998). In this book, the teacher authors reflected on classroom episodes and decisions they made as they asked students to work in small groups.

"Some groups work and some don't; why I even bother to "craft" the perfect group still mystifies me," writes Mr. M., a high school English teacher. He had asked his students "to nominate a poem that would be good for the group to write about, 'unpack,' and 'present' to the class" (Shulman et al., 1998, p. 46). His case focuses on a particular group and the four students assigned to that group: Daryl, Kara, Josh, and Elizabeth.

Daryl transferred to our school from the "weak" working-class high school in the district. He arrived on the third day of school with a recommendation and an "A" from his freshman college prep teacher; he also came speaking slang, writing run-ons, and willing to be brutally honest in his oral and written work. . . . In many ways, Daryl stuck out. He wore a cap as he slyly munched on sandwiches and sipped Cokes in the back of the class, where I've never allowed eating for fear of rodents. He said "pissed off" when asked how a particular character acted. His classmates didn't know how to react. Should they look at me? At Daryl? Or share a snickering glance with a friend? They didn't speak slang in class. Daryl also managed to read within the first week two books from the required summer reading list. . . .

With Daryl I placed Kara, one of my best students whose stellar beginning-of-the-year writing seemed to bode well for good groupwork. I searched the roll book for nice kids, whom I figured would be tolerant.

I nabbed Josh, who seemed especially mature and nice. I liked how he had complimented my independent reading list and asked for more recommendations. I also added Elizabeth, a quirky young woman, who had sworn off pants and who probably would have been just as happy wearing long skirts at the turn of the century. . . .

On the day Daryl, Kara, Elizabeth, and Josh tried to reach a consensus about which poem to pursue, I watched, growing increasingly disappointed. Were they trying to reach a consensus? Did they know how? Daryl and Elizabeth sat facing Kara and Josh. Sagging in his chair, Daryl gazed away, pointing his outstretched legs toward another group. Elizabeth, disgusted, looked down as she paged through the anthology. Across from them, Josh and Kara talked animatedly. When I stopped at their group, Kara told me the group had chosen Raymond Carver's poem "Gravy." Elizabeth complained that no one was listening to her and that she hated "the dumb poem they both want." I immediately worried that the "both" Elizabeth referred to meant that Kara and Josh were the decision makers. And Daryl proclaimed, "I really don't care which poem they want." Finally the day came for their presentation of "Gravy." I hated watching it. Kara and Josh read alternating stanzas of the poem in a self-important way, while Elizabeth, wearing a checkered apron over her long skirt, mixed up some real gravy. Daryl stood aside with nothing to do. Then, in an unrehearsed moment that distracted from the presentation, he reached for the gravy, taking a few licks. Other than that, the initial selectors of the poem, Kara and Josh, had taken over the presentation. The other two never really found their way into the project. (Shulman et al., 1998, pp. 45–47)

Why is this description hauntingly familiar and disturbing to so many teachers? One or maybe two students do all the work and make all the decisions for the group. They dominate the conversations while others feel frustrated and become disengaged. Why do the teacher's best intentions have such dire consequences for many students?

In another case, Ms. W. writes about Sam in her 2nd-grade classroom:

Sam and his family immigrated to the United States from Hong Kong when he was 5. His 1st-grade teacher's recollections of Sam's year in her class painted a grim picture of the difficulties he faced: He spoke limited English, his scores on the district language assessment measures indicated that his comprehension of spoken English was restricted, he was a nonreader, he struggled with most classroom activities, he cried often, and he suffered almost daily playground injuries. . . . I hoped Sam would receive the initial help and support from his team that he so desperately needed. . . . It was soon apparent that the group had no "magic." . . . Problems became apparent during their first cooperative task, which was to create a new invention. I told the class that each group could create any invention as long as it was useful. They had to write a description of what it looked like and how it would be used and draw a picture of it. The first step was for each group to decide what to invent. As Sam's group discussed the possibilities, Sam suggested that it would be interesting to have an umbrella that opened on command. Initially, the other members seemed interested in the idea, but later they changed the command umbrella to a flying umbrella. Sam's suggestion fell by the wayside and he was left having little or no involvement in the group's decision. . . . Later, when I asked Sam about it, he said "They changed everything I said. . . . At first they say, 'Yeah, yeah,' then they change and say, 'No, no.' They no like me."

After this conversation, I decided I needed to pay extra attention to the group's interaction. I began noticing that most often when Sam tried to explain something, the others would have a difficult time understanding him. Over and over again Sam would repeat, "no, no, I mean . . . ," but the others invariable lost patience and simply left him out of the conversation. It appeared that Sam's inability to be understood lowered his status in the group. Over time, a "pecking order" emerged and Sam was at the bottom. (Shulman et al., 1998, pp. 39–40)

Many teachers read about Sam's experiences with consternation and remember others like Sam with a sense of helplessness and grief. Ms. A. was one of those teachers. Echoing Ms. W.'s concern for her student, Ms. A. writes about Dennis, whose experiences with groupwork left her feeling at a loss.

Just a little too thin, and slightly drooped at the shoulders, Dennis was an expert at being disengaged in class and a master magician whose greatest trick was making himself invisible. His book would be open, his paper and pencil ready, but closer inspection would reveal, instead of history notes, page after page of drawings—guns, gang graffiti, and comic book heroes. . . . When students discovered that he was going to be in their group, they would shrug their shoulders and roll their eyes. They would complain to me and give Dennis bad evaluations on their feedback sheets. (Shulman et al., 1998, p. 60)

These accounts raise many issues about what goes on inside small groups. Why do the students allow one member of the group to do all the work and make all the decisions? It might make some sense in Kara's case, because she really is a top-notch student, "the group's academic achiever, who took control so she wouldn't lose control," as Mr. M., her teacher, tries to figure it out (Shulman et al., 1998, p. 47). In the cases of Daryl and Elizabeth, the two students who were arguing unsuccessfully, and unpopular young Sam, it is almost as if the pecking order of student play-and-friendship groups has invaded the classroom groups. Why aren't the students nicer and more considerate to each other? Why aren't they aware of how those like Sam must feel about having no chance to participate? Why don't they see that Elizabeth is frustrated and discouraged? Why can Dennis remain silent and invisible?

One thing is clear: The teacher who has no more tools for the planning of groupwork than an initial attraction to an idea of groupwork as a democratic and creative setting for learning is likely to run into trouble in trying out new pedagogical tools. Although the results are unlikely to be as consistently disappointing as the ones just described, careful observation of any class working under unstructured grouping and task instruction will reveal patterns of undesirable domination on the part of some students and nonparticipation and withdrawal on the part of others. In addition, there appear to be both disciplinary and motivational problems that might not be apparent in classrooms where teachers use more traditional methods of whole-class presentation or well-supervised seatwork. Although some students can successfully "hide" in whole-class settings, doing so during groupwork becomes conspicuous and salient.

Some of these disciplinary and motivational problems are closely related to our initial observations of domination and lack of participation. Some are related to the teacher's lack of success in selecting and defining a more suitable task for the groupwork setting or her failure to prepare the students in the skills they will need for groupwork. This chapter focuses on the problems of unequal participation and undesirable domination of groups by certain students.

Let us imagine that a teacher tries to compose groups so that students of more similar academic achievement or grades are placed together. She reasons that one student who gets much better grades won't take over and do all the work. Furthermore, this arrangement has the added advantage of separating friends who play rather than work, reduces the problem of social isolation like that of Sam or Dennis, and desegregates the sexes. Yet, as the teacher walks around the room and listens carefully to what is happening in each group, she finds that although discipline problems might be much improved, in most of the groups one student is doing far more talking and deciding than anyone else, and at least one student is saying practically nothing. Many students of color in predominantly white classrooms are quiet members of their respective groups. In at least one of the groups, the teacher might observe, there is a real struggle going on as to whose opinion will be adopted by the group. Their talk is not an intellectual discussion about the task but rather an interpersonal conflict over who is going to be the leader of the group.

What is the matter? Are the students just too immature to work in groups? The problem is not one of immaturity: Adults working in small groups will also exhibit problems of dominance—they will struggle over leadership in a group and will participate unequally.

BEHAVIOR OF TASK-ORIENTED GROUPS

Small task groups tend to develop hierarchies where some members are more active and influential than others. This is a *status ordering*—an agreed-upon social ranking where everyone feels it is better to have a high rank within the status order than a low rank. Group members who have high rank are seen as more competent and as having done more to guide and lead the group.

In the more than 100 four-person groups of schoolchildren Elizabeth Cohen and her graduate students studied, they rarely found that each person contributes one-fourth of the speeches on the task. Even among a group of adults who do not know each other and who have been selected for a laboratory study on the basis that they are all male, 19 or 20 years old, and white, inequalities in interaction and a status order will emerge. After the task is completed, group members are likely to agree that the person who has done the most talking has made the most important contribution to the task and has had the best ideas, whereas the person who was relatively quiet is seen as having made the least important contribution and is felt to have contributed few good ideas (Berger, Conner, & McKeown, 1974).

The very same problem occurs in groups of students who have been prepared for cooperative learning. These students may treat each other with civility, but still exhibit unequal participation and all the other signs of a status order among the members of the group. Among the developers of methods of cooperative learning, there is often confusion between what we are calling a status problem that is based on different expectations for competence and a problem of unfriendliness, aloofness, or distrust. A group can be friendly and trusting and still exhibit a sharp status order, with some members perceived as much more competent than others.

Expert Status

If dominance and inequality emerge in groups with members who are equal in status, then we should not be surprised to find these patterns in classroom groups where students have known each other on an intensive basis in what is often a competitive setting. In the classroom it is impossible to compose groups where all members have equal status. Students generally have an idea of the relative competence of each of their classmates in important subjects like reading and math acquired from listening to their classmates perform, from hearing the teacher's evaluation of that performance, and from finding out each other's marks and grades. They usually can, if asked, place each of their classmates in a rank order of competence in reading and math or subject-matter expertise. This ranking forms an *academic status order* in the classroom.

Students who have high standing in an academic subject are very likely to dominate a group given a task from that subject area—recall Kara's group in Mr. M.'s class. Kara is viewed as a very successful student in English language arts. People who are seen as knowing more about the specific topic of the group task are very likely to be highly influential in the group. In other words, they are high-status individuals. Expert status is an important idea for the designer of groupwork. If you assign a group a task from regular academic work, the student who is seen as getting the best grades in that subject is likely to dominate the group. Even if you think you have picked group members of similar academic achievement, the students are likely to make very fine distinctions about who the best student in the small group is.

As a teacher you may decide that there is nothing undesirable about experts dominating student groups, as long as the experts are on the right track for a particular assignment. If they are not, groups may miss the point of the assignment because members are unwilling to argue with the experts. Also, students who feel as if they are distinctly less expert within the group may sit back and play a very passive role, learning little from the experience.

Academic Status

Now suppose the teacher does not pick a traditional academic task from the textbook or from an online assignment. Suppose she asks her students to play a simple board game called Shoot the Moon. This board game was used in many laboratory studies to study interaction among schoolchildren under controlled conditions (for a review of these studies, see Cohen, 1982, 1993). On the board are many different paths to the moon. Depending on which square the playing piece lands on, the group stands to win or lose the number of points printed in each square on the board. A roll of a die determines how many spaces the playing piece advances. The group has only 14 turns to reach the goal in their rocket ship. For each turn, they must come to agreement as to which way to proceed on the board.

Shoot the Moon is a game of chance requiring no academic skills. There is no rational connection between reading skills and the ability to play Shoot the Moon. Yet the student who is seen as best in reading is very likely to dominate the discussion. And the student who is seen as poor in reading is very likely to be relatively inactive in this game. Reading ability, as perceived by others, is an important kind of academic status. And academic status has the power to spread to new tasks where there is no rational connection between the intellectual abilities required by the task and the academic skill making up the status order.

Rosenholtz (1985) demonstrated the power of reading ability to affect the status order in classroom groups playing Shoot the Moon. After she asked 5th- and 6th-grade children to rank each other on how good they were in reading, she composed groups with two classmates who were seen as more able in reading and two who were seen as less able. Those perceived as better readers were more active and influential compared to those seen as less able in reading. Thus reading ability, an indicator of academic status, had the power to spread to a task where reading was irrelevant.

Many students (and some teachers) see reading ability as an index of something more general than a specific skill. Reading ability is used as an index of how smart a student is. Thus, good readers expect to be good at a wide range of school tasks, and poor readers expect to do poorly at just as wide a range of schoolwork.

Rank on reading ability is evidently public knowledge in many elementary classrooms. In most of the classrooms studied by Rosenholtz and Wilson (1980), the students were able to rank each other on reading ability with a high level of agreement. Furthermore, the teacher's ranking was in agreement with the student rankings. This means that if you are a poor reader, it is not only you who expects you to do poorly— all of your classmates expect you to do poorly as well! It is an unenviable status, particularly when one thinks of how many hours a day you are imprisoned in a situation where no one expects you to perform well. Claude Steele (2010) describes vividly and compassionately the experiences and feelings of individuals who are in situations where they know they are being judged or treated in terms of a negative stereotype—a phenomenon he and his collaborators have called "stereotype threat." Even in the higher grades where reading is no longer a regular subject of study, students will still show considerable agreement on who in the class is best in schoolwork and who has the most trouble with schoolwork (Hoffman & Cohen, 1972). Just as in Rosenholtz's study described earlier, Hoffman and Cohen found that those students who were seen as better in schoolwork tended to be more dominant when playing a game requiring no academic skill in comparison to those who were seen as less able in schoolwork.

What happens when small groups of students work on tasks that require academic skills *as well as* many other intellectual skills, such as being able to visualize three-dimensional models (spatial ability) or to act out a scene with captivating flair (dramatic ability)? In this case the good reader or the student who gets the best grades in math or social studies is expert on some part of the task, but is less expert on other parts. If this were a rational world, we would expect to see different students acting as experts for different parts of the task.

This is *not*, however, what happens. Studies of classroom groups involved in tasks requiring many different intellectual abilities reveal that those students who are perceived to be good at math or science (Cohen, 1984, 1997) or good at social studies (Bower, 1990) do much more of the talking about all phases of the task than the other students. Those students who are perceived as weak in the relevant subject matter say very little and when they do participate, they tend to be ignored.

Perhaps, you may argue, these students are listened to because they really are high-ability individuals who do well on a variety of intellectual tasks. Dembo and McAuliffe (1987) demonstrated clearly that what is going on here is due to the perceptions of "high ability" rather than to some actual difference in ability. They used a bogus test of problem solving to label some students publicly as "high ability." The students so labeled also turned out to be more active and influential in small groups working cooperatively than those labeled as "average" on the bogus test. Thus, it is clear that perceived academic or intellectual ability, whether it is actually relevant to the task or not, has the power to affect both participation and influence in small groups of students.

In a series of four experiments testing stereotype vulnerability of black college students, Steele and Aronson (1995) found that black students underperformed in relation to white students in conditions where a verbal test was presented as an ability-diagnostic test—that is, that success on the test had been known to be greater for white students than for black students. Steele (2010) further explains how the pervasive negative stereotypes in a particular culture impede the performance and achievement of certain groups, for example, women who underperform on math tests, or white college students who underperform compared to Asian American students who are perceived as mathematically prodigious.

Peer Status

Why do some students who have high social standing among their peers dominate in their groups even though they are not high achieving academically? Ms. K. tells the story of Eddy and his group in her 7th-grade classroom:

One of the most popular boys in school, (Eddy) was cute, athletic, and physically mature. But academically he was insecure and anxious, usually doing just enough to pass and often announcing that he could have gotten better grades if he'd wanted to. . . . When it came to study medieval Japan, Christi, Eddy, and Roberto were teamed up again. The activities required each group to investigate some aspect of social stratification in medieval Japanese society. This particular group was to design and build a Japanese castle town, showing the ways in which even the design of the castle and the layout of the town reflected considerations of rank and power. Eddy immediately took command and Christi eagerly became second lieutenant, completely excluding Roberto. He wasn't even allowed to pick up the materials. Eddy did the building and grunted out orders: "Where's the tape? Get me something to put here. Find the scissors." Christi fetched whatever he called for and then stood silently beside him, handing him whatever was needed. There was no discussion, no investigation—just single-minded concentration on completing the product as quickly and painlessly as possible. Roberto tried to make some valuable suggestions about some of the castle details but was ignored. (Shulman et al., 1998, p. 88)

Students create their own status orders as they play and interact with each other at school and outside of school. Those who have a higher social standing have high *peer status* and are likely to dominate classroom groups. Among students, peer status may be based on athletic competence or on attractiveness and popularity, as was the case with Eddy. Newcomers to the classroom like Roberto, especially if they are not proficient in the language of instruction, are very likely to have a low social status. Those with a lower social standing are likely to be less active participants. In this way a group inside a schoolroom can reflect the world of the schoolyard, even though the task is academic and has nothing to do with play and purely social life.

Societal Status

Classrooms exhibit one other kind of status that will affect student participation in small groups. In the society at large there are status distinctions made on the basis of social class, race, ethnic group, and gender. These are general social rankings on which most people agree that it is better to be of a higher social class, white, and male than it is to be of a lower social class, black or brown, or female. (At least that is what people believe in many Western societies.)

Just like academic status and peer status, societal status has the power to affect what happens in a small task-oriented group. (For a comprehensive review of the theoretical and empirical underpinnings of this phenomenon, see Correll and Ridgeway, 2003). Within interracial groups of junior high school boys who played Shoot the Moon, the white students were more likely than the black students to be influential and active (Cohen, 1972). This happened even though the boys did not know each other and saw themselves as equally good students in school.

Likewise, other studies have found that men are more often dominant than women in mixed-sex groups; and Anglos are more often dominant than Mexican Americans who have an ethnically distinctive appearance (Rosenholtz & Cohen, 1985).

Why do these status differences affect participation? Why should some students have so much influence on tasks where they have no special competence? Why should new groups working on new tasks reflect preexisting status orders among the students? In order to intervene and modify this process, the teacher needs to understand more about how and why it operates.

EXPECTATIONS AND THE SELF-FULFILLING PROPHECY

Basic to our understanding of the way in which the process operates is the idea of a *status characteristic*. A status characteristic is an attribute (e.g., gender, computer expertise) on which people differ and for which there are widely held beliefs and agreement that greater social worthiness and overall competence are associated with the higher rank (male, computer whiz) than with the lower one (female, computer novice) (Correll & Ridgeway, 2003). Thus, a status characteristic is an agreed-upon social ranking where everyone feels it is better to have a high rank than a low rank. Other examples of status characteristics are race, social class, reading ability, physical attractiveness, and educational attainment.

Attached to these status characteristics are general expectations for competence and performance. High status individuals are expected to be more competent than low-status individuals across a wide range of tasks that are viewed as important. When a teacher assigns a task to a group of students, some of whom are higher and some lower on any of the status characteristics just described, these general expectations come into play. They lead the way for a kind of self-fulfilling prophecy to take place in which those who are higher status come to hold a high rank in the status order that emerges from the group interaction. Those who hold lower status come to hold a low rank on that same status order. Steele and Aronson (1995) posit that lower expectations internalized based on stereotypical perceptions of one's group "can play a role in mediating stereotype threat effects" (p. 809)—that is, confirming the negative stereotypes about the group.

From the start of the group's interaction, high status students are expected to be more competent at the new assignment; moreover, these students also expect themselves to be more competent. This is due to the operation of general expectations for competence described earlier. Thus, they are very likely to start participating right away.

Low-status students who are not expected to make an important contribution and who share the group's evaluation of themselves are unlikely to say much of anything. As high status students continue to talk, others tend to address their remarks to them, and one of them rapidly becomes the most influential person in the group. By the end of the interaction, this person is likely to be viewed by group members as having made the most important contribution to the group's performance. Thus, the status order that emerges from the group assignment is very much like the initial differences in status with which the group started.

Returning to the Shoot the Moon board game described earlier, when interracial groups knew nothing about each other beyond the fact that they were of different races, white students were more likely to be active and influential than African American students (Cohen, 1972). In this case, the group used race as a basis for forming expectations for competence in the game. Because in our culture people of color are generally expected to be less competent in intellectual tasks than whites, these racist expectations came into play in the innocent game of Shoot the Moon. Once this had happened, it was very likely that the white students would talk more and become more influential in group decision making than the African American students.

In accordance with Expectations States Theory (Berger, Rosenholtz, & Zelditch, 1980), a theory that explains the phenomenon of unequal power and participation in small groups, the same thing happened in the Rosenholtz groups playing Shoot the Moon. Here the students used information they had about each other's standing on the academic status characteristic of reading ability to organize their expectations for competence on the new game of Shoot the Moon. Group interaction turned out to mirror initial differences in reading ability.

In the classes that Rosenholtz studied, peer status was closely related to academic status, so that those students who were seen as influential in the informal social relations between classmates tended to be the same students who were seen as best in schoolwork. In other classrooms, students like Eddy in Ms. K.'s class will have high peer status but low academic status. Students with high peer status will have the same effect on a classroom group as students with high academic status; in either case they are likely to be more active and influential than students with either low peer status or low academic status.

A note of caution is necessary. The operation of expectations based on status does not result in the domination by high status children of every group in the classroom. Although research finds that, on the whole, high status persons are more active and influential than low-status persons, in the case of particular groups, some low-status members are more influential than high status members. There are two other factors that help to account for what happens in a particular task group. These are the nature of the task, and who participates frequently at the beginning of the session.

Studies of small-group interactions almost always conclude that some of the patterns of behavior observed are a function of the peculiarities of the task that has been selected (Alexander, Chizhik, Chizhik, & Goodman, 2009). The same holds true of classrooms. Suppose that you introduce a science task in which the group is asked to do observations of a live mealworm. Some students will be fascinated with touching and holding the worm, whereas others will be squeamish. Those who are fascinated are likely to be more active and influential than those who are squeamish. This ordering of behavior is linked to the peculiar nature of this task and may have nothing to do with the standing of the students on any of the status characteristics we have discussed. The nature of the task can also affect the total amount of interaction in the group. Some classroom tasks are intrinsically interesting and provoke a high level of interaction, while others are boring and produce only desultory talk. Still other classroom tasks may be carried out nonverbally by manipulating the material or by communicating through writing. Such tasks will have a low level of verbal interaction, but a high level of other kinds of communication.

In addition to differences stemming from the nature of the task, studies of groups show that members who start talking right away, regardless of their status, are likely to become influential. Suppose a student who is perceived as low status had been given the task of handing out the materials to the group. She might have had an advance look at these materials and so might have been able to explain what was to be done with them. Just such an event can change what happens in a particular group quite radically. Because the group would need to turn to her from the beginning to find out more about the materials, this student might have become quite active in that particular group.

Recognizing a Status Problem

What are the signs of low status behavior? As illustrated in the teachers' accounts earlier, low-status students often don't have access to the task. They sometimes can't get their hands on materials. Body language is a good indicator of status. A student without access will frequently be physically separated from the rest of the group. Low-status students don't talk as much as other students. Often when they do talk, their ideas are ignored by the rest of the group. Being treated in this way may lead to misbehavior; this is how the teacher finds out that something is amiss in the group, but scolding or punishing the low-status student will do little to remedy the difficulty.

Sometimes, teachers mistakenly see low-status students as uninvolved or disengaged. In fact, such students are simply unable to get access to the materials or the attention of the group. Some teachers attribute lack of participation to shyness, introversion, or similar personality traits. Observing groups closely and attentively will allow you to find alternative, sociological, rather than purely psychological, explanations for student behavior. Considering the overall quality of the interactions among all members of the group will help you intervene and address the detrimental effects of unequal participation.

Contextual Influences on Status Problems

Academic and peer status are powerful locally relevant status characteristics in classrooms (Cohen & Lotan, 1997b). However, the relationship between academic and peer status varies among schools, grade levels, and classrooms. The two dimensions can be positively related (e.g., students who have high academic status have also high peer status) or negatively related (e.g., students who have high peer status have low academic status). The two dimensions can also be independent of one another. We found that peer and academic status were generally positively related in earlier elementary classrooms: those who were perceived as high in academic status were also most frequently chosen as being best friends (Cohen, Lotan, & Catanzarite, 1988). In middle grades, peer status becomes increasingly powerful as an independent source of power and prestige. In some secondary classrooms, academic and peer status are negatively related. In these classrooms, being perceived as academically competent is seen as not "cool."

When the two dimensions are independent, the overall impact of status on an individual's participation in the group might be lessened because there are more students with at least one dimension in the higher state. The chances of students who have high status on both dimensions consistently interacting with students who have low status on both dimensions are smaller. Thus, the overall predictive power of status on participation is somewhat reduced (Cohen & Lotan, 1997b). Such contextual factors became particularly relevant when we address the ways in which we propose to treat problems of unequal access to learning materials and group participation in Chapter 10. The complex interaction of academic and peer status across race and class lines is evocatively apparent in Beth Rubin's study (2003) of a detracked 9th-grade program at a diverse urban high school, which notes: "For students, small groups often proved to be sites of tension and discomfort where factures of race and class came to the fore" (p. 541). Students' voices in this study are particularly poignant, as reflected by the following quote:

> The darker your skin is, the less you're respected . . . the expectation is different. They would expect me to not do as well in class and stuff like that, and when people expect that of you you kind of do what they want in a sense because it really lowers your self-esteem to the point where you're like, "I guess that's all I can do." (Rubin, 2003, p. 554)

EDUCATIONAL DISADVANTAGES OF DOMINANCE AND INEQUALITY

Why should a teacher be so concerned about patterns of unequal interaction in the classroom? After all, not all children have equal ability, so it is only to be expected that those who get better grades will be the most active in classroom groups. It is also likely that those who are social leaders among the youngsters will be looked up to, even in the classroom.

There are several good answers to this. The first has to do with learning. If you design a good groupwork task, learning emerges from the chance to talk, interact, and contribute to the group discussion. Those who do not participate because they are of low status will learn less than they might have if they had interacted more. In addition, those who are of high status will have more access to the interaction and will therefore learn more. It is a case of the "rich getting richer." In classroom research on a curriculum using learning centers, children who talked and worked together more showed higher gains on their test scores than children who talked and worked together less. Furthermore, children who had high peer and academic status did much more talking and working together than those who had lower peer and academic status (Cohen, 1984). Thus, the operation of unequal status can impair the learning of low-status students during groupwork.

The second answer to the question has to do with the issue of equity. Most teachers want to offer children equal chances to succeed in school, regardless of race, gender, or socioeconomic background. They also hope that the classroom will be a place where children who have different societal statuses will meet each other and learn that stereotypical and prejudicial beliefs held by society are not true. Teachers want children of different status levels to learn to treat each other as individuals rather than as members of particular social groups.

If status characteristics are allowed to operate unchecked, the interaction of the children will only reinforce the prejudices with which they entered school. For example, if African American children who come from poorer homes are consistently viewed in a classroom as less competent in groupwork, racist beliefs about the relative incompetence of African Americans will be reinforced, as we heard in the student's words noted earlier. If the leadership position in groups always falls to boys, it will reinforce the cultural belief that "girls can't be leaders."

This reinforcement of stereotypes is not avoided by using only whole-group instruction or closely supervised ability groups. If the students have very little chance to interact with each other, there will be no opportunity to challenge societal or cultural prejudices. Group interaction offers a chance to attack and dispel these prejudices, but the teacher must do more than simply assign group tasks. Understanding that an individual's perceived status reflects his relative ranking in a particular group and is situational rather than an individual trait goes a long way in helping teachers address the detrimental effects of status inequalities.

The third answer to the question of why unequal interaction should be a matter of concern has to do with the intellectual quality of group performance. In order to get the best possible group product, it is critical that each member have an equal opportunity to contribute. Watching videotapes of groups at work, we saw and heard some students softly and hesitantly disagree with the prevailing opinion of the group; they are on the right track and the group is not, but no one is listening to the ideas of a low-status group member. If some members are hesitant to speak up or are immediately dismissed or ignored when they do, even though they have better ideas, the intellectual quality of the group's performance suffers. A second way that status interferes with the productivity of the group is through subservience to the person who talks the most. We studied videotapes in which the group consistently turns for advice and direction to one student who, as it happens, is quite confused in her thinking, but the group persists in believing that she is the only one who has the required competence. The operation of status interferes with the quality of group performance in still another way. When two members of a group engage in a struggle over which one will be dominant, the quality of the performance almost always suffers.

From an educational perspective, what is the ideal pattern of group interaction? Over a series of groupwork assignments, one would hope that different students would play influential roles depending on their abilities, interest, and expertise; on the nature of the task; and on a number of chance factors. This is not to say that there is no such thing as differences in ability to contribute to tasks. When tasks are interesting, challenging, and varied, each one will require different abilities, and it would seem desirable for those who are strong in these abilities or who are expert in a particular topic to do more talking and explaining and to be viewed as more competent. These inequalities become a problem, however, when a student's status on a rank order that has nothing to do with the task becomes the basis for dominance in the group. For example, we can all recognize that ability in reading is a valuable skill and that readers can make an important contribution to a group task where some students have difficulty with reading. This becomes a problem when the good reader is assumed to be better at everything and thus dominates all aspects of groupwork. When ability in one area is used as an index of general intelligence and classroom competence, you are dealing with a status problem.

This chapter has posed a dilemma: Although groupwork is attractive for sound educational reasons, it can activate status problems within small groups. The following chapters, especially Chapter 10, contain specific suggestions about how to gain the advantages of groupwork without its drawbacks.

4 | Preparing Students for Cooperation

The first step in introducing groupwork to the classroom is to prepare students for cooperative work situations. It is a mistake to assume that children, adolescents, or adults know how to work with each other in a constructive collegial fashion. The chances are that they have not had enough previous successful experience in cooperative tasks working with people who are not personal friends or family members. Although many students have had varying levels of contact with cooperative learning, often they did not receive adequate preparation for that experience.

Students who are prepared for cooperation will know how to behave in groupwork situations without direct supervision by the teacher. It is necessary to introduce new cooperative behaviors in a purposeful training program. The goal of such a training program is the construction of new *norms,* collective conceptions for how one ought to behave in group settings. Sometimes norms are explicit and written down, and sometimes they are unspoken expectations or obligations for behavior.

When an individual comes to feel that he or she ought to behave in this new way, the norm has become *internalized.* Internalized norms produce not only the desired behavior but a willingness to enforce expectations for the behavior of others within the group. In cooperative learning settings, even very young students can be heard advising other members of the group on how they ought to behave. Given their role in the classroom, teachers have extensive power to establish rules and to introduce new norms for classroom behavior.

In traditional classrooms, most rules focus on individual student behaviors: Do your own work; don't pay attention to what other students are doing; never give advice to or ask for advice from a fellow student while doing an assignment in class; pay attention to what the teacher is saying and doing and not to anything else; keep your eyes toward the front of the room and be quiet. When dealing with younger students, many teachers reinforce these rules through repetition, reward, and punishment. By the time students are in high school, these rules have become internalized to such an extent that compliant students are quite unconscious of why they behave in class the way they do.

Working in groups involves a major change in traditional classroom norms. When assigned a group task, students are asked to depend on each other. Now students are responsible not only for their own behavior but for group behavior and for the product of group efforts. Instead of listening only to the teacher, they are asked to listen to other students. In order for the group to work smoothly, they must learn to ask for other people's opinions, to give other people a chance to talk, and to make brief and sensible contributions to the group effort. These are examples of new norms that are useful to introduce before starting groupwork. Because these new behaviors involve interactions among students, the norms governing these behaviors need to be shared and internalized by all the students in the class. (See also Lotan, 2006.)

Studies of groups with no special preparation for cooperative learning suggest that if students are not taught differently, they will talk about specific procedures and will not discuss ideas or articulate their own thinking (Webb, Ender, & Lewis, 1986). If teachers want more productive and higher-level discourse, the students will need to learn specific skills for discussion and for working with each other. These are not an automatic consequence of cooperative learning. Some students have no strategies for dealing with disagreement and conflict other than physical or verbal assault.

Many teachers, particularly in secondary schools, feel so much pressure to cover curriculum that they hesitate to take time to prepare students for cooperation. This is not a wise decision: In the long run, more time is lost through disorganized group behavior than would be spent on advance training.

GETTING STUDENTS READY FOR GROUPWORK

Students need to understand your purposes in introducing small groups and why groupwork skills are important. Surprisingly, some students do not realize that adult life calls for working with people who are not close friends. Sometimes students feel that the instructor is trying to force them to be friends with classmates assigned to their group. When told that in the work world many important tasks are accomplished in small groups of people who are not personal friends, such as research teams, firefighting personnel, nursing teams, committees, and construction crews, they are still doubtful. Confirmation from parents or other family members about how adults work might make them more willing to accept membership in groups composed by the teacher.

Preparing students for cooperative groups requires you to decide which norms and which skills will be needed for the groupwork setting you have in mind. These norms and skills are best taught through exercises, games, and activities referred to as skillbuilders. People rarely learn new behaviors or convictions about how one ought to behave through lectures or general group discussion alone.

The remainder of this chapter will provide the principles for a program designed to get students ready for productive groupwork. Appendix A contains detailed instructions for a number of skillbuilders that have worked well for many teachers. What if none of these particular activities exactly fits the skills and norms needed for your training program? Once you see the principles on which they are based, you can adapt the activities described or make up some of your own.

One note of caution about the skillbuilders: Don't judge their suitability for your class by whether or not they seem too easy for your students. The point of the activities is to learn how to work together. The tasks themselves are just a vehicle for new skills and norms, not an end in themselves. They should not be too complex; otherwise students will be distracted from group processes and will become too involved in the activity for its own sake. In each case, the key to learning lies in the combination of the experience and the discussion that follows. The teacher assists the class in reflecting on important features of what has happened and in developing key insights about the relevance of this experience to the forthcoming groupwork.

Responding to the Needs of the Group

Responsiveness to the needs of the group and its members is a skill required of any kind of cooperative task. If students are oblivious to the problems experienced by peers, the group will not function properly, the group product will be inferior, and the interaction will not provide the necessary assistance for all its members. It is necessary that students learn how to become aware of the needs of other members of the group and to feel responsible for helping them for the sake of the group product.

One of the best ways to teach this skill is with a group exercise called Broken Circles. It was developed by anthropologists Nancy and Ted Graves (1985) based on the classic exercise called the Broken Squares problem (Pfeiffer & Jones, 1970). In Broken Circles, a puzzle cannot be satisfactorily solved until group members become aware of problems being experienced by others and are willing to give away their pieces of the puzzle in order to attain the group goal.

Each member of a group is given an envelope containing pieces of circle. The task of each group is to form circles of equal size. The task is not completed until each individual has before him or her a perfect circle of the same size as that formed by others in the group. There are specific limitations on the interaction: No speaking is allowed. Members may not ask for or take pieces from other persons. They may only give fellow members pieces that they may need. Detailed directions for this exercise and follow-up discussion suggestions appear in Appendix A (pp. 193–197).

The challenge lies in the fact that exchange of pieces takes place between members before the goal is achieved. For all but the easiest version of this exercise, some of the envelopes given to each group contain pieces that will produce a circle without exchange. However, if the person who receives such an envelope is unwilling to break up his complete circle and share with others, the group will not be able to complete the task. What often happens in a group is that one of the more competitive members quickly finishes a complete shape and then impatiently waits for the others to solve their problems, gazing around the room oblivious to the struggles of other members of the group—quite unaware that he or she is the cause of the group failure.

By eliciting ideas during the postgame discussion of what made for successful or unsuccessful cooperation in the group, you can help the students gain insights about sensitivity to the needs of others and to the act of sharing. Ask them how they could have cooperated more fully. This task is an excellent analog to many cooperative tasks: the individual becomes concerned with giving rather than with taking or showing off individual achievement.

Do not lecture students on what they are supposed to learn from the experience. Allow them to arrive at conclusions through your questions and the discussion that follows. Then, when they have been able to develop the important insights, you can point out how cooperation in this situation relates to cooperation in the planned groupwork. Education is not magic—always make the connection between the new behaviors and the situation when you want the students to use their new awareness or skills.

Follow-up Experiences. Often it is necessary to design a follow-up experience if the groups are exhibiting problems in being responsive and sharing. An advanced version of Broken Circles (see Appendix A, pp. 196–197) allows the same class to do the exercise at a later time. Or you can provide a supplementary experience involving sharing pieces of a jigsaw puzzle, as also described in Appendix A (pp. 197).

Other skillbuilders that can be used to teach the same lesson include a workout with a relatively large beach ball where the group is given the task of keeping the huge ball in the air and bouncing it for so many minutes. Here, too, the success of the group will depend on everyone's efforts. Creating a mural together or putting together a complicated puzzle can teach or review the same point about cooperation. As with the first activity, it should be followed by a discussion in which the students have a chance to draw the connections between cooperation demanded by the exercise and their own behavior in the groupwork setting.

Teaching Specific Cooperative Behaviors

Your training program will deal with specific behaviors that are required by the groupwork setting you have in mind. Start by analyzing your groupwork task. Will it be a small discussion group where everyone must come to consensus before producing a group product? Will it be a working group where students help each other in a collegial fashion, but are responsible for their own product, such as a completed write-up or a laboratory report? Will the task be a purely verbal one involving values and opinions, or will the task involve students showing each other how things work with manipulative materials? Will the task involve creative problem solving in a situation where there are clearly better and worse answers?

Different groupwork tasks require different cooperative behaviors. To illustrate, let us contrast the behaviors called for in two groupwork settings: learning stations or centers and small discussion groups. In the learning station format, the instructor sets up different tasks in various stations in the classroom. These might be science experiments, math problems using manipulatives, or examining primary source documents in social studies. Tasks are typically multimedia and call for a variety of problem-solving behaviors, with more than one way to solve each part of the problem. There are clear standards and criteria by which one can assess the group's performance and its products as more or less successful. Students are expected to work together to help others at their station; at the same time they are expected to turn out individual reports or products that the teacher can examine and use as a basis for assessment of individual progress or for individual evaluation.

A key behavior at learning stations is helping other students. Helping others is not as simple as it sounds; the most common response is to help by doing the task for the other person. Students need encouragement in asking each other questions. They need to realize that this is a legitimate and recommended behavior at learning stations. Furthermore, they need to know how to answer each other's questions; instead of telling the "right answer," students learn to give a full explanation. Webb (1991) found that students who received only the answer learned less than those who received an elaborated explanation.

When there is an individual product, there is a distinction between the students' finding out what others think and deciding for themselves what they are going to include in their own final report. Students need not only to be encouraged to consult with others but also to make up their own minds in creating their individual product. Finally, if students are to have a productive interchange at the learning station, they will need some practice in listening actively. Both the questioner and the answerer must know how to listen and respond attentively.

Although many questions concerning manipulative tasks can be answered by physical demonstration with materials, nonverbal communication is too confining as the only method of communication. Younger children need practice in *telling how* as well as in *showing how* things can be done. Younger children also need to learn new ways in which to act politely in a collegial setting; when someone gives you assistance, you thank them or show them your appreciation in some way.

Required behaviors for small discussion groups differ to some extent from those required by learning stations. Here the task is one of verbal exchange as well as the requirement that the group reach some kind of a consensus. For example, you might ask the groups to arrive at some interpretation of literature or drama, use the assigned readings to answer a discussion question, apply what they have learned about nutrition to plan a meal, create a pantomime or role play illustrating an idea, create a short conversation using new words and sentence frames in a foreign language class, improve the grammar and sentence structure of a composition written by a classmate, or propose a solution to a social or political problem.

The basic set of required behaviors includes, at minimum, the norm that everyone contributes and that no one person dominates the group. In addition, discussion requires listening skills. There is a tendency for some members to be so concerned about saying their piece that they don't listen to what someone has just said. Not only do people have to listen to each other, but they need to learn to think about what the other person has said. Lack of listening and reflection on what others have said will result in a disconnected discussion and often in a failure to reach consensus.

While some older students need to learn to be concise in sharing their ideas, many younger students need to learn to give reasons for their ideas. If the group is asked to come to consensus, then students will have to learn how to pull ideas together and to find out if the group is ready to decide what to do. Young people are often unaware that coming to a collective decision involves some procedural discussion about how and when the group will narrow down to a decision. This is evidently learned in formal club and committee settings; even high school students do not engage in as much procedural talk as adults.

Skills for High-Level Discourse. Cooperative learning can stimulate the development of higher-order thinking skills, many of which are the focus of recent curricular frameworks and standards. Students can hypothesize, analyze, generalize, seek patterns, and look for logical consistency in the context of a demanding group task. Students often demonstrate their thoughts by stating their conclusions or by illustrating their thinking with manipulatives. However, they might find it difficult to articulate their thinking, or to communicate the logic by which they reached their conclusions. In watching such groups, we can infer that the students are engaging in higher-order thinking, but we would have difficulty proving it on the basis of what they say. Students will engage in higher-level discourse when they are specifically asked and instructed to do so.

The importance of articulating one's thinking and clearly communicating ideas to others increases exponentially as students move into secondary school. Unless the students can communicate scientific ideas, analysis of a social problem, or the logic behind a deduction in mathematics, they will have difficulty with advanced coursework in these subjects. Thus, despite reluctance to place so much emphasis on purely verbal intellectual production that puts some students at a disadvantage, you may decide that all students should have access to training and experience in these skills of discourse as early as possible. How to develop the linguistic proficiency of students who are in the process of developing their proficiency in the language of instruction will be addressed in Chapter 7.

Rainbow Logic is an example of a skillbuilder specifically designed to help students communicate their deductive thinking and spatial reasoning (see Appendix A, pp. 203–205). In this exercise the grid designer, out of sight of the group, creates a pattern of colored squares on a 3 × 3 grid, following the rule that all of the squares of the same color must be connected by at least one full side. It is the task of the group to deduce this pattern through asking a series of questions such as, "Are there blue and yellow squares in the top row?" The goal is for the players to be able to give the location of all colors on the grid after as few questions as possible. In order to achieve this goal, it is necessary for the group to *discuss and decide* before asking the grid designer a question. In the course of the discussion, students should share the logic of their thinking. An observer is utilized to record how often players give reasons for their suggestions and whether the group really discusses suggestions before coming to a decision. In this way, the students are making their thinking explicit in order to share the rationale for their ideas.

As a teacher, you will think about the kind of interaction you would like to hear when you listen in on the group conversation. Because it is important that the group discussion be articulate and thoughtful, consider using a specific skillbuilder designed to teach the kinds of "talk" you want to hear. In this case, you do not have to actually teach the words you want to hear. Rainbow Logic is a good example of a skillbuilder that does not prescribe particular words, but encourages the students to learn to put their own thought processes into words. Any exercise that forces students to practice giving reasons for their ideas will have the same effect.

Skillbuilders have also been developed to promote the use and application of subject-specific group discourses. For example, to promote "science talk" in high school classrooms, Holthuis (1998) developed a skillbuilder in which students worked in small groups to analyze data— in this case, copies of checks written by two people over the course of about 20 years. Students were asked to construct claims about events in these individuals' lives based on the information garnered from the checks. As with all skillbuilders, a critical component is the follow-up discussion in which the teacher identifies, labels, and reinforces when students made claims that were well supported by evidence, when and how students justified their conclusions, and when, like scientists, they changed their theory or claim in the face of sufficient contradictory or anomalous evidence.

Mathematics educators (e.g., Yackel & Cobb, 1996) describe social norms and sociomathematical norms that govern interactions in the inquiry-oriented mathematics classroom. Engaging in mathematics requires that students explain their arguments and justify their solutions, and listen to and make sense of their groupmates' explanations. Sociomathematical norms are the subject-specific norms that state the mathematically appropriate and valuable contributions as well as the mathematically acceptable and effective arguments, explanations, and justifications.

Use of Social Teaming Principles. Detailed instructions for skillbuilding exercises designed to teach behaviors such as those just described are included in Appendix A. When you recognize the simple principles behind the construction of these exercises, you can create training experiences for these and for any other skills you decide are important for the kind of groupwork you have chosen.

Bandura (1969) and others have developed some relatively simple principles of social learning through extensive experimentation. These are extraordinarily useful whenever one is introducing new behaviors to children or adults. These principles may be summarized as follows:

1. New behaviors are labeled and discussed.
2. Students learn to recognize when new behaviors occur.

3. Students are able to use labels and discuss behavior in an objective way.
4. Students have a chance to practice new behaviors.
5. New behaviors are reinforced when they occur.

If a skillbuilding exercise you develop meets the requirements of these five principles, you will have a very good chance of seeing the students make frequent and correct use of their new skills. Actually, they are learning more than the new behaviors; they are learning that these are effective ways to behave if they want a good group product. Furthermore, they are learning that these are desirable and preferable ways of behaving in groupwork situations. In sociological terms, they will be willing to enforce these new norms on their peers in the group.

Let us illustrate the use of these five principles in a skillbuilder called "Master Designer," which is described in detail in Appendix A (pp. 198–200). The exercise requires a set of seven geometric shapes also known as a tangram (illustrated in Appendix A). Each of the four persons in a group needs a complete set. The fifth member of the group is the observer. One person takes the role of the master designer and creates a design with the shapes. The master designer then instructs the others as to how to replicate the design without showing it to them. Group members cannot see what the other members are doing, but they may ask questions of the master designer.

Master Designer illustrates three new behaviors. It shows students how to help other students do things for themselves. It illustrates how a group can be dependent on the master designer for explaining how a project should be done. And by virtue of another of its rules—after the master designer has certified a member's design as correct, that person may also help others by explaining how—it shows students that cooperation can lead to the group's success.

Before the exercise begins, the teacher introduces the new behaviors and assigns them labels: "Helping Students Do Things for Themselves," "Explaining by Telling How," and "Everybody Helps." These labels also appear on a poster that remains on display for the groupwork that follows the training. In accordance with the social learning principles listed earlier, assigning labels helps to fix the new behaviors in the students' minds; playing their parts provides them with the chance to practice the new behaviors. In subsequent rounds another student can take the role of master designer, thus giving others a chance to practice explaining and helping.

The job of the observers is to watch the group and check off every time they see two of the three new behaviors for example, Explain by Telling How and Everybody Helps. After each round, the observers report how many times they saw the new behaviors. According to the principles of social learning, the observer role teaches students to recognize new behaviors when they occur and to discuss them with the correct labels.

It is very important to prepare the observers for their role. You cannot assume that students will automatically be able to recognize the new behaviors you have in mind—the words may have a very different meaning for them than for you. Discussing what the behaviors are and how to look for them is an essential step if everyone is to gain a needed awareness of what behaviors you are talking about. When the observers later report what happened in the groups, you have an opportunity to reinforce the new behaviors. In this way the exercise uses all five of the learning principles listed earlier.

The Four-Stage Rocket (described in Appendix A, pp. 206–209) embodies the same learning principles. A technique developed by Charlotte Epstein in her book *Affective Subjects in the Classroom* (1972, pp. 48–57), this exercise for small-group skills has become a general favorite among practitioners of cooperative training. It can be adapted to teach a variety of needed skills for different kinds of group tasks. Other activities are presented in Appendix A for the two common formats of learning stations and discussion groups. Guess My Rule (Appendix A, pp. 200–202) can be used with 2nd-graders as well as with older students, whereas Rainbow Logic (Appendix A, pp. 203–205) and Four-Stage Rocket (in its original form) are more suitable for middle school and high school students and can be used for adults as well. The exercises in Appendix A are self-explanatory.

Further Training. During the course of using groupwork in your classroom, you will see some loss of training, some slipping back to old ways. When this happens, there are a number of strategies that you can use. The simplest is to listen in on groups; when you hear that they are not giving reasons for ideas, you ask, "Are you giving reasons for your ideas?" Or when they are not really discussing decisions before making them, you can ask: "What is the overall strategy or plan for this group? I will be back in a few minutes and you can tell me what you plan to do." You will be surprised to find that after repeating these queries for a number of sessions, you will hear the students asking these same questions of each other.

Another valuable strategy is to circulate and take notes while the groups are in operation. Note good examples of use of the desired behaviors and skills, as well as failures to use them and the ensuing consequences for the functioning of the group. Bring up these observations during wrap-up or before you begin the next day's session. If there have been failures of cooperation, ask the class what members of the group could have done to make the group work better.

Sometimes you will decide that serious problems in the behavior of the groups necessitate more time and attention to promoting cooperation. When this happens, take time to review important behaviors that make for a successful experience. Ask the students if they have noticed any difficulties they are having in the groups. Can they think of any way to solve these problems? What are some of the new behaviors that might help? Make a public list of these behaviors. Tell the groups to repeat or extend an assignment they have already carried out. Appoint an observer for each group. The groups will work for 5 minutes while the observer watches for use of specific recommended behaviors. Then stop the groups and allow each group to discuss with the observer what was seen and what can be done to improve the quality of the group process. There is no need at this point to go back to exercises that are not directly related to the work at hand. The group itself has the capacity to be self-critical and to correct its problems.

During group processing, older students can work without the observer role. The entire group can undertake to reflect on the behavior of its members. Then the group members can discuss how well they are doing and how they might increase key cooperative behaviors. Research has shown that problem solving on a complex computer simulation problem was superior with a combination of the teacher giving specific feedback on cooperative behaviors and the students having a chance to reflect on how the group was behaving with respect to specific skills (Johnson & Johnson, 1990). This treatment produced better results than either large-group discussion of cooperation or groupwork with no processing.

The secret of successful pretraining in cooperation, feedback from the teacher, or group processing is the *use of very specific behaviors*. For example, Huber and Eppler (1990) asked 5th-graders to rate their own cooperative process on general dimensions, such as friendly–hostile and hardworking–careless, and to discuss for 5 minutes what went wrong during the last session and how they could improve cooperation next time; this strategy had no effect on achievement. Apparently, this method did not provide students with sufficiently specific information on what was missing in their behavior and on what behaviors would make things go better.

The behaviors must not only be specific, but they should also be *directly relevant to the goal of the group.* This is why general human relations training programs that emphasize sensitivity, receptivity, openness, and reciprocity are not recommended here (Miller & Harrington, 1990). Compare these very general qualities of interaction to the behaviors that Johnson and Johnson (1990) selected for groups working on a computer simulation: summarizing the ideas and information of all group members, encouraging active oral participation of all members, and checking for agreement among members each time a decision is made. Each member was assigned to monitor one of three social skills and made sure that all members used that skill.

There are additional skills, especially for group projects, that become more important as groups attempt longer-term, more ambitious projects. Lists of helping and troublesome behaviors for improving group process skills are provided in Appendix A (pp. 208–211). Ask colleagues or other adults to use an observation tool while the group repeats or extends an assignment. The observers can report to the class as a whole or to their own groups. This should be followed by a discussion of whether or not the students feel these behaviors are important for achieving a better group product. The students should also discuss alternative strategies of using helping behaviors and avoiding troublesome ones. Choose those behaviors from the list you think will be useful for your class; don't feel that you have to address every single one.

Special Norms for Group Behavior

Equal participation is probably the most important norm to teach when training students to discuss, to make decisions, and to do creative problem solving. When students feel that everyone ought to have a say and receive a careful hearing, the problems of inequality and dominance discussed earlier can, in part, be addressed. If group members have internalized this new norm and have acquired some skills for discussion, students with high status are less likely to dominate the group.

Prevention of Dominance. In a laboratory study, Morris (1977) demonstrated the effectiveness of training procedures in preventing unwanted dominance in creative problem-solving groups. Here are the norms for cooperative problem-solving behavior Morris presented to the participants in his study:

1. Say your own ideas.
2. Listen to others; give everyone a chance to talk.
3. Ask others for their ideas.
4. Give reasons for your ideas and discuss many different ideas. (1977, p. 63)

In order to train groups to use these norms, Morris gave them a challenging survival problem to solve. This task, adapted from survival problems developed by Jay Hall (1971), is called Shipwreck. It requires the group to imagine it is a crew of a ship sinking near a tropical island. Eight items are available to take with them from the ship. The group is asked to rank order items according to how important each is for the group's survival.

After discussing how research has shown that groups do better than individuals on creative problem solving, Morris introduced the task and instructed the group they were going to work as a team and that they would be evaluated on how well they worked together. He explained the four behaviors that make a good team effort.

To teach the group to be self-critical and to evaluate group processes, he interrupted them after they had arranged four items. He used the following discussion questions:

1. Is everyone talking?
2. Are you listening to each other?
3. Are you asking questions? What could you ask to find out someone's ideas?
4. Are you giving reasons for ideas and getting out different ideas? What could you ask if you wanted to find out someone's reason for a suggestion? (Morris, 1977, p. 157)

He then allowed them to finish the task and presented them with another similar survival problem. This research was able to show that the teaching of norms for equal participation prevented the high status students in these groups (those who were seen as better at reading) from dominating the interaction.

These norms influenced behavior on a third and different task, even though it was unrelated to the survival problems and nothing was said about using these new behaviors. Students assumed that this was the best way to behave in a cooperative task. In other words, the norms had begun to influence group behavior on a new groupwork task without the adult in charge having to say anything.

How did this intervention work? Sociologically, the training introduced a new norm for equal participation along with some group process skills. Because these groups were initially unequal in reading status, we may assume that better readers thought they were going to be more competent on the survival problem. The treatment did *nothing* to interfere with the operation of these expectations for competence.

If that was the case, then why were high status students less active in the treated groups than in the untreated groups? Even though the better readers may have thought they were more competent at the survival problem, the treatment told them that they would hurt the group effort unless they let everyone talk. Thus, the new norm interfered with the process at that point where different expectations turn into different rates of talking in the group.

When students in the treatments condition were asked about who had the best ideas in the group, they tended to pick the better readers. Thus, we see that although the inequality in talking was reduced in the treatment group, status problems were only partially treated.

Although this treatment has only a partial effect on status problems, it is a safe, simple, and pedagogically sound way to remind the members of your class who tend to dominate small groups that others can and should contribute. Appoint an observer in the group to monitor the use of the desired behaviors. After the reports from the observers, carry out a class discussion using the questions listed earlier. When you are ready to assign a groupwork task requiring creative problem solving, remind the class of the four features of group process that Morris (1977) stressed.

Effective Group Functioning

When the members of a group are confronted with a challenging and uncertain task that will require a group product, they face a fundamental problem: how to decide on the final nature of that group product, and how to divide the labor in order to carry out the work. Suppose that a group is tasked with designing a skit to dramatize the conflict between Martin Luther and Pope Leo XI. What form should that skit take? Who should write it? And who gets to play the parts of Martin Luther and Pope Leo XI? These are all questions that must be answered if the group is to have a credible product to present to their classmates.

Although it doesn't seem sensible to an outside observer, students will often try to move ahead without developing any general plan or strategy. Someone will say, "I think we ought to make a gold crown for the pope." "I can cut up these pieces of paper that will look like indulgences for sale," says another person. Soon the group is busily engaged in making props, having evaded both the substantive historical questions and the issue of what form the skit will take. Given enough time, this group would eventually shape the skit, but in the school schedule there is not enough time to work this way. It is essential, if the group is to finish its job within time constraints, that they start by discussing the historical issues and then develop a plan or strategy.

Teachers can assist this process by creating a specific norm for effective group functioning: *Consider the issues and develop a plan or strategy for creating your group product.* This will not have much meaning for students until they have some examples. Examples you take from listening in on their interactions can be very useful. You can either report strategy sessions you overheard, or you can ask groups to share with the class how they created a plan. You can intervene when groups are floundering, and ask them to discuss the issues and come up with a plan. Be sure to return to the group to hear their plan.

A second common problem is often found in groups of secondary school students. When faced with making a group decision, they will take a vote rather than have a full discussion and develop a consensus. They may not even comprehend the concept of building a consensus. The drawback of voting on a plan of action is that those who are voted down then have no stake in the group product and will very likely withdraw from participation. In addition, votes often short-circuit a discussion of the intellectual issues involved. Members are too focused on the actions they will take and do not take the time to gather all opinions and examine the intellectual resources provided by group members or the materials given by the teacher.

You can introduce the norm of developing consensus in connection with the norm concerning plans and strategies. You can discuss with students what happens when instead of a full discussion, a vote is taken on what the group should do. You may want to introduce the concept of compromise. In her 7th-grade classroom in Pittsburgh, California, Diane Kepner had students practice consensus building by asking them to reach consensus on three specific items of food to have for a classroom party. After 10 to 15 minutes, groups reported to the class their chosen items and discussed how they had reached their decisions. In a second step, representatives from each group came together as a panel before the whole class to negotiate and decide on the final selection of items. The third step was critical: she discussed the group processes, such as negotiation and compromise, that were used, and the implications of these strategies for consensus building in small groups in general.

When the groups are in operation, you can move around listening to the discussions. When you hear a group approaching a vote, you can ask, "Does everyone agree? Have you taken into consideration everyone's suggestions?" This will usually have the effect of opening up the conversation once more and emboldening those whose opinions have been ignored to make their case more strongly. Most of the time, you are not present at the critical moment when the group is taking a vote. Instead, you realize that a group is making no progress and will not complete their task successfully without your intervention. Ask them what they are attempting to do and how they reached that decision. According to Diane Kepner, they will often report having taken a vote. Then Kepner advises a teacher to say to those who lost out on the vote, "What will it take for you to feel comfortable with the group decision?" This opens the way for compromise and improved motivation to participate for all group members.

COOPERATION AND ANTISOCIAL BEHAVIOR

Vigorous disagreement about how to solve a problem, or about the social issues under discussion, is one of the positive features of cooperative learning and should be encouraged. Students learn as a result of being exposed to conflicting views; they are forced to justify their own views and come to the realization that there is often more than one legitimate perspective on a problem. Johnson and Johnson (2009a) have described the instructional power of intellectual conflict and shown convincing evidence for its contribution to learning.

However, some students do not know how to handle disagreement. They may engage in personal attacks or "putdowns," they may even hit each other, or they may get up and walk away from the group, feeling that their ideas have been rejected. Teachers are understandably distressed. How can students proceed with the content of the cooperative learning lesson if they have so few strategies for working together? Such behavior may be common in classes where there are many students who have had little experience with negotiation and too much experience with verbal and physical violence.

Other common problems, particularly with students in the middle grades, are physical and social rejection of some members of the group. They may quite directly say that they don't want a particular student in their group; or they may indicate their rejection with body language. The student may be barred from the materials with elbows and turned backs. Rejection may take the form of nonresponse to any of that person's contributions. The group may act as if the person were invisible.

Diane Kepner, now a retired teacher, worked closely with us for many years. She had been trained in conflict resolution techniques (Kreidler, 1984; Rosenberg, 1983) and applied work from this field to antisocial behavior within cooperative groups in her 7th-grade classroom. Central to her interventions was the observation that conflict escalates with a cycle of blaming: "He told me my ideas stink"; "He called me a bad name"; "She told me to sit down and shut up"; and on up to "He pushed me first." If students learn to translate these blaming statements into "I feel" statements in which they express honestly how they felt in response to the other person's statement or behavior, it has a remarkable way of defusing the conflict. For example, a student might say, "When you told me that my ideas stunk, I felt like no one in this group wanted to hear anything I had to say—ever again." This provides an opening for the other person to explain more carefully the basis for his negative evaluation of the first person's ideas, and the path is opened to normal conversation once more.

Because this is not a "natural" way for most people to talk, give students the chance to practice translating blaming statements into "I feel" statements. Kepner also trained her students to follow the "I feel" statement with a positive request such as "I'd like you to wait until I finish before you start talking" instead of the negative statement "Stop interrupting me." Positive requests should be specific and constructive rather than vague and negative in requests for changed behavior in others. The communication worksheet Kepner used, entitled Conflict Resolution Strategies for Groupwork, is in Appendix A (pp. 211–214). She had created specific examples of troublesome behavior in small groups so that students could practice "I" statements and positive requests.

Once students had mastered these concepts, Kepner was able to intervene in conflict situations, asking students to think about how they might replay what has happened in the group using alternative ways to express distress and disagreement. When members can talk to each other in a more constructive way, they are often able to move ahead with the groupwork. Kepner cautioned that these interventions will not work if the source of the conflict is some serious difficulty between students that is of long standing, or is a product of an acute conflict that is currently taking place in the school. If students could not put this antagonism aside in order to work together in the classroom, she changed the composition in the group, or in the case of such serious problems as gang conflicts, she turned to her colleagues and the administration for advice and support.

It is not only what people say to each other that causes so much harm; it is also their body language that signals rejection, dislike, and anger. Many students are not aware that they are sending messages with their bodies. Kepner advised talking with students about what an important form of communication this is. Body language includes facial expressions, posture, and gestures. She explained that messages that are received may be misunderstood, and that a complaint of "she's giving me looks" may have no actual basis in hostility. She then divided the students into groups and told them they were going to be given a situation to act out with only a minimum of talking. The rest of the class then determined what the message was through the interpretation of their body language.

Kepner selected the following situations, as examples from her experience, of what often goes wrong among students in groups:

- Two members sit beside each other and hold or turn the book, the task card, or the computer screen so that the other members of the groups cannot see it;
- Two group members sit across from each other and form a wedge to exclude a third member as they write and talk about their project;

- Group members actively discuss while one member withdraws;
- During a discussion, group members show by facial expressions and other movements that one member's contributions are never accepted;
- As one member joins the group, another member shows that he or she wants nothing to do with this person;
- During a presentation to the class, one person shows that she or he does not want to be associated with the rest;
- During preparation for a skit, one member of the group is treated as if he or she cannot do anything right.

To follow up this exercise, Kepner observed groups in operation. Upon spotting one of these nonverbal problems, she said to the group, "Take a look at yourselves and how you are sitting and working. What are you communicating to each other?" She then left it to the group to figure out what is wrong and how to correct the problem. Like Diane Kepner, many teachers apply conflict resolution techniques developed in recent years to help students manage interpersonal issues that arise in interactions with their peers.

NORMS AS A PRACTICAL CLASSROOM TOOL

Once you have completed a successful training program, the fact that new norms have been internalized is of considerable practical importance. Much of the work that teachers usually do is taken care of by the students themselves; the group makes sure that everyone understands what to do; the group helps to keep everyone on task; group members assist one another. Instead of the teacher having to control everyone's behavior, the students take charge of themselves and others.

Many educators think of training for cooperation as a kind of moral socialization; they wonder whether this is the function of schools when there are so many other objectives to be realized through public education. Although there is evidence that cooperative training will have these socializing effects, there are entirely different grounds for arguing that cooperative training is worth the time it takes from ordinary instruction. Cooperative training allows you to gain the benefits of group instruction—benefits in terms of active learning and improved achievement outcomes. If the training results in internalized norms, it has the added benefit of transferring those norms to any groupwork situation where you remind the students that the norms are relevant and useful. Most important, it frees you from the necessity of constant supervision and allows you to use your professional skills at a much higher level.

Figure 4.1 is a summary of the norms, helpful behaviors, and skill-builders discussed in this chapter.

Figure 4.I. Norms, Behaviors, and Skillbuilders

Norms Required for Productive Groupwork	Behaviors	Skillbuilders
Responding to the needs of the group	• Pay attention to what other group members need.	Broken Circles
	• No one is done until everyone is done.	Broken Squares
Learning to help, ask questions, and explain	• Discuss and decide.	Rainbow Logic
	• Give reasons for your suggestions.	
	• Explain by telling how.	Master
	• Everyone helps.	Designer
	• Help others do things for themselves.	Four-Stage Rocket
	• Find out what others think.	Guess My Rule
	• Tell why.	
Preventing dominance	• Everyone gives information.	Shipwreck
	• Make a plan.	Space Ship
	• Agree on strategies.	Alligator River
	• Describe accurately and in detail.	
	• Say your own ideas.	
	• Listen to others; give everyone a chance to talk.	
	• Ask others for their ideas.	
	• Give reasons for your ideas.	

5 | Planning Groupwork in Stages

The planning process starts with your answer to a fundamental question: How will students work together to learn what they need to know and be able to do in the language or languages used in the classroom? Your answer determines the nature of the training program for cooperative skills. Cooperative training, one of the first steps of your overall plan, is described in Chapter 4. In this chapter, we describe the next steps you take as you get yourself and your students ready for successful groupwork.

Your decision about the learning goals leads to a process of backward planning (Wiggins & McTighe, 2005). First, you design tools to assess the group products and the performance of the individual group members. You create or adapt the learning tasks that the groups will complete. You collect the resources and materials needed. Next, you plan the physical layout of the classroom. You decide how the groups will be composed and how you will assign students to the groups. Finally, you make a plan to evaluate the overall outcomes of the lesson or lessons you so carefully prepared. Quite a bit of effort is invested even before the students start their groupwork tasks. Fortunately, if your design is a successful one, you have a useful procedure for next year's class as well as a basic format that can be replicated with different tasks for this year's class. By developing at least one of these designs each year, you can, before long, assemble a fine array of successful experiences as part of your repertoire. You can also collaborate with colleagues and create a bank of tasks easily accessible through shared networks. (See also complexinstruction.stanford.edu.)

STRUCTURES FOR WORKING TOGETHER

How students will work together depends on your objective for using groupwork and on the kind of interaction in which you want your students to engage. What are your main goals for the planned lesson or lessons? Is it the development of skills such as mastering the technical aspects of writing (e.g., spelling, punctuation, capitalization), memorizing dates, labeling diagrams, reviewing for a test, or deciphering the key on a map? Or are your goals for your students to understand an abstract idea that can be recognized and addressed in a variety of settings, to apply a mathematical concept, to grapple with ethical dilemmas from different perspectives, or to plan a scientific experiment and make an argument based on evidence? What are your language goals, and how will students develop mastery of content as well as proficiency in using academic and discipline-specific language? Although many teachers use groupwork with all these learning objectives in mind, groupwork is particularly advantageous in providing opportunities for students to learn more deeply, develop oral and written language proficiency, and perform at high cognitive levels. These goals are advanced strongly in the recently released curriculum standards and frameworks (see Chapter 2).

The type of interaction you expect to see and hear when you listen in on groups is related to your decision about the learning goals. When groups are working on more routine tasks, you probably want to hear students asking questions and patiently helping each other with clear and detailed explanations. You want to see students showing each other how to do things or questioning each other in preparation for a quiz. Bilingual students can act as interpreters to students who have not yet acquired the language of instruction. In many cases, your expectation is that the higher-achieving student will be helping the students who need support when you cannot reach everyone who needs assistance.

Desired interaction in groups working on conceptual objectives does not consist of academically stronger students assisting weaker ones. Instead, you want to hear an exchange in which people are engaging with each other's ideas and in which each person's contribution becomes input for any other member of the group. In many cases, you also hope to hear higher-level, discipline-specific discourse where members articulate their strategies, assumptions, conclusions, and general reasoning. There can be a playful quality to the interchange in which group members are creating physical models, pointing out patterns, and using their imaginations. They are willing to risk "far-out" hypotheses and suggestions in order to stimulate the thinking of others. Participants are not overly constrained by trying to find the right answer or to guess what the teacher has in mind. How to orchestrate this kind of interaction among students with varying levels of proficiency in the language of instruction will be discussed in more detail in Chapter 7.

Once you have decided on your learning objectives and the kind of interactions you want to hear and see, you have set the stage for the way you will structure the groups and the group task. In the case of more routine tasks, collaborative seatwork is a common pattern: Students are given an assignment that they might ordinarily do as individual seat-work, but are told to work together and help each other. This design will work *only if* students are truly motivated to assist each other and are able to give high-quality explanations. Failure to meet these conditions will leave poor achievers without the help they need to complete the task (Webb, 1991). Collaborative seatwork is an example of a *limited exchange model of working together.* The major need for interaction lies in supplying information on how to proceed and information on specific content; and the information is likely to flow unidirectionally, from academically higher-achieving students to the struggling students.

Turn-taking is another example of limited interaction that is suitable for routine tasks. Partners may take turns in quizzing each other on spelling, items on a list, or historical dates. Group members may take turns in saying what they think is the correct answer and giving their reasons. Students may even take turns playing the role of the teacher and summarizing the main points of the lesson while other students play the role of the "learner" whose job it is to ask probing questions and encourage the leader to explain better. When the measure of success is how well students retain information on a test, this kind of structured oral discussion has been found to be markedly superior to simple discussion (Yager, Johnson, & Johnson, 1985). Although groupwork might not be essential for routine tasks, it can benefit many students, particularly those who provide help to their peers by explaining, modeling, and practicing these basic academic skills (Webb & Farivar, 1999).

In the case of less routine and more challenging conceptual objectives, the pattern of working together needs to be based on an *equal exchange model.* To create equal exchange you will need a task that is "groupworthy," where no one person could easily and with limited time complete the task alone. When working on a groupworthy task, members will find it necessary to exchange ideas freely and continuously to achieve the learning goals set earlier. If one person can do the task alone, then there is no motivation for a free exchange of ideas, and the only issue is whether the person who knows how to do the job will help those who don't. To achieve equal exchange you will also want to avoid dividing the labor among participants too sharply because if everyone has their own job to do, there is no need to talk and exchange ideas.

To maintain an equal exchange, you will strive to create a situation that encourages as much talk among the members of the group as possible. Research has shown that when the group task consists of a problem with an uncertain solution, the success of the group depends on the amount of talking and working together (Cohen, Lotan, & Leechor, 1989; Cohen, Lotan, & Holthuis, 1997). Thus you want to select patterns of working together that will not constrain but rather enhance the amount and the quality of interaction. Features of groupworthy learning tasks and how to craft them are described in detail in Chapter 6.

In a review of research on what makes small groups productive, Cohen (1992) concluded that improvement in various measures of learning depends on matching the pattern of working together with the desired learning outcome. For relatively less ambitious outcomes, the limited-exchange model, with its focus on acquiring information and correct answers, is adequate and often superior. For the development of higher-order thinking skills, deeper, more intricate, and less constrained interaction is more productive. Nystrand, Gamoran, and Heck (1991) make a similar distinction between groupwork tasks that are only collaborative seatwork and tasks that permit the students to define their problem and to produce knowledge on their own. On a test of understanding of literature that included conceptual questions, they found that 9th-grade classes spending more time in cooperative groups that demanded production of knowledge scored significantly higher on the test than classes spending less time in such groups. In contrast, collaborative seatwork, the most common pattern, was distinctly unhelpful in improving students' ability to deal with conceptual questions. In a study of 64 middle and high school English classrooms, Applebee, Langer, Nystrand, and Gamoran (2003) found that discussion-based approaches in the context of high academic demands were effective across a range of situations for both high and low achieving students. Through the discussions, the students internalized the knowledge and developed the skills necessary to engage in challenging literacy tasks on their own.

Holding Individuals and Groups Accountable

Regardless of which structure of working together you choose, the issue of accountability is central and needs to be addressed explicitly and early on. Your students will be successful in groupwork if you hold individuals and groups accountable through formal and informal assessments of both the process in which they engage *and* the products of their collective as well as individual work. Formative and summative assessments are the mechanisms by which groups and individuals are held accountable for engagement and high-quality performance.

What will you do to encourage students to relate to one another like true members of the same group? Assigning a single task to a group is not enough. Even though everyone has the same goal, some people will sit back and let others do the work. This is known as the "free rider" or "social loafer" problem. If you try to solve this problem by giving everyone an individual assignment and telling them that they should work together and help each other, it is very likely that the group will break down into individuals doing their seatwork. In this scenario, students who complete the task might or might not share their ideas and their product with struggling group members. Another common way to solve this problem is to divide the labor and give each person a part of the task, telling the group that they cannot achieve the group goal unless everyone does his or her part. Although this solution has the advantage of making sure that everyone contributes to the group goal, it has the disadvantage of providing little or no motivation for people to help each other and not much basis for free and unconstrained interaction.

The solution to this dilemma is ongoing formative and summative evaluations to support both *individual* and *group* accountability. A review of the research indicates that the best results are achieved when the design for groupwork includes both of these features (Cohen, 1992; Abram et al., 2002). Individuals are expected to complete an individual product based to a great extent on their participation in the group. Students can complete this individual product during groupwork time. It can take the form of individual performance on a quiz based on the academic content of the group activity, or it can be homework based on the group activity. Students need to know that an individual product will be required after each and every groupwork experience and that this product will reflect the content of the group's work.

In addition to the individual product, the group will be held accountable for its collective activity. One way to do this is to require the group to turn out a product that reflects its exchange, such as a presentation to the class, the creation of a physical model, the results of an experiment, or a group report. Often groups are asked to reach consensus on a dilemma or a problem. Reaching consensus and reporting on the process can be considered a group product as well.

In reviewing different cooperative learning methods, Slavin (2010) found that two elements must be present for a method to be effective: group goals and individual accountability. Groups must be working together to achieve some goal or to earn rewards or recognition. Furthermore, the success of the group must depend on the individual contribution and achievement of every member of the group. To enhance the development of students' basic reading and mathematics skills, four methods of cooperative learning based on Slavin's conceptualization have been developed at Johns Hopkins University: Student Team Achievement Division (STAD), Teams-Games-Tournament (TGT), Team Assisted Individualization (TAI), and Cooperative Integrated Reading and Composition (CIRC). The effectiveness of group rewards does not mean that it is impossible to hold individuals accountable or to motivate them to participate without such rewards. Group rewards seem to be more important for the kinds of collective or collaborative seatwork tasks described earlier as examples of a limited exchange model, where it is necessary to motivate those who could do the task by themselves to interact and to assist those who are struggling. Some practitioners use group grades to hold groups accountable. Whereas in some contexts grades might motivate students to put out more effort, group grades, like other extrinsic motivators, are often perceived as unfair by students (and their parents) and detract from the many benefits of cooperative groupwork (Kagan, 1995).

Group rewards seem unnecessary for achievement when using the equal exchange model, where students are interdependent and motivated to complete a challenging and interesting group task that requires everyone's contribution for a good outcome (Johnson & Johnson, 2009b). Most students care about making an engaging presentation and being recognized by their peers. They don't want to look foolish and unprepared. Several studies have documented major conceptual achievement gains as a result of motivation by intrinsically interesting and challenging group tasks. To create individual accountability, individual reports were required or individuals were responsible for some portion of the final product (Cohen, 1991; Sharan et al., 1984).

In addition to holding groups and individuals accountable for the respective products, you will recognize the need to hold individuals accountable for the ways they work as a group and as individual members of the group. Is the group functioning smoothly? Do you see evidence of cooperative norms in action? If so, let them know. If not, suggest they stop and discuss strategies for working more productively together. Has the group discussed and designed a plan of action? If so, commend them. If not, alert them to the disappointments and sad consequence of not finishing the task on time.

DESIGNING THE TASK

As explained earlier, during groupwork, students can engage in two kinds of tasks: routine, well-defined tasks or open-ended, uncertain tasks. Routine or well-defined tasks follow clear and detailed procedures and precise steps to arrive at a correct answer or a predictable solution. Students can be successful at such tasks by conscientiously following instructions, applying familiar algorithms and formulae, and/or locating and memorizing information.

Alternatively, a groupworthy task can provide opportunities for students to access the instructions and the information required to engage in the task, facilitate equal-status participation, and allow students to demonstrate the multiple intellectual abilities and the different academic and social skills they use to complete the task successfully. More information about the concept of multiple abilities and its importance will be provided in the discussion of treatments for status problems in Chapter 10.

With early-elementary-grade students, the group task, along with a brief orientation and a concluding wrap-up, may be sufficient to accomplish your instructional objective. For example, students can learn about map coordinates by locating where each of the members of the group lives using the coordinates on a local map. With older students, the task at hand may require background information or prior knowledge, certain intellectual skills, and appropriate use of academic language. In these cases, the group task cannot carry all the burden of instruction. Instead, the group activity is used in conjunction with textbooks, large-group discussion, lectures and presentations, work on computers, teacher demonstrations, and skillbuilding exercises.

The groupwork can be a culminating activity that allows students to synthesize and apply what they have learned in exciting ways. Alternatively, groupwork can be used to teach central concepts that are difficult to grasp through reading, lecture, searching for information on the web, or discussion alone. For example, the concept of a system is both central and highly abstract in teaching life sciences. Students can discover the difference between a collection of objects and a system by taking apart and putting together a flashlight, by connecting animals and plants to form a food chain, or by creating a three-dimensional model out of a pile of castoff objects. When older students have difficulty in reading textbooks, groupwork in an introductory phase can help the students learn to become familiar with the central concepts through manipulating objects and discussing by using some new vocabulary and discipline-specific talk. Subsequently, reading more complex texts becomes less challenging for struggling readers.

If the conceptual objective is demanding, then no single group assignment will probably be sufficient for the students to gain a fundamental grasp of the essential idea. For many years, the staff of the Program for Complex Instruction has experienced success with the use of multiple tasks in simultaneous operation in the classroom. The tasks all reflect a central "big idea" or concept and each task represents the concept with different materials and a different kind of product. For example, in a 7th-grade social studies unit developed by Rachel A. Lotan, Jennie Whitcomb, and Gerald LeTendre, the essential question of the unit concerns ways in which historians use historical artifacts to learn about earlier historical periods, in this case, about the age of the Crusades. Different groups of students study floor plans and pictures of ruins of a Crusaders' castle in Syria, listen to recordings of two medieval songs, analyze excerpts from Pope Urban II's appeal to the masses, and examine disparaging representations of half-human infidels from the *Crusaders' Handbook*. Students spend several days on this project, so they experience the historical sources in each of the media: text, visuals, music, art, and architecture. Individuals write reports of their answers to the questions the group discussed.

Each group presents products that require a variety of intellectual abilities. After discussing the floor plan of the Crusaders' castle, students design and build a model of a castle and explain how it can be defended against potential invaders. After listening to the songs, students write a song about current events that echoes the purpose of the music to which they had listened. They perform a skit imagining how the *Crusaders' Handbook* might have been used to recruit naive villagers. As students present these products, the teacher stimulates a general discussion on the different sources and how historians might use them to learn about the Crusades. More examples of groupworthy tasks can be found in the next chapter.

SETTING THE STAGE

By now you have realized that groupwork requires careful planning and preparation. An orientation session focuses the students on the major concepts underlying the activities and prepares them for the challenges of working together. Task cards with instructions and discussion questions, resources, and materials are made available to each group. In bilingual settings, task cards are often provided in both languages used in the classroom. Before students can begin groupwork, you need to decide on the size of the groups, who will be assigned to each particular group, and on the physical layout of your classroom. Unless you have thought these things through in advance, you will rapidly find yourself trying to be in six places at once, straightening out the various problems. Finally, your plan for a wrap-up will encourage students to link their experiences in groups with your instructional objectives.

Planning an Orientation

In a general orientation session, you might decide to introduce the central concepts with a short lecture, with a demonstration of scientific phenomena, with a video accompanied by a discussion, with a freewrite, or with another teacher-directed activity. If the students need to develop considerable levels of prior factual knowledge before they can carry out the group task, it may be wise to develop an introductory lesson before the work in groups.

The orientation can also be used to remind students of cooperative norms and roles that will be of particular importance for these activities. Avoid an elaborate discussion of interpersonal and role skills in the orientation. One of the common mistakes is to try to place too great a burden on the orientation, often making it too lengthy. You need an analysis of which components can be done in advance and which components can be left to the instructions on the task card or to students figuring things out. Remember that an orientation is only that; it's best not to preteach the content of the group task. Students need to explore the questions or conduct the inquiry you had planned in the first place.

Orientations have still other purposes. If you have created a rich multiple ability task, this is the time to implement a status treatment (see Chapter 10) by discussing the multiple abilities required by the activities. Orientations can also motivate students through building connections to current events or to their personal concerns.

Size of Groups

Groups of four or five seem to be the optimal size for productive group discussion and effective collaboration. This group size allows members to be in physical proximity to hear the conversations and be able to establish eye contact with any other group member. If the group gets larger, chances are that one or more members will be left out of the interaction almost entirely.

A major argument in favor of larger groups is the need for more people for a long-term project; the larger group then divides into task forces to accomplish subgoals. In addition, when equipment is expensive or hard to come by, having fewer, but larger groups may be more practical. However, the challenge in this design is for the committee-of-the-whole to develop consensus on what the subtasks will be and on who will serve in the various subgroups. The teacher may have to check on the process of these large decision-making groups to ensure that everyone has had their say and has a feeling of ownership over the final decision. Remember, as the group gets larger, arranging times and places for group meetings and activities becomes more and more difficult.

Groups that are smaller pose difficulties of their own. In a group of three, two persons often form a coalition, leaving the third feeling isolated and left out. For certain tasks, a pair of students is an ideal group size. The limitation of pairs is that if the task is a challenging one requiring different and multiple intellectual abilities and other skills, some pairs might not have adequate resources to complete the task or might be short on fruitful ideas and creative insights.

Composing Groups

Groups working on groupworthy tasks need to be mixed as to academic achievement, gender, language proficiency, and other status characteristic such as race or ethnicity. This heterogeneity can be achieved by composing groups and assigning students or by allowing students to choose groups according to their interests in special topics that the groups will be studying. The mix in any single group does not have to represent the proportion of minority students, English learners, or gender balance in your class. Mechanically ensuring that each group has equal numbers of males and females or one or two students of color has the disadvantage of making the basis of your decision clear to the students. They will tend to focus on their fellow members as stereotypical representatives of their race or gender and are much less likely to respond to them as individual persons (Miller & Harrington, 1990).

In her study of an untracked 9th-grade classroom where groupwork was used consistently, Rubin (2003) describes some of the drawbacks of this effort, despite the teacher's best intentions:

> In spite of the teachers' belief in a "multiple intelligences" approach, small groups in the detracked classroom were nevertheless built with an eye toward balancing "strong" and "weak" students as defined in a traditional academic sense. "I do build it from the weak kids up," Mr. Apple told me. "I don't build it from the strong kids down." In this way, the markers of competence constructed in the whole class context made their way into the small group context. Students who were competent readers and writers and who kept up with their assigned work were positioned as experts, and those who were seen as having lower skills were placed with their more highly skilled peers, with academic assistance as the implicit goal.
>
> A second feature of a balanced group was racial diversity. Group work fulfilled the democratizing role for the core teachers by bringing "kids who are different" into proximity with each other . . . Mr. Apple pointed out that constructing groups around racial and socioeconomic difference could be "tricky, especially if Blacks are the racial minority, you're always separating them . . . there will be one Black kid in each group." In the Cedar High context, having one African American student in each group usually meant that that student did not have any close friends in that group, and often meant that that student was also positioned as a "weak" student. This exacerbated the correspondence between race and achievement that loomed large for both students and teachers at Cedar High. (pp. 552–553)

Note that this teacher still sees his students uni-dimensionally and generally as "strong" or "weak" based on a narrow measure of academic achievement. It seems that his strategy in composing the groups does not reflect his proclaimed belief in "multiple intelligences."

As you continue to use groupwork and recompose groups, students will have the chance to work with everyone else in the class at least once if not multiple times, so the occasional group that is all female or all male will not do any harm. More important, avoid groups that are homogeneously low achieving and thus might lack academically relevant skills and resources for the assignment.

Allowing friends to choose each other for work partners is usually not a good idea. Students should think of groupwork in terms of work rather than play, and there is clearly a tendency for friends to play, rather than work, when assigned to the same group. Furthermore, some students who are social isolates will not be selected or will actively be rejected for group membership. Teachers sometimes feel that secondary school students will be resistant if they are required to work in groups that are not of their own choosing. You can prevent this by orienting the class to the purpose of the groupwork and by being transparent, consistent, and efficient in your assignments.

In composing groups, there are students whom you will view as needing extra support. A student who is still learning the language of instruction will need an interpreter until he is able to communicate in a consistent way. A student who is not yet performing at grade level in basic skills required for the task is another example. Students who have great difficulty in working with others should also be placed in groups with special care. These are often students who will bother, annoy, and distract their fellow students to get attention, even if that attention is negative. At the younger ages, children who have difficulty with monitoring their own behavior often represent a challenge in their interactions with classmates as well as with the teacher. Place such needy individuals with at least one person who can be helpful. Children who have difficulty focusing and working at a steady pace should be placed in a group with someone who can work with them interpersonally and prevent them from disrupting and distracting.

As the students gain practice in reading, discussing, and writing in the group setting, you will note that some students who have had problems in the past develop to the point where they can function independently and productively. A label of "problematic student" should not be used as permanent or as indicative of unchanging characteristics of the person. Similarly, avoid seeing some students as "natural leaders," as that might preclude opportunities for others. With proper training and your insistence that they play their assigned roles, most students are able to develop and perform leadership functions. Being successful in leadership roles will contribute to being recognized as competent and contributory by their peers—a status-equalizing process in itself.

Students have clear preferences as to whom they want to be with in a group. They know they could benefit from working with others who are perceived as academically strong. They would also choose to work with others who are socially attractive. In the study quoted earlier, Rubin (2003) asked the students about their priorities for group membership. With great acuity, she documents their answers:

Students wanted group members who were academically competent, fun to be with, motivating, and respectful. Many of these attributes were in conflict with the criteria that the teachers used when configuring small groups. Students based their judgments about with whom they would want to work in small group on how their peers displayed themselves in the whole-class context, on the stereotypes drawn from the particular school context, and on their previous experiences with individuals in small-group settings.

One quality of a good group member was academic competence. Students' definitions of academic competence in small-group setting were consistent with the earlier discussion of what made a good student. Thus a good group member would be someone who is "always reading" (Grant), who "does the work" (Kiana), who does not "play around" (Mike), who "actually works" (Sasha), and who does not "like to mess around" (Tiffany). . . .

Some students came into the small-group setting bearing reputations as "bad students": students who "don't really pay attention in class" and "don't do their work" (Grant), "don't want to learn" (Kiana, Sasha, Mike), "don't even try" (Sasha), and who are "rude" (Kiana, Mike). This was a difficult position to hold in a group setting and often led to a reduction in responsibility for those students.

Another characteristic of a good group member was that she or he be "fun" to work with. This was consistent with the more social and intimate setting of the small-group participant structure. Sasha told me that she wanted to work with "someone who could joke around. When you work really, really hard, after a while you get really, really punchy, and you just want to stop and joke around."

Some students spoke of desiring group members who were "motivators" and could keep the group moving along. These students were the "groupmakers" and they were in demand. Grant told me he would like to have in his group "somebody who's kind of social and sort of a leader. I might pick Sasha. She's good at that. . . . Somebody who'll just keep us all working on the same thing and not let us go on to something we're not supposed to do." (pp. 556–557)

After you have gained confidence in using groupwork and given students' awareness of the intellectual importance and the social value of the different group members, you might want to make group assignments a public and open classroom event and use *controlled randomness* (Lotan, 2006). "No hidden agendas" would be the motto of this seemingly oxymoronic method. Many teachers use pocket charts on the wall to signal to the students their group assignment and group role for the day, or write or project their names on the wall or on a whiteboard. The labels on the rows and columns of the chart inform the students which group they are in and what role they will play. The use of roles is discussed in Chapter 8.

Before the start of a groupwork activity, you might take a few minutes to compose the groups while the students are present in the class. After shuffling them like a deck of cards, you can start placing students' name cards into the different pockets. After distributing all the names, you can review the groups that emerge. Now will be the time to make well-justified changes. For example, you might acknowledge that a newly arrived immigrant student will need a translator for the next few weeks and the student who can serve as a translator needs to move to a new group. You might want to separate two close friends who tend to socialize rather than work when placed together in a group. Alternatively, you might separate two students who are known to be engaged in a drawn-out quarrel, acknowledging that for now it could be too hard to address the deeply felt animosity these students feel toward each other. An open and random assignment to groups symbolizes that the teacher sees students as being competent and able to contribute to the task in many different ways rather than exclusively through reading, writing, and calculating quickly. When students complete group tasks, they bring to the table many different abilities—all to be acknowledged as intellectually valued. By ranking students on a scale from "strong" to "weak" and by, intentionally or unintentionally, transmitting that ranking to his students as the criteria by which groups were formed, Mr. Apple in the previous description fundamentally contradicted his stated belief in the intellectual competence of all his students.

Waste no time in letting students know their group assignment. Put project assignments and table numbers up on the board or on a wall. The labels on the rows and columns of the chart immediately inform the students which group they are in and what role they will play. Figure 5.1 presents a sample chart.

Classroom Ecology for Groups

Discussion groups need to be seated so that everyone can see and hear everyone else, preferably around a table. Irregular seating arrangements will result in very little interaction among those who have to twist around or sit in uncomfortable positions to see and hear each other. Station the groups as far apart as the room will permit so that they will not be disturbed by the conversation in the other groups.

If you expect group members to work with manipulative materials, additional books and resources, computers, or mobile devices, space considerations are important. Group members need adequate space to work. Lack of work space can result in disengagement and general failure of the projects. If members do not have adequate room to lay out their task, they may find themselves unable to solve the problems;

Figure 5.1. Group and Role Assignments

Group #	Facilitator	Reporter	Checker	Materials Manager
1	Anita	Jose	Julie	Annalise
2	DeJuan	Erick	Atiya	Miriam
3	Joan	Yani	Hanh	Rudy
4	Luke	Danisha	Gerald	Lilly
5	Ruth	Tran	Ellie	Ma'Kiya
6	Antonio	Edmund	Miguel	Vip
7	Laney	Doug	VanAnh	Christopher

materials tumble off the table, students jostle each other for space, and constructions don't fit together.

Work stations often require rearrangements of the tables and chairs from their usual formation. Take into account traffic flow as well as the amount of workspace required. If tables are placed so that they block the free flow of traffic, students will constantly be disturbing one another. It is a good idea to map out your classroom arrangement and consider carefully how people will move about. If your classroom furniture is inflexible and unsuitable, perhaps you can borrow another more appropriate room for groupwork.

Noise is often a special problem for open-space schools. If students are working at learning stations, a fair amount of productive noise is to be expected and is a sign of functioning groups. It is advisable to consult with neighboring teachers and administrators in advance of scheduling groupwork.

All curricular materials, resources, and tools should be reviewed to make sure that they do what they are supposed to do. Check for scissors that don't cut and magnets that don't magnetize. Although it may seem sensible to keep things like scissors and glue at a central location, setting them out at each learning station where they will be needed is more efficient when possible. With decentralized materials, there is far less rushing to and fro, with its distracting consequences.

Teachers of elementary students are well aware of safety issues like sharp tools or the use of heat and fire. The usual solution is to station an adult to supervise these activities directly. This is a costly solution in terms of using up scarce adult resources. As an alternative, discuss strategies for dealing with potentially dangerous materials in your orientation. Another solution is to appoint one of the children as a safety officer, with a clear understanding of what he or she should watch for and when to call for an adult.

Setting up work stations with instructions and materials sounds like too much work for an already very busy teacher. It is! The students can be trained to do the work of setting up these stations; they can move the furniture and set out the materials needed. If the teacher lists or illustrates what will be needed on the activity card, the student in charge of setting up can get the materials from cupboards or storage areas, provided that these places are properly labeled (with illustrations or symbols for nonreaders). Another successful pattern is for teachers to prepare a box or a bucket filled with the materials and the activity cards for each center. The person in charge of materials can pick up the box, distribute the materials, and ensure that everything is returned in proper order after the task is completed. You should not have to spend time and effort to clean up after the work is done; students will cheerfully carry out these tasks if it is made clear that this is part of their job. First-graders can do an excellent job of cleaning and setting up; they appear to relish the responsibility. Remind them of one of the norms: Everybody cleans up!

Sometimes, students will want to read and learn more about the topic of their group task. Make resources easily accessible, especially with students who need to be encouraged to dig further for information, search on the web, or read books on subjects of their interest. Place relevant books, computers, or mobile devices close by the learning station where the students are working on a particular topic. If everybody needs certain reference materials or mobile devices, put these on a cart so groups can easily move it around to the different work stations. Display pictures, maps, costumes, and objects near the work stations to stimulate students to ask questions, think more, and dig further into the subject. A great advantage of this strategy is that if one group has finished its work before the others, the materials for obvious extension of the activity are all prepared. You can, with a few minutes of discussion and questioning, help the group to push the investigation further with the materials at hand. As students learn to gather information on the web, be sure to teach them how to distinguish between reliable and less reliable sources of information.

Planning a Wrap-Up

Wrap-up is an essential part of groupwork. When the students report on their work in the groups, they share with the class what they learned. When each group is doing the same task, each group can be given a different question or report on a different aspect of the task to avoid repetition and boredom. You can weave these reports together through questions and discussion. Teachers with whom we worked invented several other successful strategies. They ask the class to compare and contrast what different groups did with the same task. When tasks are open-ended, groups will come up with different products and different ways of getting to the product. After each report, they use informal discussion groups to prepare questions or comments they think will be stimulating. All the reporters may convene at the front of the room as a panel of experts. Reporters are encouraged to ask groupmates for additional and/or more specific information. You might also define and then enforce a reasonable time limit for the report. Above all, *vary* the way you handle wrap-up to keep it interesting and engaging. Students can also learn how to conduct peer assessment by using the evaluation criteria included in the task card. Many teachers value the development of this particular skill for students.

ASSESSMENT *OF* LEARNING AND *FOR* LEARNING

How will you assess the quality of the group product? How will you know what your students have learned? Should you give a group grade, an individual grade, or no grade at all? How can you gauge the relative contribution of each member—and how and why would that matter? Should you grade students on their social skills, their effort, their level of participation, their mastery of the academic content, or on all aspects together? Weighted or not weighted?

Although the social and affective outcomes of groupwork are highly desirable, it is the academic potential of this pedagogical strategy, its potential to narrow the achievement gap between racial and ethnic groups and groups from different social-class backgrounds, that is the most important goal of groupwork (Cohen & Lotan, 1997a). As mentioned earlier, Abram et al. (2002) found that providing students with specific criteria as to what makes an exemplary group product will improve the quality of the group interaction as well as the quality of the group product. Students' substantive exchange of ideas and their willingness to be self-critical about what the group was creating enhanced the quality of the group product. The high-quality products reflected the group's learning, which then led to the enhanced academic performance of individuals.

It is necessary to disentangle the issue of learning from the issue of giving grades and marks, also the distinction between assessment *for* learning and assessment *of* learning. For many teachers, the need for students to receive feedback on their work is fused with the responsibility to assign grades, in spite of very convincing evidence that generally students will not pay attention to feedback if a grade is attached to it (Black & William, 1998).

Start with the assumption that groups and individuals need to have some way of finding out if they are on the right track in solving problems. They need to know how what they have done measures up to some set of intellectual criteria and what they can do to improve their product. This is assessment *for* learning and it needs to be considered quite apart from grading.

There are many ways to provide formative feedback for learning. Some groupwork tasks have the happy quality of a built-in evaluation of success. Consider a task like building a machine, constructing a device that works, or designing an electric circuit that makes an electric bulb light up. The students can see for themselves whether or not they are successful. If they are unsuccessful and consequently frustrated, you can help them, *not by showing them how to do it properly,* but by encouraging them to try some new strategies, to go back to the activity card, or to try out the ideas of all the members of the group. Don't hesitate to let the students struggle; this is a good way to grasp more abstract concepts. We all learn from our mistakes.

It is not always necessary to evaluate whether students have grasped the ideas after each groupwork task. Some students may not yet get the idea in completing just one task but may suddenly begin to understand it in another setting. If you become overly concerned too early in the process with whether each student is mastering the content of each groupwork assignment, you will find yourself insisting that students get the right answer to every task, thus short-circuiting the necessary process of inquiry.

If you want to know whether or not students are making some progress, you can and should examine the individual reports included in each group task. Students will benefit greatly from specific feedback clearly stating what they did well or what could be improved. Give a reason why you think this is so. Avoid nonspecific phrases such as "very good," "great," or "fine." If you have chosen rich multiple-ability tasks that have no simple right answer, then different students can learn different things from the same task. If the tasks have this open character, you will not necessarily use standardized criteria to provide feedback to individual students. Let students know that some of them might still be confused about key concepts or are making dubious assumptions in solving a problem. Sometimes students will write two meager sentences when you expected a well-organized paragraph. You can ask the students to do the activity again, to rewrite or amend the report. Even though students have received help from other group members in writing their report, they can be held accountable for what they have written. Writing with help is better than no writing at all.

Individuals may also receive feedback when you talk to the class as a whole:

> "I noticed that Jose was able to pull the whole group together by pointing out that people were not all talking about the same question."
>
> "When Alonso asked for help, Lila asked what she could do to help."
>
> "I saw today that Jeremy created a model that helped the group figure out a way to solve their problem."

How can a group product be evaluated? You can provide feedback to the group, remembering that it should always be honest, clear, and specific about what the group did well and where it could improve. General comments such as "Great job!" may make the group feel good but they will do very little to promote learning. Be sure to point out important areas of confusion in the presentations. You may not want to launch into an extensive correction of their misconceptions right then, but you can point out that there is a misunderstanding and that you expect the next group that has this group task to work out some alternative way to understand the phenomenon. If you find it difficult to listen to the presentations and to prepare your feedback simultaneously, then take notes and provide feedback on group process and products at the beginning of the next class session.

You can pick out a group that, according to its presentation, has obviously grasped the central idea or has a product illustrating an important concept, and ask members of the group to provide additional explanation of what they have learned. This has the double function of reinforcing the learners, and if you are having different groups carry out different tasks, it can prepare the rest of the class for their turn at this particular activity. Hold a discussion during a wrap-up in which group members discuss how well they have done on using cooperative behaviors featured in the training program. Remember that the class needs feedback on their group process as well as on their products.

Peer Assessment

During any group interaction, there will be a constant process of peer evaluation. This is an unavoidable part of group interaction. One of the advantages of groupwork is that many students can help extend your power to teach by providing feedback to peers. Of course, you may want to include some training on giving constructive feedback as part of your program. Sometimes peers can be merciless toward one another.

If the criteria for evaluation are clear, students can learn to evaluate group products. If each group displays its work in some way, students can be taught what criteria are legitimate and how to give specific feedback: what went well and what needs improvement. This strategy enables the group to obtain feedback at the same time that it teaches a valuable intellectual and social lesson to the class.

Students can also evaluate how well they have done during the group process. Use the techniques of observation and self-assessment described in the section on training during groupwork (Chapter 11) for constructive peer evaluation.

Testing and Grading

Some proponents of cooperative learning recommend giving a group grade for a group project. This has the effect of making individuals dependent on the group effort for a satisfactory evaluation. It has the drawback of making the peer evaluation process rather harsh. If one group member is perceived as incompetent at the task, the group is likely to forbid him or her to have any part in the product. The student who is perceived to have the most relevant knowledge will be encouraged to take over the task. It is therefore preferable to provide feedback on group products instead of grading them.

Some teachers feel that unless the group product is graded, students will not be motivated. If the task is challenging and interesting, and if students are sufficiently prepared for skills in groupwork, students will experience the process of groupwork itself as highly rewarding. Knowing that they might present their product publicly and that they will receive feedback on their product from the teacher and from their peers will also help motivate them to complete the task.

Should groups compete with each other for grades or prizes on their group product? Competition has the effect of increasing the motivation of students; for that reason, many teachers cannot envision groupwork without external rewards. Offering competitive rewards, however, may have negative effects on the perceptions that team members have toward other teams, specifically causing them to be perceived as less personally attractive than when there is only cooperation without competition (Miller, Brewer, & Edwards, 1985; Johnson, Johnson, & Maruyama, 1984). In a socially and ethnically diverse classroom, the negative effects of between-group competition may well offset the advantages of within-group cooperation in improving intergroup relations (Cohen, 1992).

Competition will aggravate the problem of status within the group because low-status students will be seen as harmful to the group's chances of winning, and it will encourage the students to believe that learning is not intrinsically rewarding but that one ought to be paid for such drudgery by something external to the learning task itself. If the tasks are rich, as has been suggested, there will be no need for such crutches to provide motivation. If the tasks are more routine, such as those found in collaborative seatwork, the mild form of competition advocated by Slavin (1983) may well be used to solve the problem of motivation. In his STAD method, the scores of students are based on the amount of improvement individuals show in comparison to the last testing; thus, the team is not penalized for members whose entering achievement level is low. On the contrary, these may be the team members who will show the most dramatic individual learning gains, not only because they have received help, but also because group pressure keeps them working.

Following any series of groupwork tasks designed to teach certain skills or concepts, you can design an examination to test the individuals' grasp of those concepts. This will provide the formal occasion for grading. Use groups to prepare for the exam; students who have worked through the tasks will be well prepared to help each other.

We urge you not to grade or evaluate students on their individual contributions to the group product or their level of participation. Even if it were true that a student contributed almost nothing, it is never clear that the student is at fault. Other students may have acted to exclude him or her from the process. Because the individual's lack of participation may be a consequence of a status problem, it is unfair to blame the victim for the group's low expectations of him or her. Alternatively, something about the task instructions or the group process may be at fault. It is better to look on such an event as a failure of the groupwork technique rather than as a failure of the individual student. Moreover, telling students that their individual contributions will be evaluated will have the effect of making low-status students unwilling to risk active participation (Awang Had, 1972).

By separating the necessity for feedback in the learning process from the grading issue, the problem of what to do becomes much less difficult. Feedback can often be accomplished by peers as well as by teachers. It can take place while the groups are at work, in individual conferences with the teacher, or during a wrap-up. Including a wrap-up each day at the close of a groupwork session is invaluable for feedback on both process and product.

Teachers can meet their responsibilities for giving grades by evaluating some individual products of groupwork and by testing students for their grasp of the basic concepts the group tasks were designed to teach. Properly designed groupwork can produce major gains, even on standardized achievement tests.

A NOTE ABOUT TIME

While making detailed plans, you estimate how much time each phase will take. How much time will be needed for pretraining? Will the students have time for their first groupwork experience after the orientation? If the orientation goes on too long, the students will be frustrated by having to end the groupwork too early, or there will be no time for wrap-up. Planning groupwork for approximately 50-minute periods in middle and secondary schools is particularly challenging. Teachers often decide to devote one period to orientation and a general warm-up activity. They devote the second period to the groupwork, along with the preparation of individual reports, and the third period to presentations and wrap-up. Classes on a block schedule might be an advantage. Making a realistic time schedule for each phase (and sticking to it) is an indispensable management tool.

6 Crafting Groupworthy Learning Tasks

Rachel A. Lotan

As explained in the previous chapter, during groupwork, students can engage in two kinds of tasks: routine, well-defined tasks or open-ended, uncertain tasks. Routine or well-defined tasks follow clear and detailed procedures and precise steps to arrive at a correct answer or a predictable solution. Students can be successful at such tasks by conscientiously following instructions, by applying familiar algorithms and formulae, or by locating and memorizing information.

Alternatively, a groupworthy task provides opportunities for students to access the instructions and the information required to engage in the task, facilitates equal-status participation, and allows students to demonstrate the multiple intellectual abilities and the different academic and social skills they use to complete the task successfully. More information about the significance and the importance of the concept of multiple abilities will be provided in the discussion of treatments for status problems in Chapter 10.

Attention to the following design features will help you craft intellectually rigorous and academically challenging learning tasks. Groupworthy tasks

- are open-ended, productively uncertain, and require complex problem solving;
- provide opportunities for students to use multiple intellectual abilities to access the task and to demonstrate intellectual competence;
- address discipline-based, intellectually important content;
- require positive interdependence and individual accountability; and
- include clear criteria for the evaluation of the group's product and of the individual report.

OPEN-ENDED, UNCERTAIN TASKS

Educators describe as "open-ended" the kinds of tasks that social scientists call uncertain or ill-structured tasks (Qin, Johnson, & Johnson, 1995). When learning tasks are open-ended, students grapple with many uncertainties and ambiguities. Depending on their framing of the problem, students devise different plans, explore multiple paths, and often come up with legitimately different solutions, at times with no solution at all. When working on groupworthy tasks, students find ways to manage dilemmas and to solve authentic problems. Groupworthy tasks require that students describe and share their experiences, and express and justify their personal beliefs, values, and opinions. In such activities, students analyze, synthesize, and evaluate; they discuss cause and effect, explore controversial issues, design experiments and build models, strive toward consensus, and draw conclusions. Often, when seeking solutions to open-ended problems, members of the group need to articulate the conditions under which a solution becomes optimal, and therefore is the right solution for a particular group. Alternatively, group tasks might have one correct answer but multiple ways of arriving at the answer or representing the answer. By assigning open-ended tasks, teachers delegate *intellectual authority* to their students and thus make their students' life experiences, opinions, and points of view legitimate components of the content to be learned (Lotan, 1997).

Surprisingly for many teachers and students, a mathematical problem can have a number of legitimately right solutions. For example, a middle-grades unit that deals with area and perimeter poses the following question:

> We have three rather large tables with the following dimensions: 1.8 m long × 1 m wide × 0.75 m high. How many guests can we invite to a festive, sit-down dinner?

"It depends," seems to be the quickest and shortest answer. Before they can figure out their correct answer, the groups have to make some decisions: Will the tables be placed in one straight line, in a T-shape, or in a U-shape? How much elbow room (in centimeters) will be allowed for adult guests and how much for children? Some groups might come up with additional considerations: should there be a separate kids' table, for example? After intense deliberations, students can calculate the perimeter for the agreed-upon arrangement of the tables, divide by the allowed elbow room, and find the number of guests who will comfortably enjoy their dinner. Although each group comes up with a correct answer, chances are that the answer will vary from group to group, as the groups will probably come up with different preconditions (Lotan, 1997). Further work on groupworthy tasks in mathematics can be found in Featherstone, Crespo, Jilk, Oslund, Parks, and Woods (2011) and Horn (2012), two highly recommended resources.

Groupworthy tasks in science are radically different from cookbook-style lab activities. Rather than strict directions to prevent potential mistakes and designed to lead students to "discover" the right answer, groupworthy tasks allow students to engage in the practices of the discipline. Melissa Meloy, Liz Beans, and Adrian Cheng (2012), chemistry teachers and graduates of the Stanford Teacher Education Program, designed a task to introduce students to the concept of balancing chemical equations. Students were given two kinds of gummy bears: red gummy bears with two toothpicks and white gummy bears with three paperclips, also called "the Halloween arrangements." These arrangements were to be rearranged into sets of white gummy bears with six toothpicks and red gummy bears joined by two paperclips called "Thanksgiving arrangements." The rearrangements needed to result in a balanced chemical equation. The overall transformation can be written in the form of a balanced chemical equation as follows:

$$6 \, GrS_2 + 2 \, GwP_3 \rightarrow 2 \, GwS_6 + 3 \, Gr_2P_2.$$

Here is the teachers' analysis of how this task is open-ended:

While our task does not have multiple answers since there is only one correct numerical answer to what students need in order to complete the transformation from the Halloween to the Thanksgiving arrangement, our task has countless pathways to arrive at that answer. For example, students could mathematically attempt to calculate what they need prior to working with the gummis. However, the group could also immediately begin disassembling the gummis. Other groups may choose to begin construction right away and approach the problem of what parts are missing later. How the group chooses to disassemble and reassemble the gummis is also left to the group. For example, students could take everything apart, then begin to build Thanksgiving gummis, or they could convert from Halloween to Thanksgiving gummis one at a time. Unlike routine tasks, students are given a very specific task but with no guidelines of a particular process that they must use in order to complete the task. Rather, students must consult with each other to determine the most appropriate strategy for tackling the problem, and because each group has different strengths and needs, the most appropriate strategy will also be different. (Meloy et al., 2012, pp. 13–14)

The outcome of this task was very positive. The teachers reported that from the individual and group assessments they found

that a conceptual understanding of the task was shown from most students, even for the students [who struggle the most academically]. The transfer of content from a task that was not specifically chemistry related to concepts in chemistry did occur. A correlation existed between how groups scored on the participation rubric and their score on the poster rubric. The higher level of equitable participation resulted in a higher quality end product. (Meloy et al., 2012, p. 46)

Finding the delicate balance between uncertainty that is productive and sparks creativity and uncertainty that is debilitating and leads to insurmountable confusion is a challenge. Make sure you actually try to perform or respond to the task yourself or, if possible, pilot it with a group of students or colleagues.

MULTIPLE ENTRY POINTS AND DEMONSTRATIONS OF COMPETENCE

In addition to routine versus uncertain tasks, educators distinguish between unidimensional and multidimensional tasks. Unidimensional tasks are tasks that focus mainly on the development of traditional academic skills such as decoding text, filling in blanks, memorizing dates, and computing quickly. Such tasks are usually completed individually with paper and pencil, on computers, or with mobile devices. Because they require a narrow range of abilities and a limited array of skills, unidimensional tasks mostly result in uniform success for some students and uniform failure for others. Students are quick to conclude that some students are "smart" and others are "dumb." These perceptions have grave implications for creating a rigid status order in the classroom that has been shown to affect participation and learning as well as students' academic self-perception (Cohen, 1997; Rosenholtz & Simpson, 1984; Rosenholtz & Wilson, 1980).

In contrast, multidimensional tasks require many different cognitive abilities and social skills for their successful completion. Multidimensional, groupworthy tasks allow students to make significant contributions to the group effort and the group product by using their intellectual capacity and their diverse repertoire of problem-solving strategies. As they design experiments and build models, create murals and compose ballads, perform scenes from plays and interpret poems, or engage in authentic dialogue about topics that matter, more students have more opportunities to express intellectual competence and intellectual diversity. By crafting groupworthy tasks requiring multiple (intellectual) abilities, you set the stage for more students to demonstrate their "smarts."

As more students contribute to the group's efforts, you, the teacher, as well as their peers will be able to see and recognize them as intellectually competent. When you publicly recognize the student's intellectual competence and his important contributions to the group's success, you are addressing a status problem. As described in Chapter 10, such interventions contribute to changing the social system of the classroom and making it a more equitable place (Cohen & Lotan, 1995). Multidimensional, multiple-ability group tasks are a necessary condition for these interventions.

Groupworthy tasks rely on resources that incorporate and support multiple representations of the academic content of the task. Multiple representations of information support multiple forms of learning and the development of multiple literacies, which in turn lead to deeper and more sophisticated understandings (Eisner, 1994). Different resources and hands-on materials attract more students and entice them to participate, thus opening additional avenues to gain access to the learning task. Some students might be lured to the task and might respond more readily when using algebra rods, microscopes, and probes, or searching for information and resources on the web. Students who are still learning to read might be drawn to the task by examining and analyzing a photograph, a map, or a video clip. A graph, a matrix, a cartoon, or a diagram might provide crucial information that has traditionally been conveyed exclusively through the text related to the activity. Multidimensional tasks provide many opportunities for students who are still learning the language of instruction to access the task, participate actively in the work of the group, and demonstrate what they know and are able to do. Using real objects, manipulatives, or three-dimensional models helps language learners in attending to and supporting verbal information. Many students who are discouraged by traditional assignments show improvement not only in comprehension and analysis but also in some of the basic skills of reading and writing when given the opportunity to access and work on the task with different materials and in different ways. (See also DeAvila, 1981; Neves, 1983.)

Sarah Carlson and Ariana Dumplis (2012), history teachers and graduates of the Stanford Teacher Education Program, designed a groupworthy task for an 11th-grade U.S. history class. The project focused on the question "Was immigration worth it for the Chinese and Irish? Why or why not?" It invited students to engage with the historical materials in a nuanced manner by weighing the reasons for immigrating and the potential benefits against the potential hurtful experiences in the United States. The two teachers wrote:

The breadth of materials (pictures, poems, songs, cartoons, manifestos) provided multiple entry points for students and ways for students to use multiple abilities to complete the task. We designed the activity so that throughout the discussion and task students could show their smarts in a variety of ways: imagining life in different time, making detailed drawings, interpreting political cartoons, explaining ideas clearly, analyzing an issue from various perspectives, making connections between ideas, working with others to complete a task. . . . We also designed the task to ensure that students could demonstrate knowledge in two distinct ways, by creating a detailed drawing, and writing a short text to create a portrait of life in a different time. (pp. 3–4)

DISCIPLINE-BASED, INTELLECTUALLY
IMPORTANT CONTENT

Well-designed, groupworthy activities address a big idea, invoke a central disciplinary concept, or speak to an essential question. The Stanford Global Climate Change Curriculum (pangea.stanford.edu/programs/outreach/climatechange), developed by an interdisciplinary team of science teachers, educators, and climate scientists, is an example of a curriculum organized around central concepts and big ideas of climate science, an emerging discipline. One of the main goals of this curriculum is to provide middle school and high school students with opportunities to learn about climate change and global warming. It focuses not only on the content of the discipline—what we know about climate change—but also its epistemological basis, that is, how we know what we know. Students are introduced to the scientific phenomenon of climate change and its societal implications. They work with authentic data, use the discourse of science by examining evidence and scientific claims, discuss the scientific consensus surrounding these claims, and explore the benefits and costs of various mitigation and adaptation strategies.

The following descriptions and examples illustrate some of the activities included in this curriculum. Working in groups to understand the Earth's energy budget, students design and conduct a lab experiment to test the effect of carbon dioxide on the atmosphere's temperature. In another activity, students analyze the data showing the current and projected effects of climate change on both physical and biological systems. They examine global temperature data from 1880 to 2000. (See Figure 6.1.) After they work together to interpret the graph, they use these data to make a claim supported by evidence. In another activity, students examine the evidence for glacier thinning around the world. Students analyze and interpret the data to answer the following questions: Based on the graphs, what claim (conclusion) can you make about the impact of climate change? What is your evidence for this claim?

The curriculum unit concludes with a performance task that asks students to examine and propose mitigation strategies to reduce carbon dioxide emissions in their communities and globally. Studies have documented the positive outcomes of implementation of this curriculum in middle schools and high schools. Researchers consistently found that classrooms with higher levels of student interactions had higher

Figure 6.1. Global Ocean and Atmospheric Temperature

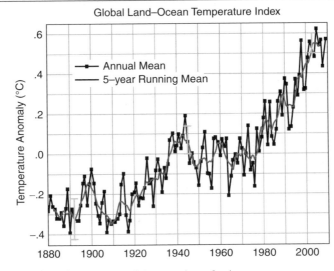

Source: http://data.giss.nasa.gov/gistemp/graphs/

achievement gains on curriculum-specific pre- and post- assessments (Holthuis, Lotan, Saltzman, Mastrandrea, & Wild, in press).

POSITIVE INTERDEPENDENCE AND INDIVIDUAL ACCOUNTABILITY

By definition, groupworthy tasks create and support interdependence among members of a group. Proponents of cooperative learning agree that positive interdependence is the essence of collaboration (Johnson, Johnson, & Holubec, 1998). When your students work on a well-defined, concrete group product, they become interdependent. Furthermore, when you are able to generate a sense of urgency for finishing the task on time, and when you insist that they create a quality product and prepare a concise and thoughtful report, students will increasingly rely on one another to understand and complete the task.

Although interdependence is built into rich groupworthy tasks, holding each student personally accountable for contributing to the group's success and for mastering the concepts embedded in the activity is essential. Although often overlooked or forgotten, written reports completed individually after a group activity can ensure such accountability. Furthermore, when students work on a concrete product and have access to quality conversations about the ideas that lead to that product, they develop their mastery of the content and are able to write about the ideas embedded in them. Cohen, Lotan, Abram, Scarloss, and Schultz (2002) found that the quality of the group discussion and of the group product predicts average group performance on final written assignments.

EVALUATION CRITERIA FOR GROUP PRODUCT AND INDIVIDUAL REPORT

Thinking about the ideas about assessment for and of learning put forth in the previous chapter, how will you assess the quality of the group product? As mentioned before, we found that providing students with specific criteria as to what makes an exemplary group product will improve the quality of the group interaction as well as the quality of the group product (Abram et al., 2002). When students exchange ideas, self-assess as a group and as individuals, and assess the work of their peers, the quality of the group product is enhanced. Scarloss (2001) documented the relationship between students' enhanced interactions and sensemaking, stronger-quality group products, and ultimately higher-quality final unit essays written individually. In other words, more and deeper discussions predict better group products, and for students in these more interactive and more productive groups, stronger performance on individual assignments.

Evaluation criteria provide specific guidelines as to what makes a good product. By including evaluation criteria on the task card and on the individual reports, you are giving students a clear idea of what they will be evaluated on and how they should evaluate their own efforts. Evaluation criteria are specific to the task but do not take away or limit its open-endedness. They reflect the use of multiple abilities and reinforce the use of the multiple-ability curricular materials. The criteria also draw the students' attention to the connection between the activity and the big idea or the central concept.

For example, in one of the 6th-grade social studies units designed for the Program for Complex Instruction, students study the ancient Egyptian belief system regarding the afterlife. One of the activities of the unit focuses on a ceremony called "the weighing of the heart." After reading about and discussing the ceremony and its symbolic meanings, the activity directs students to develop a skit depicting the journey into the afterlife and the weighing of the heart ceremony. Evoking important gods and deities, the students are asked to discuss some of the virtues and some of the sins of the deceased believed to determine whether he would pass into the afterlife.

The evaluation criteria for the skit are as follows:

- Skit includes at least 2 sins, 2 virtues, and 1 spell.
- Skit gives good reasons for whether or not the deceased entered the afterlife.
- Skit is well rehearsed and believable.

INSTRUCTIONS TO THE GROUP TASK

Much of the burden of explaining what students are supposed to do are placed on written instructions in the form of activity cards or task cards for all but the youngest children. Being able to refer to written instructions, after hearing the main ideas in your orientation, allows the group to figure out what to do for themselves. The task card is a physical representation of your delegation of authority to the group. It conveys to the students the message that a task, a problem, or a dilemma has been assigned to which they need to come up with a response.

Crafting the task cards requires a delicate balance. On the one hand, task cards need to be clear enough and include sufficient detail so the group can proceed without your assistance. On the other hand, the task needs to be open-ended and uncertain enough to generate rich conversations. The solution to the problem posed to students cannot be immediately obvious. By declining to give a quick answer to requests for help from the group and by encouraging them to solve some of the problems, you can help students learn that they have the capacity to deal with uncertainty for themselves.

The most common error in writing instructions is to provide too much detail, as if teachers were instructing an individual on how to carry out a technical task step by step. This approach, designed to provide as much certainty as possible, has a numbing effect on group discussion because there is little left to discuss. Needless confusion also comes from adding too much text or too many alternative ways of explaining things. You want to pose questions for students that will stimulate them to discuss, to experiment, to discover, to use trial and error, and to develop solutions for themselves. Often task cards that have too much text or too many directions that involve the minutiae of the process rather than substantive questions overwhelm the students. Even the youngest students rise to the challenge. Don't hesitate to use big, interesting words; as long as someone in the group can read them and as long as someone knows what they mean or can look them up, the group can function very well. An excellent example of instructions with just the right level of productive uncertainty is taken from the Measurement Unit of the *Finding Out/Descubrimiento* curriculum (De Avila & Duncan, 1980). One of the activity cards accompanies an inflatable model of a stegosaurus, a string, and a metric ruler. It says: "Measure the waist of the dinosaur." The 1st- or 2nd-graders are left to imagine where the waist of the beast might be as they figure out that the only way to measure is to put a string around the "waist" and hold it up to the ruler.

In working with older students who can handle more written information, curriculum units for complex instruction often have a couple of resource cards or references to specific websites in addition to the activity card. For example, in a unit on the visual system, students are instructed to build a better eye that will have superior capacities to that of the human eye. They are to prepare a presentation to a potential developer of this eye, describing its advantages and special features. On the resource card is information about the eyes of animals and humans that may prove useful. The resource card, however, does not contain the answer to questions posed on the activity card. Otherwise the resource card will remove all the productive uncertainty from the task.

Other kinds of uncertainty are unproductive for the learners. Suppose that you have not made clear that you expect the group to prepare a presentation for the class. This lack of clarity in your instructions will lead to a serious misfiring of your plans. The criteria for some of the more common group products (e.g., a poster, a skit, a presentation, a visual) can include some standardized elements accompanied with specific criteria for the particular activity. However, avoid micromanaging the presentation through the task card.

Figure 6.2. Curriculum Components

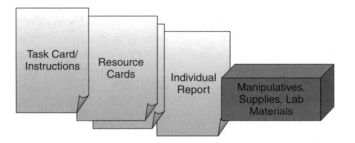

Students, particularly younger ones, will be fascinated by the resources and the manipulatives provided with the task. Figure 6.2 represents the different parts of a groupworthy task. Acknowledging this fact, you need to remind them that reading and understanding the instruction before plunging into the task will be most useful. Supply one or at most two sets of instructions; if there is one for everyone, students will try to read silently and there will be no discussion.

The task card, resource card, and individual report shown in Figure 6.3 are from a unit called "Discovering Poetry." Developed at the Program for Complex Instruction, the activities of this unit focus on the power and effects of poetic devices. As the students read, explain, interpret, and analyze the different poems, they become familiar with some fundamentals of poetry: sound, rhythm, and repetition; metaphors and similes; visual patterns.

A NOTE ABOUT TIME

The rationale provided for the design features as well as the examples described have implications for teachers' work. It is evident that the design and implementation of such tasks require considerable expertise and significant investment of time and effort. Groups of teachers who teach similar subjects and/or similar grade levels need to work together collegially to create groupworthy tasks—a groupworthy task in itself. Teachers can also use the design features as criteria for analyzing and evaluating published curricula and learning

Figure 6.3. Poetry Unit: Task Card, Resource Card, and Individual Report

Unit: Discovering Poetry

Discovering Poetry

Metaphors and Similes
Task Card

Read Hughes' poem, *Dream Deferred* and discuss the following questions:

- Hughes selects vivid images to create his similes and metaphors. What senses does he appeal to? What are some of the feelings you get from the images?

- What is the difference between a **simile** and a **metaphor**? Which images use similes and which use metaphors? W[...] feel?

- What kinds of dreams might Hughes be r[...]

As a group, create a collage or a mobile that illus[...] *Dream Deferred*. Use different shapes, images, c[...] inspired by the poem. Be ready to explain your c[...]

Evaluation Criteria for Group Project:
- The collage/mobile uses **at least** four different shapes
- Explanation includes a description of how each of the collage/mobile relate to the poem.

©Program for Complex Instruction/ Stanford University

Unit: Discovering Poetry

Discovering Poetry

Metaphors and Similes
Individual Report

Dream Deferred

What happens to a dream deferred?

Does it dry up
like a raisin in the sun?
Or fester like a sore—
and then run?

[...]Hughes (American, 1902-1967)

[...]m Deferred which images use similes, which use [...]s make you feel?

[...]rt:
[...]similes and one of metaphors, and describes the feelings

[...]mplete sentences.

[...]ord University

Unit: Discovering Poetry

Discovering Poetry

Metaphors and Similes
Poetry Card

Dream Deferred

What happens to a dream deferred?

Does it dry up
like a raisin in the sun?
Or fester like a sore—
and then run?
Does it stink like rotten meat?
Or crust and sugar over—
like a syrupy sweet?

Maybe it just sags
like a heavy load.

Or does it explode?

Langston Hughes (American, 1902-1967)

©Program for Complex Instruction/ Stanford University

tasks proposed for groupwork. Working together to craft groupworthy tasks has the potential of being a powerful professional learning activity for teachers interested in expanding and strengthening their repertoire of pedagogical strategies for their academically and linguistically heterogeneous classrooms.

7 Groupwork and Language Development

Rachel A. Lotan

In this chapter, the emphasis on language serves to remind you that developing students' oral and written proficiency in the language(s) of the classroom is part of maintaining equitable interactions. The introduction of new standards and new assessments with challenging language and literacy demands makes engaging in meaningful discourse and producing high-quality written work necessary for student learning. For students who are still in the process of learning the language of instruction, doing so is imperative.

What will your students know and be able to do using the language or languages of instruction as an outcome of their work in groups? What do students need to know and be able to do academically and linguistically in order to access the group task and to participate actively in small groups and in whole-class settings? How will students demonstrate what they have learned and what they have accomplished? How will you develop their capacity and skills in *listening*, *speaking*, *reading*, and *writing*? As introduced in Chapter 5, these questions guide the planning, implementation, and evaluation of groupwork in your classroom.

PERSPECTIVES ON LANGUAGE IN EQUITABLE CLASSROOMS

Like the range of academic achievement or the skill level of your students, their oral and written language proficiency is a dimension of classroom heterogeneity. As an outcome of officially administered language tests, some of your students might be formally classified as English learners. They might find it difficult to express their mathematical thinking orally or in writing using conventional mathematical discourse, although they have solved the problem correctly. Others, while seemingly fluent speakers, still need to build up their skills and productive uses of classroom language. Some students are native speakers of English, yet perform below grade level in reading and writing. A good number of students, some of them bilingual or multilingual, have met the content standards associated with your assignments. Your goal is to ensure that all students, irrespective of their academic achievement and their still-developing linguistic proficiency, gain access to the learning task, can participate actively, and will be able to demonstrate what they have learned. You recognize that students can serve as academic as well as linguistic resources for one another. You decide to use groupwork.

First, consider the following: Students in your classroom are appropriately competent speakers of the language and its varieties spoken in their homes and communities. They use the dialects, registers, accents, and cultural signifiers with which they are familiar. They connect, they communicate, they express their thoughts and their feelings, they describe their interests, and they voice their needs. They have language. They act with language.

Your responsibility is to expand and to deepen your students' linguistic repertoire so that they can use language to communicate effectively with a number of different audiences for different purposes. (See also Valdés, Bunch, Snow, & Lee, 2005.) You do so by modeling and explicitly describing the forms and functions of language used in academic settings and content areas. You use appropriate vocabulary and make the "big words" accessible to students with colloquial, everyday expressions and explanations. You listen attentively and acknowledge students' developing understandings, even if they are not initially using technical or "academic" vocabulary. You provide feedback and reflect with your students on the language practices of the classroom and of the subject you teach. You design an environment and learning tasks in which students use language purposefully and unrelentingly. They *listen* to instructions and explanations; they *speak* to ask questions and justify their conclusions. They collaborate with others to gather, evaluate, and communicate information. They *read* and interpret complex texts. They *write* cogent responses to prompts and demonstrate their thinking through literary essays and scientific reports. As such, all students are perennial learners of the subject matter and of the language of the classroom.

Second, consider your perspective on language in general and language in the classroom in particular. Viewing language only as a vocabulary list, a system of grammar rules, and pragmatic conventions limits effective teaching in academically and linguistically heterogeneous classrooms. It distracts from noticing what students are learning and doing well. Your students' use of language depends upon and indicates active engagement as learning and constructing understanding occur through interaction with peers, with adults, with text, and with real objects. Because learning is a social activity, language is a venue for accessing content, a tool for participating vigorously, and a resource that mediates oral or written performance. Thus, during groupwork, focus more intensely on meaning than grammatical correctness.

Researchers agree that learners acquire language when they are exposed to language-rich environments where they can actively engage in authentic conversations and negotiations with adults and with peers who are native or native-like speakers of the language (Valdés, 2011). The quality and the quantity of the language students hear and read influences the kind of language acquired and the speed with which it is acquired. In addition to such language input, learners need multiple and different opportunities for meaningful output, that is, speaking and writing. Like many other scholars, Cazden (2001) suggests that the optimal environment for language learning might be one in which students engage in problem solving and interdependent tasks, where they manipulate real objects and talk about them. Gibbons (2002) extols the benefits of varied participation structures, including groupwork, for language learning and development. You create such an environment as your students work in small groups engaged in groupworthy tasks.

Bunch (2013) proposes that teachers could benefit from "*pedagogical language knowledge* that is integrally tied to the teaching of the core subject area(s) for which they are responsible" (p. 299) rather than knowledge about language as expected of second-language teachers. Recently, the importance of such pedagogical knowledge, skills, and practices has been recognized in the newly developed and widely adopted teacher performance assessments required for initial licensure. In these assessments of their teaching, candidates are asked to identify and support the language demands of the learning activities and also to analyze students' language use as they develop understanding of the subject-matter content. (See edtpa.aacte.org/ and pacttpa.org.)

For open-source resources that support language development and learning in the content areas, see ell.stanford.edu.

As they work in groups on tasks that promote learning, students use language that is both colloquial and formal. Some features of this language are common for most subject areas; others are discipline-specific features. For example, Lee, Quinn, and Valdés (2013) identify key features of the language of the science classroom related to the science and engineering practices put forth in the Next Generation Science Standards (NGSS Lead States, 2013). The teacher uses language as she explains and presents to the whole class and communicates with small groups of students, individual students, and parents by using both colloquial and disciplinary language and terms. She does so when she gives instructions, checks for understanding, facilitates discussions, describes models, and evaluates students' responses. In science classrooms, like their teachers, students act with language to describe, explain, propose ideas, or construct an argument based on evidence. They listen to and comprehend questions and explanations offered by others and by texts, ask for clarification, communicate their ideas orally and in writing, and respond to critiques and critique explanations of others. Because we *act* with language, using verbs to emphasize the practices as well as the discourse of the discipline clarifies to students what they can learn, do, hone, and, in due course, demonstrate successfully.

The key practices associated with the Common Core State Standards (National Governors Association Center for Best Practices & Council of Chief State School Officers, 2010a) for mathematics and the language needed to perform the tasks associated with them are closely related to those just described. These practices include modeling with mathematics, reasoning abstractly and qualitatively, and, as in science and engineering, responding to critiques and critiquing explanations of others. Like in science classrooms, in mathematics classrooms the teacher gives directions, checks for understanding, guides processes, presents to the whole class, facilitates small groups, and guides individual students. Students participate in discussions, make sense of word problems, and describe their reasoning. Working in small groups increases the frequency with which students engage in these practices, as well as the quality and the depth of such engagement. Working in groups also poses significant cognitive, linguistic, and social demands. Identifying the language demands associated with the development of these practices in the context of working with peers is an initial task for the teacher. Along with the demands, working in groups also offers inviting opportunities and affordances (Greeno, 1994; Van Lier, 2000) that, when acted upon, further develop language and deepen academically rigorous content. In the rest of this chapter, I will describe examples of what students do linguistically to be successful academically.

LANGUAGE DEMANDS AND AFFORDANCES IN GROUPWORK

What do students need to do with language to understand instructions, to figure out the flow of the activities before, during, and after working in groups? How does working in groups provide opportunities to *listen, read, speak,* and *write*? How do students negotiate the floor, how do they gain and maintain airtime? How to they clarify their thinking? How do they ask for more information? How do they report on the group's work? How will they demonstrate their smarts and their accomplishments?

What activities do students engage in as they *listen, speak, read,* and *write* to

- access the learning task,
- participate in the work of the group, and
- demonstrate what they have accomplished?

Access to the Learning Task

To engage in the academic demands of the learning task, students need to *listen* to and *comprehend* the teacher's instructions. Sadly, one of the main reasons for limited student engagement is difficulty in understanding instructions to the task. During groupwork, as group members *read* and discuss the task card collectively, they clarify information, repeat instructions, restate the questions and prompts for discussion, translate, and organize the information in various ways. As students listen, these additional sources of language input and the shared responsibility for reading the task card and the resources increase the likelihood of understanding what they are supposed to do.

Structurally, a greater proportion of students have opportunities to *speak* during groupwork as compared to whole-class settings where, legitimately, only one student speaks at a time. More students have opportunities to ask clarifying questions or seek further explanations. They can ask for definitions of new vocabulary words or idiomatic expressions and practice using them in the context of grappling intellectually and linguistically with the task. You can model and encourage students to say:

- Can you explain it again?. . . . Please repeat what you just said. . . .
- I have a question about what (you/the teacher/Tim) just said.
- I don't know what X means. Let's look it up. . . .

Paraphrasing and summarizing are additional ways in which students can confirm that they understand the task or what their peers are saying.

- I hear you saying that. . . . Do I have that right? Is that correct?
- In other words, we have to. . . and then we will. . . .
- Did you mean to say. . . ?

In addition, students might take notes as they *listen* or *read* the instructions. They can *write* a summary of the main points addressed in the clarifying discussion.

Participation in Group Interactions

Physical proximity, eye-to-eye contact, and a sense of familiarity facilitate *listening* and *speaking*. A convenient ratio of conversation partners lowers the affective filter (Krashen, 1985), the mental block that inhibits language production in stressful situations such as being called upon unexpectedly or sitting for high-stakes tests. Following well-established discussion norms and assurances from the teacher that mistakes are expected and respected reduces anxiety and creates a comfortable level of physical and intellectual safety. While engaged in groupwork, students serve as academic and linguistic resources for one another. These affordances boost rates of speaking, participating, and contributing.

Language and Group Roles. Language functions such as giving directions, monitoring participation of others, and providing feedback are associated with the various group roles and provide opportunities for students to practice and develop their linguistic proficiency. You can introduce and solidify grammatically appropriate forms through sentence starters and sentence frames. These are particularly beneficial as English language learners take on specific group roles. For example, the facilitator says:

- Who will read the directions?
- Does everyone understand what we need to discuss and do?
- How much time do we need for each part of the task? What else do we have to do?
- Let's get back to work! . . . We have ___ minutes left to finish up.
- What's the question for the teacher? Can we answer it for ourselves?

The resource manager can say:

- What other sources of information do we need?
- Which words should I look up?
- Here is the definition of . . . .
- What else do we need to complete this assignment?

As described in Chapter 8, the reporter organizes the group's report. The reporter can prompt the group's thinking by asking:

- What is our final product supposed to be?
- What do we want to show in our report? What do we want to say?
- How shall we present it to the class? I will take notes.
- What is the big idea/essential question for this activity?
- How are we addressing the big idea/essential question/ discussion questions in our report?
- How are we putting it all together?

The role of the reporter might be particularly challenging, even intimidating, for students who have limited proficiency in the language of the classroom. However, as students come to realize that the report is the responsibility of the group rather than of the reporter alone, they will be willing and ready to contribute to the language of the report as they do to its content. As the group rehearses the report under the guidance of the reporter, additional opportunities for language development arise. Students move from the often informal, less precise interpersonal talk as they work on the task to more formal, presentational language as they prepare the report. In his analysis of students' talk during groupwork, Bunch (2006, 2009, 2014) distinguishes between the *language of ideas* and the *language of display* to show how students use different modes of communication and address different audiences during groupwork. Often, the reporter *writes* down the main points of the collaboratively drafted report or even prepares a paragraph or two to be *read* to the class. Preparing a high-quality report is more than using new vocabulary and grammatically appropriate sentence structures. It offers potentially fruitful opportunities for students to plan for and practice the academic discourse characteristic of formal presentations. Most important, for students who are learners of the language, such public demonstration of growth in their ability to *speak*, *read*, and *write* can and should be recognized by the teacher and used as a perfect opportunity to recognize their intellectual competence and contributions. (See Chapter 10.)

Language in Group Interaction. Beyond the language used as they perform the different group roles, groupwork is a particularly appropriate setting for developing the language of group interaction. Teachers often ask students to use specific language as they

- explain why or how by using logical connectors (because, consequently, as a result of), temporal (first, second, then, next), or comparative ones (more . . . less, rather, instead, also);
- connect reasons with what needs to be explained or to evidence (As a result of . . . ; This is why . . . ; As a consequence of . . . ; One reason for . . . is; another reason is . . . ; This argument is supported by/is based on . . . ; We know this because . . . ; When we look at . . . , we can see that . . .);
- respond analytically to complex texts and ideas (By saying . . . , the author implies that . . . ; The protagonist felt . . . , because he . . . ; The story ended abruptly, consequently . . .); and
- persuade (There is little doubt that . . . , therefore we need to . . . ; Let's improve our report by including more detail. . . .).

Other examples of important language frames for active group participation are:

- acknowledging other group members' ideas: My ideas are similar to . . . ; I agree with . . . and would like to add . . . ;
- offering a suggestion: Maybe we could . . . ; What if we . . . ; We could try . . . ; and
- disagreeing: I don't agree because . . . ; I see your point and I think . . .

Examine the disciplinary practices recommended in the core curriculum standards and list the language demands associated with those practices. For example, what language will students use to describe a model in science, identify bias in a historical source or give reasons for a particular position or point of view, communicate their reasoning while solving a word problem in mathematics, or interpret and explain an author's use of figurative language of poetic imagery? As you make the list, be sure to model the language in the classroom and explicitly draw students' attention to the ways you use it in different contexts.

Holthuis, Lotan, Saltzman, Mastrandrea, and Wild (in press) describe how the teachers who participated in the NASA-sponsored Global Climate Change project identified the elements of a well-constructed scientific argument and modeled using evidence to make a specific and coherent claim. The following transcript documents Teacher L's discussion of a graph that shows the rise in the level of carbon dioxide (CO_2) over time. She models how to use evidence and engages with the student about the elements of a claim:

T: What is the evidence for the change in climate that we see here?
S: CO_2 has increased.
T: (Referring to the Y-axis) This is temperature.
S: Oh, temperature.
T: Average annual temperature has increased. How much?
S: Point 8.
T: 0.8 degrees C. Over the period of when?
S: (Inaudible)

T: 1880 to 2000. So that is a good statement of evidence, right? So I've said what my graph shows, I've talked about what the trend is, I've said how much the trend has covered, and I've told you what years I was looking at. So, when [you] present evidence, that's the kind of statement that I'm looking for. I want a very concrete statement that has all of those pieces, if possible.

In another exchange, the teacher pushes her students toward greater specificity and clarity:

T: What claim do you guys make?
S1: Over here the events are increasing.
T: Are they increasing equally in all parts of the globe?
S2: Yes. Oh, not equally, but all increasing.
T: So, what areas seem to be more affected? (Brief silence.) So you guys aren't making a claim, you're making a generalization . . . so, a claim should be more specific. So looking at that, you need to have a more specific statement . . . if you weren't presented with this information, what statement could you make about this to base that . . . ?
S2: More extreme . . .
S1: More populated areas.
S2: More populated western areas.

Demonstrating Intellectual Competence and Growth

Increased rates of interaction with peers are excellent opportunities to recognize students' intellectual and academic growth and enhanced competence to use the language of the classroom. Those who *listen* come to appreciate the contributions of those on whom they rely to complete the learning task. Those who *speak* give voice to their ideas and opinions. Hearing others read the task card and discussing the resources after someone read them enhance the reading skills of developing readers and language learners. When language learners attempt to *read* in small-group settings, their progress is recognized by peers. Often the group's discussion and work on the group product serves as a scaffold for *writing* the individual report or the final unit essay.

During groupwork, you can hear students describe their thinking:

- I/we found that . . . ; I/we discovered that . . .
- Lisa agreed with me that . . . ; My idea is similar to X's . . .
- I imagine/estimate/guess/hypothesize/predict that . . .
- In my/our opinion . . .

When completing individual reports or final unit essays, students provide convincing reasons, they appeal to the thoughts and the emotions of an imaginary or real audience, and they argue for or against a position. The following are the writing prompt and excerpts from a two-and-a-half-page final unit essay of a 7th-grade student identified as "limited English proficient" at her school.

Prompt:

Challenging the Authority of Institutions: The Reformation—Final Essay

You have just finished studying the Reformation. By participating in group discussions, preparing your products, and making your presentations to the class, you learned about the ways individuals and groups challenged the authority of institutions. People living during the reformation used new art forms, emerging technologies, and personal and collective appeals to persuade individuals in positions of power to make changes. Write an essay in which you try to persuade members of your family either to join or to oppose Martin Luther and his supporters in their campaign against the church. You may use your individual reports to help you write the essay.

Excerpts

We need to challenge the authority of the church. Now, we might be at risk of getting excommunicated from the church because we're challenging the church but the Pope is wrong and Martin is right. I believe that we should follow him because the sale of indulgences are (sic) wrong, tithing is totally unfair, and because of the way us peasants are being treated.

I think the sale of indulgences are (sic) wrong. We shouldn't pay for forgiveness. God is the only one who can forgive us. Martin Luther said that [quote from Martin Luther's text]. . . . He also said that [quote] . . . So you see, I agree with Martin Luther about indulgences.

Secondly, I believe tithing is totally unfair! The Bible plainly says that the money should be given to God and passed on to his own. I mean, the priests, the Pope and the church are the wealthy and rich ones in town, while we peasants are poor and living in smelly old shacks. . . . So, as I conclude from this, the money from tithing should go to God and passed on to his own, and the remainders should be given to the poor.

Lastly, the peasant's (sic) aren't being treated right. Many of them are discontented with poverty because they are poor. They should be able to hunt, fish, own their own land, cut their own wood and they should have freedom. . . .

We should follow Martin Luther because he is right. We should follow him because of the following reasons: Indulgences are wrong, tithing is unfair, and because the peasants are being treated badly. So, my family, we need to follow Martin Luther, and we need to challenge the institution and the authority of the church. (6/18/0; Period 4)

The student wrote persuasively, passionately, and courageously. The teacher recognized the student's strong statement of a position on the issue and the evidence provided to support that position. The student concluded with a well-grounded appeal to the family. She demonstrated effective organization following a five-paragraph structure. She shows overall strong mastery of the mechanics of writing.

In a study conducted at Gerona Middle School in California's central valley, Bunch and Willett (2013) describe and analyze in great detail how groupwork, and in particular complex instruction (Cohen & Lotan, 1997a), provided opportunities for students to make sense of the academic and linguistic demands of their school work, and develop their writing skills to demonstrate their ability as "productive makers of meaning" (Bunch & Willett, 2013, p. 158). Importantly, teachers can learn to recognize this kind of meaning making in student writing, even when students are still in the process of developing English. Based on a study in the same setting, Bunch, Lotan, Valdés, and Cohen (2005) describe the kinds of supports provided to the students as they negotiate the intellectually challenging and academically rigorous curriculum. In addition to textual support for struggling readers and writers in the form of notations in the margins of the text on the resource cards, multiple drafts and revisions, and consultations with peers and with the teacher, teachers made the essential features of an academic explanation and persuasion explicit (Figure 7.1).

Figure 7.1. Persuading (While Speaking OR Writing)

To *persuade* is to state a position and attempt to get others to agree. When we *persuade*, we

- Take into consideration the beliefs and opinions of our audience.
- Include sufficient support for our opinions.
- Respond to the "other side" of the argument.

To *persuade* effectively, we use the following techniques:

- Providing reasons for our argument
- Stating facts
- Giving examples
- Appealing to the emotions of the audience
- Presenting the argument against our position and pointing out the weaknesses of that argument

---

After an analysis of a model essay, the teachers led the class as a whole in writing a sample introductory paragraph, and introduced sentence starters. As the year progressed, these supports were gradually reduced so that by the final unit, students were writing their own text, assisted by marginal guidelines and rubrics.

Because groupwork enhances academic achievement and language development, you will find that all students and especially language learners experience more instances of academic success. As explained in Chapter 10, recognizing language learners' intellectual competence, rather than magnifying their limitations in using the language of the classroom, will contribute greatly to furthering equal-status interactions in the small groups. It will make your classroom a more equitable place.

Language Development and Mastery of Subject-Matter Content

Arellano (2003) conducted a study investigating the processes by which bilingual students acquired academic English and learned social studies content in a classroom using complex instruction. She found that the students she observed showed significant growth in the knowledge about the social studies content they studied as measured by gain scores on multiple-choice unit tests, and in the oral and written language skills in English they needed to demonstrate that knowledge. In her analysis of student talk during small-group interactions, Arellano found that, over time, English learners increased their use of complex language functions such as explanations and justification. As they practiced making presentations, these students developed discourse strategies that made their language more explicit and increasingly appropriate for formal audiences. In examining the written products, Arellano found significant growth in their writing ability both as they completed their individual reports and as they composed the final unit essays. The students focused on central ideas, included supporting details and evidence, and showed development in their use of organizational patterns of the essays. In her final discussion, Arellano emphasized the crucial role of the teacher in creating a classroom environment where she was able to challenge her students cognitively and linguistically.

In her study, Swanson (2010) describes the use of groupwork, groupworthy tasks, and a focus on developing writing to support middle-grade students both mathematically and linguistically as they grapple with the concept of integers while writing integer story problems. By using manipulatives, images, posters, and word walls, students built conceptual understanding of mathematical concepts such as positive, negative, sign, operation, and opposite and developed their ability to engage in mathematical discourse orally and in writing.

To examine the conditions under which students accomplish the dual goal of developing language proficiency and mastering subject-matter content, researchers at the Program for Complex Instruction at Stanford collaborated with a team of 7th- and 8th-grade teachers from Gerona Middle School in California's central valley and supported them in the use of complex instruction in their linguistically and academically heterogeneous mainstream classrooms (Lotan, 2008). We found that there were significant learning gains in both content knowledge and use of English for academic purposes by students in all four language proficiency designations: English-Only speakers, Redesignated Fluent English Proficient, Limited English Proficient, and Transitional. For all four units of the social studies curriculum, the average end-of-unit posttest scores were significantly higher than the average pretest scores for the sample as a whole, as well as for the students in the four different language designation groups. Analyses of the final unit essays showed that students understood the "big idea" of the unit, mastered the content, and used persuasive strategies and disciplinary discourse to communicate in English about their academic tasks.

A significant finding of this study made the connection between the level and quality of student interactions during small-group work and students' performances in English at both the individual and at the group levels. Our detailed classroom observations documented sustained and consequential interaction related to the content of the groupworthy tasks. Students engaged in "social studies talk," learned and used vocabulary and specific terms of art related to the discipline, and rehearsed and practiced reports using presentational language. The interaction in the groups served as the bridge from oral to written language as students were preparing their individual reports as well as their group presentations. We found that the proportion of presentational talk in the small group was a predictor of the student's use of persuasive strategies in their individual end-of-unit essays. Furthermore, on the average, the number of individual reports completed by each student was related to all individual achievement measures.

Providing students with opportunities for language development and age-appropriate, intellectually challenging content is a primary concern for teachers, policymakers, and scholars interested in equitable educational outcomes. Although still a timely and highly contested political issue, this chapter suggests that reaching that goal requires a comprehensive approach to changing the educational experiences of students in academically and linguistically heterogeneous classrooms. (See also Michaels, O'Connor, & Resnick, 2008.) Intellectually challenging, age- and grade-appropriate curricula and meaningful assessments, language-rich and content-rich classroom environments, and equal-status participation in small groups and in wholeclass contexts are necessary conditions. Your careful planning of the curriculum and thoughtful orchestration of the social system of the classroom can equip all students to participate in academically and linguistically productive and equitable interactions.

8 Group Roles and Responsibilities

Here are two illustrations of groupwork in which students have different responsibilities for managing the work of the group. The first is a group of five 4th-grade students from an academically and ethnically heterogeneous classroom using complex instruction, a structured approach to groupwork. The facilitator is reading the activity card with instructions on growing a salt crystal garden.

> *Facilitator:* What kind of changes do you see? Write what kinds of changes you see on your worksheet. If the base dries up, add 2 tsp. of water and 1 tsp. of ammonia. OK? Do you understand what we are supposed to do? [The group members smile and nod. The facilitator places the activity card face down.] OK. What is the name of the center? [Group laughs. Several members raise their hand, and the facilitator recognizes one girl.]
>
> *Girl:* Salt Crystal Garden?
>
> *Facilitator:* You got it. [Puts card back in plastic box and directs the materials manager to hand out materials. The manager lays out the materials and hands out role badges to the facilitator, the person in charge of clean-up, and the checker who checks to see if all the worksheets are done.]
>
> *Materials Manager:* Who is the reporter?
>
> *Reporter:* I am. [He takes the role badge offered by the materials manager. The group spends about 5 minutes looking at the pictures on the activity card and working with the materials.] Hey you guys, before you begin, I have to write down the answers to this question on the reporter worksheet: What do you predict will happen in this science experiment? And don't just tell me what you predict. I have to write down why

you made this prediction. [The group, hesitantly at first but more excitedly as they go on, begins to talk about how they think salt crystals will form, just like in the picture.]

The second illustration is from the written report of a team of beginning high school teachers. One of the pair worked as the teacher and the other functioned as observer. The observer is reporting on Mike Leonard's geometry class.

This is a casual and friendly group of students who appear to relate well to each other and to their teacher. Mr. Leonard begins the lecture with a short review of last night's homework. This work covers skills needed in today's groupwork. He uses an overhead projector; the class has many questions. Mr. Leonard then goes over the assignment. Each member has at least one equation of a line for which he or she must find three ordered pairs in the relation, draw the graph of the relations, find the slope of the graph and find the y intercept of the graph. The group has the responsibility of writing an explanation of the y = ? Mr. Leonard has placed graph paper and a straight edge on each desk before class.

He now reads and explains information written on the board. This includes a list of behaviors expected in the role of facilitator: (1) makes sure everyone participates; (2) makes sure task is completed in 20 minutes; (3) gets help from teacher if entire group cannot answer a question.

The groups have been prearranged so that students already know their group and their location. The facilitator's role is a rotating one; and today's facilitators are given tags to indicate their special function. One person has the role of grapher who must graph all equations on one set of axes and label them neatly.

Next, Mr. Leonard asks the students to get into their groups and begin work. It is apparent that he has trained his students well beforehand because it takes less than a minute for all the students to be in groups and involved in the task. Once in their group, certain students are still unclear as to what the task involves, but other members explain it to them. All the students certainly seem to be engaged in their work. Even those that Mr. Leonard has described as "academically weak" seem involved and active. Some students need help in understanding how to find ordered pairs and in graphing lines; they receive explanations from other members of the group. The facilitators start out by leading, but as time goes by the other students are doing as much directing and "facilitating" as the person assigned to that role.

The students begin by clarifying the task among themselves and by choosing someone to play the role of the grapher; they then move into their separate tasks, working out their lines and points. The graphers are interested in pushing everyone to complete and pass the graphs on to them so that they can finish their job. In the last phase, the collective group discusses an explanation, while the graphers produce their summary graph. The assignment is done in twenty minutes. Mr. Leonard now puts up on the board the graphs from the groups—all are correct. He writes the equations on the board and proceeds to ask questions. Interestingly, several groups are able to give variations on the correct answers. This takes ten minutes, and there are still five minutes left to hand out a review sheet for the test tomorrow and an evaluation questionnaire on the groupwork. (Kinney & Leonard, 1984, pp. 9–12)

EFFICIENT AND EFFECTIVE GROUPS

How do the groups in the previous two illustrations avoid problems of nonparticipation and interpersonal difficulty? The secret of their success lies partly in their teachers' thoughtful planning and preparation and partly in the way members have something specific to do. When each person's job is given a name and is accompanied by a list of expected behaviors, group members have been "assigned specific roles to play." Members feel very satisfied with their part in the group process in groups with different roles and/or jobs to do; such groups can work efficiently, smoothly, and productively. The use of roles alleviates problems of nonparticipation or domination by one member. Roles, like cooperative norms, contribute to the smooth functioning of groups, thereby allowing the teacher to observe, provide feedback, and push the students' thinking by posing challenging questions.

In the complex instruction classrooms described earlier, the roles students play are not included in the written instructions because they are not part of the task that the activity card describes. Instead, roles like facilitator and reporter relate to *how the work is to be done*. For example, the facilitator is checking whether members of the group understand what is to be done; the reporter is stimulating scientific thinking and discussion about the task. We refer to these as the "how" roles. In addition to playing a "how" role, everyone fully participates in the discussion, in the creation of the group product, and in the preparation of the group report. Everyone completes an individual report. Through the assignment of "how" roles, the teacher delegates to group members many of the tasks that the teacher ordinarily does: keeping the group on task, ensuring good social relations, organizing the clean-up, and summarizing what has been learned for the class as a whole.

When each group member is doing a part of the job, there is a *division of labor*. Mr. Leonard's assignment is an example of such division of labor: each student has to do one equation, but the results of all equations are necessary to the final product. When a specialized part of the assigned task has a name and specific expectations for behavior, we call it a "what" role. "What" roles refer to the substance of the group's assignment as opposed to how the group goes about its business. The grapher is an example of a "what" role; in order to complete the task the grapher has to take everyone's equation and graph it into one final product. Notice that Mr. Leonard combines this with the "how" role of a facilitator who makes sure that everyone participates, sees to it that the job gets done on time, and seeks the teacher's help if necessary. Some teachers have combined "how" roles with the roles students take on in reciprocal teaching (Palinscar, Brown, & Campione, 1989), such as questioner, summarizer, or predictor.

"HOW" ROLES

The roles used in complex instruction helped to ensure a high-quality discussion and a group product that was on track and on time. By having a materials manager, only one person moved about the classroom gathering the needed materials. The clean-up person directed the group in wiping down the table so that the teachers did not have to pick up after the children. The facilitator helped those students who could not read the instructions to the task and saw to it that people carried out their roles. Finally, the reporter organized the report by requiring the whole group to discuss what he or the group would report to the class. Thus, he ensured a thoughtful presentation based on a thorough exchange of ideas.

Leadership Roles

There are advantages to the use of leaders. In the adult world of work, there are very few leaderless groups. When one person is an appointed leader, there is less jockeying for influence among the members than in leaderless groups because the status order is clear (the leader is in charge);

the leader is seen as legitimate, that is, backed up by the person in charge, the teacher. When not every decision has to be made by consensus, the group's operation is quicker and more efficient. The teacher has it well within her power to appoint group leaders for each of the collective task groups. Furthermore, the teacher has the authority to say exactly what the group leader has the right and duty to do with respect to the group.

From an educational point of view, the use of a strong leader has some drawbacks. Group members may have very little to do with each other and may simply respond to the leader's directions. If the task involves a group discussion, a strong leader is likely to dominate. Members will tend to listen more to the group leader concerning the content of the task, even though other group members may have more valuable ideas. Furthermore, if the leader is constantly saying whose turn it is to talk, the amount of interchange between group members is greatly reduced. A leader with the power to direct discussion and to make final decisions will often cause the group to give up and to let the leader do the whole task. Watch out for situations where the role of group leader is taken away from the legitimately assigned group member. The problem of unwanted domination becomes even more disruptive.

Limited Leadership Techniques

How can a teacher gain the efficiency of a leader without sacrificing the active learning that takes place during creative interchange? If the leadership role is properly structured, one can have the benefits of creative interchange and the efficiency of a leadership role for a short- or long-term task.

A facilitator who acts as a limited leader is not a boss with executive decision-making rights. Everyone in the group needs to understand that the facilitator does not have control over the decision or the content of the discussion. Instead, the role is limited to functions such as seeing to it that everyone participates, keeping the group on task and away from irrelevancies, and/or making sure that the group makes clear decisions in the time the teacher has allotted. Facilitator roles can be tailored for particular tasks and classes.

The use of such a clearly defined, yet limited leadership role has the advantage of efficiency because one member is in charge of the group process. It has the added advantage of preventing status struggles and domination by members of the group who have high academic or social standing. No doubt something in the way of a free and full exchange of the well-trained leaderless group is given up, but like so many decisions in designing groupwork, there is a trade-off in the relative advantages and disadvantages of each strategy.

Research on complex instruction has demonstrated that the use of facilitators boosts the rate of talking and working together in the group (Zack, 1988). When the facilitator asks if everyone understands the activity card, the group often engages in a good discussion of what they are supposed to do and what strategies they will employ. Also, conversations will take place as help is delivered so that people are not left on their own to struggle with the task.

Group Moderator

A group moderator can ease interpersonal conflicts that arise, can be attentive to the feelings of individual members, and can encourage members to compromise and discipline themselves to help maintain the group. You can adapt the moderator role differently for different age groups. The youngest students may only be able to comment favorably on other's ideas. A version of the moderator role could include the following responsibilities: Make sure communication lines are open; encourage positive responses; discourage "putdowns." With somewhat more mature students, the group moderator can learn how to address many of the socio-emotional needs that arise during groupwork and use previously introduced conflict resolution techniques.

Roles for Older and Younger Students

With more mature groups that have the task of synthesizing individual productions into a written or oral report, an excellent specialized role is that of summarizer (or synthesizer). The summarizer works with a laptop, an iPad, a mobile device, or poster paper in front of the group, noting key ideas under discussion. The summarizer is not merely recording; she leaves out irrelevant issues and highlights disagreements between ideas that will need to be resolved. The advantage of this role is that it tends to depersonalize disagreement; the argument is between *ideas* rather than between individuals who proposed the ideas. The group gains objectivity. Those who are unwilling to say negative things about each other's ideas when face to face are able to be objectively critical when faced with ideas separate from persons.

Another useful role for more mature students is that of resource person. This student is responsible for helping the group to use the materials relevant for discussion. Some teachers introduce material in a short lecture accompanied by a handout or references concerning the major concepts. In the groupwork task that follows the lecture, the groups are asked a series of questions that requires them to use and to apply the concepts. The resource person uses the handout or the textbook, or searches online for answers to questions raised by the group during the discussion.

A recorder can provide the group with notes, a diagram, or a summary of the discussion. This is particularly useful in helping individuals finish their reports as well as in creating the group report. The recorder can also make sure that everyone completes an individual report.

The reporter is a frequently used role for younger and older groups of cooperative learners. Unfortunately, it rarely achieves its full potential. Unless the role is properly developed, the reporter struggles, in the final minutes of group activity, to think of what to say. The resulting product may be so scanty that the class has no clear idea about what this group discovered. Or the report may bear little resemblance to the actual conversation of the group. Teachers often complain that reports are boring and repetitive and that the audience becomes restless and inattentive.

To prepare a successful report, the reporter holds a discussion with the group about what is to be said. Clarify to the students that the report as a whole is the group's responsibility. The reporter is the spokesperson for the group and the organizer of the report. The group may decide that several people should participate in the report. The reporter who is hesitant to speak in public or whose oral proficiency in English is at a beginning level may request that other group members accompany or assist him in presenting the report. If the group product is a role play or the presentation of a concrete construction, the reporter may act as announcer or narrator, briefly summarizing the activity to introduce the presentation to the class. When the reporter has the opportunity to rehearse the report with the group, the quality of the report is greatly enhanced. You might specify a format or structure, clarify the necessary elements, and set a reasonable time limit for a concise yet clear report.

In a study of the reporter role, Ehrlich (1991) experimented with stopping the group for a formal discussion similar to that held by the reporter in the first illustration in this chapter. The reporters were given a special form and time to discuss with the group the answers to a set of questions in preparation for their report to the class. The enhanced reporter's job was to encourage the group to think and talk together and, as a group, to answer questions on the special form. These questions were timed at the beginning of the task, in the middle, and at the end. They were designed to encourage scientific thinking. For example, the group was asked to specify their predictions for the science experiment, their observations, the inferences from their observations, and the extent to which their predictions were supported by their observations. Fourth-grade classes receiving this treatment were compared with classes using the same curriculum and techniques for cooperative learning, but with no special preparation or form for the reporter role. Classroom observations revealed that students interacted more frequently when they used the reporter form than when it was absent. On a criterion problem-solving task at the end of the year, groups from classes that had experienced the enhanced reporter role demonstrated more behaviors that indicated scientific thinking. These behaviors included asking thinking questions, requesting justification, predicting, hypothesizing, inferring, and concluding. Ehrlich felt that 4th-graders were the youngest students who could manage these challenging discussion questions.

In an experimental study of the use of evaluation criteria for the group product and for the individual report, Abram et al. (2002) found that in classrooms using clearly articulated criteria, students spent more time evaluating their products and discussing content than students in classrooms not using evaluation criteria. This self-assessment and on-task talk was in turn significantly related to student learning, as indicated by a final unit essay.

Young children enjoy playing roles that entail clear responsibilities. The children preparing a salt crystal garden at the start of this chapter illustrate the set of roles used by teachers of 2nd through 5th grades for *Finding Out/Descubrimiento,* a bilingual curriculum designed by De Avila and Duncan (1980) to develop thinking skills in the context of math and science activities. The system of classroom management Cohen and her graduate students created for this approach was the initial version of complex instruction: heterogeneous groups of four or five children assigned to each of five or six learning centers. All classrooms use facilitators; teachers select from the other roles on the following list to suit their own situations and address the needs of a particular task:

> *Facilitator:* Sees to it that everyone gets the help he or she needs to do the task; is responsible for seeking answers to questions within the group; teacher is only queried if no one in the group can help.
>
> *Checker:* Makes sure that everyone has completed his or her individual report.

Setup: Is responsible for setting up all the materials at the learning center. These are stored in such a way that a child can easily gain access to the materials needed. Pictures help to tell the child which materials will be needed and where they will be placed.

Materials Manager: Is responsible for getting materials and resources and putting them away properly.

Safety Officer: Is responsible during tasks involving heat or sharp edges for supervising others and for notifying an adult of potentially dangerous situations.

Reporter: Is responsible for organizing the group report and its presentation to the class.

DIVIDING THE LABOR

There are so many ways to divide up the work within groups and between groups that the actual limit is set only by the teacher's imagination. To provide an idea of the possibilities, let us present three examples.

Constructive controversy, developed and evaluated by the Johnsons (Johnson & Johnson, 1985, 2009b; Smith, Johnson, & Johnson, 1981), illustrates a method in which an elaborate use of "what" roles and shifting division of labor successfully foster higher-level discussion leading to conceptual understanding. In one study of constructive controversy, students worked in four-person groups over several classroom sessions. First, two-person pairs, having been provided with relevant information, prepared opposing sides of a debate concerning conservation versus economic interests on the proposed reintroduction of wolves into Minnesota. Within the pairs each student played a relevant role, such as farmer or rancher. Second, the pairs presented their opposing sides. The opposite pair was motivated to listen very carefully because the third phase required the pairs to switch sides and argue the issue, using the information that had been presented. In the final phase, the entire group had to arrive at a consensual view of the issue and write a group report. In quality of discussion and on a test of understanding, this method was found to be superior to either conventional debate or simple discussion groups.

A second possibility is the expert technique: Divide the class into groups, with each group asked to prepare the answers to a different set of study questions. Students are told that they must make sure that each person in the group will be able to function as an expert on the answers to his or her set of questions in the second phase. For the second phase, divide up the experts so that there is one expert for each set of questions in each group. Then instruct the group to go over all questions, with the resident expert acting as discussion leader for his or her set of questions. This is an adaptation of Aaronson's Jigsaw Method (1978). We would recommend it only for classes where students are fairly adept in reading. Otherwise, an "expert" may experience public embarrassment because he or she is unable to master the study materials in the time allotted.

As a third possibility, break up the task so that each person plays a different and complementary role; a technical group such as an airplane crew or an operating room team operates in this way. People work together very closely, but each has a different job to do—all examples of "what" roles. Cohen used this method with success at the Center for Interracial Cooperation, a summer school where students made movies in interracial groups (Cohen, Lockheed, & Lohman, 1976). The roles were divided into camera person, director, story writer, actor, and so forth. Over the weeks of the summer school, each student played every role. For the interracial situation, this technique had the great advantage of teaching the students that if given the chance to play a specialized role, different people can make very different and creative contributions to the group.

Dividing the labor and the use of "what" roles have two special problems. The first is getting help for the persons who cannot play their specialized role unaided. Many teachers try to solve this problem by selecting those students who have already shown success in performing particular roles such as story writer, actor, or illustrator. However, this strategy has the unfortunate effect of pigeonholing people and not allowing them to expand their repertoire through trying new roles. The second problem is that of maintaining group interaction and an exchange of ideas. If everyone is doing their job, there may be no basis for interaction.

The technique of constructive controversy uses roles such as rancher and farmer, but each side of the controversy works in complementary pairs to use written materials and to build a case. Thus, a struggling reader could receive assistance. Second, the group has a final integrating phase in which everyone collaborates equally to propose a final report, thus solving the problem of ensuring interaction.

In the second example, the expert group provides assistance to any member who is not confident of playing the expert role for the second phase. The group rehearses some of its members if necessary. Thus, no one who is supposed to be "expert" is left to flounder. Although students play specialized roles as experts on particular questions in the second phase, they work together as a leaderless group in the first place, thus ensuring exchange of ideas.

In the third example of the movie crew, the task is one in which the roles work very interdependently. They must interact extensively while they work and while they view the results of their attempts at filming. Moreover, the roles rotate so that no one is pigeonholed as an actor, a camera person, or a director.

ASSIGNING ROLES

How can you make sure that students will accept roles that you assign and will be willing to play them? The following might help ensure the effectiveness of role assignments:

- Make the assignment of the job to a specific member of the group public knowledge. Other group members will recognize that you have given this person the authority to act as facilitator, reporter, or materials manager.
- Rotate role assignments so all group members eventually play all roles.
- Specify in great detail what the person playing the role is supposed to do and what the role responsibilities are.
- Make sure that all group members know what the responsibilities of each role are.

Many teachers found it useful to describe the expected behaviors for each role and display them prominently in the classroom. This will help to clarify the role; it will also make everyone understand that the facilitator (or any other role player) is only doing what the teacher has directed. When this is done, even the most timid student will be willing to step forward and be a facilitator if you ask, and group members will treat that person with respect.

Strong, clear assignment of roles is particularly important for leadership roles. Suppose the facilitator tries to quiet down someone who is doing too much of the talking: "I think the group understands what you've been saying; we need to hear some other ideas." Unless the target of this remark understands that the job of facilitator involves giving everyone a chance to contribute, she is likely to view such a remark as a personal insult. The object of all this clarity, specificity, and publicity is to have group members understand that the leader is behaving in a certain way only because he or she is expected to do so as part of the job. As described in Chapter 7, the language functions and forms associated with certain roles support language development for students who are beginning or early intermediate language learners.

In selecting students for leadership positions, don't try to pick people on the basis of "leadership quality." Give everyone a chance to experience the role of facilitator at one time or another. Because teachers often believe that few students have the capacity for leadership roles, they tend to pick the most academically successful student or the most popular student. Socially high status leaders are sometimes picked for a practical reason: Teachers sometimes worry that unless they win over such students, they might be a source of trouble during the groupwork.

It is true that under ordinary classroom and playground conditions only a few students are capable of persuading others to do as they say. But the conditions in groupwork are different in important ways. The facilitator does not have to assert leadership in an informal group. Instead, the facilitator has been *assigned* to play a specific role in a specific group by the teacher. Under these conditions a student with ordinarily low or middling status in the classroom will have little difficulty in guiding a group. If the role is clearly and publicly defined, and if students are properly prepared for any skills that will be called for (see following discussion), a wide variety of students can be excellent facilitators.

The opportunity to play such a role is a much-needed boost to the status of many students in the classroom who are perceived as timid, mild, or ineffectual. It is especially important that girls get the chance to play leadership roles; on average, fewer girls than boys are spontaneously seen as leaders by teachers or by peers (Lockheed, Harris, & Nemceff, 1983). When they were given the chance to play the role of facilitator in cooperative learning, Leal (1985) found that girls were just as likely to be seen as leaders as boys. When there are only few minority students in the classroom, appointing one of them to play a leadership role is important in combating the sense of powerlessness they may feel in a classroom with few students like themselves and in a school with few teachers or administrators of their racial or ethnic background.

When a low-status student attempts to play the role of a facilitator, you will sometimes see group members literally take the role away and play it themselves. As mentioned already, watch out for this occurrence, and be careful not to let it happen. Hold students accountable for playing their own roles and not usurping those of others. It is easier to do this when everyone is wearing a badge indicating their particular job in the group. Then you and everyone else know who is supposed to be doing what.

If you let the group choose their own roles, they will tend to give whatever they perceive as the most desirable and powerful role to the student with the highest status. Because you don't want to reinforce the status order that already exists in your classroom, this is obviously not a good idea. Make it clear that everyone gets a chance to play every role through systematic rotation of jobs. The easiest way to do this is through the use of a chart (see Figure 5.1) where the labels of rows represent the various roles. Students can see that you are systematically moving their names down the chart with each new group assignment or every day of a multi-day unit, so that they play new roles each time.

DEVELOPING ROLES

Roles have become very popular with teachers who use cooperative learning. However, we often find that students are not playing the assigned roles. Why does this happen? As they move around the room, many teachers forget or avoid checking whether or not roles are being well executed. Also, often students don't feel comfortable or able to behave in the new and different ways specified for their position. Roles take much more development and learning than many teachers imagine.

The younger the student, the more time it takes to develop clarity and skills for the group roles. Younger children have had much less experience in playing a variety of roles than older students and adults. Playing these roles is related to drama; therefore it helps if students have some standard phrases to get started. For example, a facilitator can say, "Does everyone understand the activity card?" A moderator can ask if everyone feels OK about the decision the group has reached. In an initial discussion of roles, the class can develop some scripts under your direction. Students need a chance to practice these new behaviors, so you can have students pretend they are in groups and practice their roles.

Older students might show some resistance to the formality of roles, arguing that they inhibit the free flow of their work. Explain to them that adult work groups use similar roles to further their work. This will go a long way toward convincing them that learning how to fulfill the responsibilities embodied in these roles will be useful.

Discussing the roles during the wrap-up is a good way to reinforce them and point out to the students how they contribute to the smooth functioning of the group. Observe how people are playing their roles and take notes as you move around the room. Raise issues for class discussion based on your notes; bring out good examples and examples illustrating the need to develop some alternative strategies if things are not working the way you expect. Write the new strategies down and provide practice opportunities. Do not hesitate to point it out if people are not playing their roles and to ask the group to take care of this problem.

Training Facilitators

Suppose that you want a facilitator to ensure a rich discussion. Typical 5th-graders rarely have a clear idea of what a good discussion is, and they might lack productive strategies for persuading group members to change their behaviors. Therefore, unless you are quite sure they know how, it is wise to train the potential facilitators to carry out their jobs.

Wilcox (1972) documented how to train 5th- and 7th-grade students from inner-city classrooms to be successful facilitators. In her study, students in groups led by trained student leaders were significantly more active and had greater exchange of ideas than students in groups with untrained student leaders. The interaction in groups with untrained student leaders was highly variable; some seemed as good as groups with trained student leaders, whereas the interaction in other groups left much to be desired.

Wilcox (1972) chose to train student leaders who were neither the most nor the least socially powerful members of their classrooms. Those students selected as trained student leaders were given the job of helping the group in meeting the three criteria for a good group discussion:

- Give everyone a fair turn.
- Give reasons for ideas.
- Give different ideas.

During the initial training session groups leaders were told the following:

> There are different ways a person can be a leader. Different people have different ideas about what it means to be a good leader. Some people think being a leader means telling everyone what to do practically all the time. Some people think a good leader means letting everyone do just as he pleases—not interfere with their fun. And some think—and this is my idea too—that a good leader is in between these two. I think being

a good leader means being part of a good group—talking with the other members—letting everyone tell his ideas—being just like the other members—so long as everything is going okay.

But if things are not okay, then the good leader knows how to help his group. When wouldn't things be going okay? (Children may suggest, and if not, trainer mentions the silent group, the non-participator, the monopolizer.) If someone in the group never gives anyone else a chance to talk—or if one person doesn't talk—a good leader can help by asking questions—or reminding the big talker that someone else needs a chance. We'll talk about how to do this without making others angry. But remember—the good leader uses these ideas only when they're needed. Most of the time the good leader is just like everyone else in the group listening and taking turns talking. (Wilcox, 1972, p. 145)

Wilcox rehearsed with the leaders how they could get the group to adhere to the criteria. The students then role-played a discussion such as they would lead. They were directed to stop the group discussion after about 5 minutes and ask members to evaluate how well they were doing by the criteria on the suggestions chart.

Note the way Wilcox (1972) stressed a limited leadership role, so that the student leaders would not become dominant, particularly in the area of the final group decision. She made sure they would recognize undesirable leader behavior by making a special training film, but there are less elaborate ways to accomplish this objective. One might role-play the leader who dominates the group discussion, or ask one of the students to play this role, or one might videotape a simulated session with an overly dominant facilitator.

This is not the only way to train facilitators. However, it does illustrate the importance of clearly defining the role and carefully preparing new skills. Regardless of the age of the students, the instructor should always try to achieve this kind of clarity and should stop to analyze whether or not appointed facilitators have the skills necessary to carry out the role.

LONG-TERM PROJECTS

For long-term projects, it is possible to use leaderless groups for selected phases. Keep in mind that consensus groups with no formal leadership and no division of labor are very costly in terms of interpersonal relations and the level of social skills required. They are likely to exhibit status problems where one person dominates the group or status struggles in which several persons grapple for dominance. Therefore, only short-term use of such leaderless groups is recommended.

If the project is of a long-term nature, one possibility is to pull out those stages or phases of the task in which exchange and creative problem solving are most critical. These particular stages can have a leaderless group structure, while all the rest of the project can benefit from combinations of division of labor and special roles for different group members, including leadership roles. Recall that creative interchange will not be accomplished without some sort of special training and socialization of norms for behavior during group discussion.

Two of the stages of a long-term project that benefit from creative interchange are the initial planning session and the integration of the final product. Obviously the project's outcome is largely determined by the depth of the analysis of the problem and the quality of decisions. If the students are discussing a social studies project on Pueblo dwellings, their final report or presentation is only as good as their analysis of which important materials are to be gathered and which activities are to be carried out by individual group members. At a more advanced level of scholarship, if the group is asked to do some library or online research on one aspect of a particular theme in order to write a group paper, the quality of that paper is dependent on the initial intellectual analysis and the subsequent synthesis and organization of the final product.

In addition to this primarily intellectual reason for desiring a thorough and open discussion of the initial plans for the project, there is an important social-psychological reason for making everyone an equal and full participant in the initial planning phase. Unless members feel that they have a strong stake in the decisions made, they are likely to lose motivation when difficulties develop in carrying out their tasks. If, in contrast, all feel that they have had a fair chance to contribute to initial plans and have accepted the group's decision after arguing the issue fully and accepting or compromising in some reasonable fashion, there will be fewer if any members who let the group down by failing to do their jobs. Other members will feel free to say, "You took part, and you agreed that this was a reasonable way to do the job. So now you have to do your part!"

When the pieces of the final product have been assembled, the group is ready for another phase that requires an open interchange. A leaderless group can be used once again at this time. Particularly if the group has been through a period where members have been on their own, researching or creating materials for the final product, the group needs to learn what each member has found out. Although some of this process can take place through reading and examining the production of individual members, major intellectual benefits come from evaluating, analyzing, and synthesizing what each person has learned. This discussion can cause the group to look at the problem in new and different ways. Integration is a challenging task intellectually as well as interpersonally. Criticism and evaluation from others are never easy to take, but they are essential for a good final product.

During the middle phase, when the labor has been divided, people can go about their business in a fairly independent way. At this stage, it is desirable to have a leader who acts as a center for group communication and who keeps everything moving forward.

Group Investigation

Group investigation, initially developed by Sharan and Hertz-Lazarowitz (1980) and further refined later (Sharan & Sharan, 1992), is a sophisticated method for long-term projects using planning groups, division of labor, and "how" roles for group management. Repeated evaluations in heterogeneous classrooms have shown that it is particularly effective in teaching concepts requiring higher-level cognitive skills and in producing more cooperative and altruistic behavior (Sharan, Hertz-Lazarowitz, & Ackerman, 1980; Sharan & Shachar, 1988; Sharan & Sharan, 1992). In group investigation, students act as creative scholars, researching and building their own knowledge. In order to achieve these goals, they must work together closely. Good group process is ensured in various ways: building commitment to the group and its project, use of division of labor, and group process skills. If your objective is to enable students to construct their own knowledge, and if you have been successful on short-term tasks with skills for group process and with the use of "how" roles and the division of labor, you may wish to plan such a long-term project. Remember that group investigation demands the combination of all of these strategies as well as skillful support and supervision by the teacher.

9 The Teacher's Role: Letting Go and Teaming Up

Question: What is your most important insight about teaching that you wish you had known during your first 2 years of teaching?

Answer: To let kids do more and me do less. This has been a hard lesson to learn over the years. I use a lot of cooperative learning, hands-on activities, and inquiry in the class and it was difficult for me to learn to step back and let it all happen.

(Paul Martini, Woodside High School science teacher, Woodside, California)

Groupwork changes a teacher's role dramatically. No longer are you a direct supervisor of students, responsible for ensuring that they do their work exactly as you direct. No longer is it your responsibility to watch for every mistake and correct it on the spot. Instead, authority is delegated to students and to groups of students. The students are in charge of ensuring that the work gets done efficiently and effectively, and that their classmates get the help they need. They are empowered to make mistakes, to find out what went wrong, and to explore what might be done about it. "In my classroom, mistakes are expected, respected, and inspected," say teachers who have become comfortable with delegating authority.

This does not mean that you have given up your position as an authority in the classroom. On the contrary, you are the authority who gives directions for the task; you set the rules; you train the students to use norms for cooperation; you assign students to groups; you delegate authority to those students who are to play special roles; and, most important, you hold the groups accountable for the product of their work. As a matter of fact, you cannot give up authority if you don't have it in the first place. This chapter discusses what letting go during groupwork means for your role.

Groupwork is easier planned for and done with the aid of a colleague, a student teacher, a mentor, or another support provider. Designing and evaluating groupwork tasks is a classic case of creative problem solving where "two (or more) heads are better than one." Considering that teachers have responsibility for their own classrooms and often have limited opportunities to work closely with a colleague, you may feel that this is an impractical recommendation. Addressing this problem is the second topic of this chapter.

DELEGATING AUTHORITY

When you stand in front of the class and instruct the students in a whole-class setting, when you assign individual seatwork and walk around the classroom overseeing performance, when you divide up the class into reading groups and sit with one group while they take turns reading aloud or answering your questions, you are using direct supervision. Even when in preparation for groupwork you gather the class together and provide an orientation, you are using direct supervision.

When groupwork is under way, however, and groups are working and talking together using the instructions on the task card you have prepared, then your authority has been delegated. You cannot possibly be everywhere at once trying to help six or more different groups. Moreover, having students talking and working together is essential as a strategy for managing heterogeneous classes. When they are trained to help each other, perhaps by reading or by translating for students who are learning the language of instruction, students serve as academic and linguistic resources for one another and use each other to understand and complete the assignments.

When students are working on uncertain conceptual tasks such as inquiry and creative problem solving, talking and working together are necessary for achievement (Cohen, Lotan, & Leechor, 1989; Cohen, Lotan, & Holthuis, 1997). Students will be encouraged to work with each other to deal with all the questions and problems involved in these tasks. Research has shown that all students, but particularly individuals who are reading below grade level, benefit from interacting with other students on challenging tasks (Leechor, 1988; Schultz, 1999). Unless you are successful in delegating authority to groups, your students will not gain these benefits of talking and working together. In that case, you will find that groupwork is unmanageable.

An Effective Management System

Teachers are often surprised to discover how smoothly students of all ages can operate on their own in properly designed groupwork. The secret of successful management of such complex instruction lies in clarity—the students' thorough understanding of how they are supposed to behave, what they are supposed to be doing, and where they can turn for help if problems develop. The same is true for a traditional classroom; The difference is simply that with groupwork, students have to take more responsibility for their own behavior and for the behavior of others in their group. They should not be turning to the teacher for constant direction, evaluation, and assistance; they should draw upon their peers instead.

Clarity is attained by having as simple a system as possible. In addition, much clarity is achieved by training in advance for roles and for cooperation, as well as by the careful planning process and curriculum design recommended in the preceding chapters. All these management techniques operate to control student behavior in a constructive and productive manner without having to tell them what to do directly. There is no need to control individual students' behavior with systems of points or rewards; the teacher's job is to make the groups and the instructions operate to address any discipline problems that arise.

The steps for developing such a management system are briefly summarized as follows:

1. Cooperative norms are to be taught as recommended in Chapter 4 so that students will know how they ought to behave and will expect and insist on these behaviors from others.
2. Students need to know which group they are in and where that group is supposed to meet; a minimum amount of time should be wasted in getting across this vital information. Table numbers are helpful.
3. Public and specific information as to who is to play what role and what specific behaviors are expected should be available as described in Chapter 8. Name and role charts are helpful.
4. Each group needs to have clear instructions for the task and criteria for assessment of their product available to them as they

work; this will do much to prevent students from having to turn to you as a source of knowledge.

5. Students need to know and understand the learning goals of the activity. Brief orientations as well as visuals clarifying those objectives are helpful.

For many groupwork situations, these five considerations will be quite sufficient for most everything to go smoothly. You may also want to select a set of fundamental norms and keep these posted. We recommend the use of the following norms:

- You are expected to complete each group activity and individual report.
- Play your assigned role in the group responsibly.
- You have the right to ask for help. You have the duty to assist.
- Help other group members without doing the work for them. Explain by telling how.
- Everybody helps.

When you use collaborative seatwork, the written worksheet or assignment directs the students as to what you want them to do. When tasks are groupworthy and conceptual, task cards or activity cards are highly recommended. (See Chapter 6.) The task cards are a physical representation of your delegation of authority. By giving the students the card, your message becomes clear: "This is the work you are required to accomplish. Do your best!" Without the task card, students rely on directions from the teacher, who frequently interrupts the group to give directions and to assist in the work. The teacher is concerned that the students get the "point" of the activity and tries to prevent the group from making errors while engaging in inquiry or in a lively discussion. This situation greatly reduces the amount of talking and working together and thus the learning of the group. The group has no chance to achieve its own insights, and individuals who are lost are unable to use other group members as resources.

"No Hovering"

Following a short orientation, you delegate authority to groups to carry out their task. It is of critical importance to let them make decisions *on their own*. They might need to make some mistakes on their own.

They are accountable to you for their work. Let go and allow the groups to work things through without you overseeing every step. Trust that they will rise to the occasion and learn to solve some problems for themselves.

Many teachers in traditional classrooms, when they are not lecturing, spend the bulk of their time guiding the students through various tasks. They show and tell how to do the assignments. They redirect students who appear to be disengaged from their work. They answer many questions that come from individual students.

This kind of direct supervision will undermine the management system you have worked so hard to put in place. If you are available to solve all the problems, students will not rely on themselves or on their group. Because of their past experiences with supervision, whenever students see you hovering nearby, they will stop talking to each other and look to you for direction. If the teacher attempts direct instruction while the students are engaged in the groups, the result will be less talking and working together and therefore less gains on measures of learning. These connections between classroom management and learning gains have been documented in numerous research studies on complex instruction (Boaler, 2006; Cohen & Lotan, 1997a; Schultz, 1999).

Avoid rushing to the rescue at the first sign of difficulty in a group. Redirect the group to its own resources by refraining from answering questions unless the entire group has been consulted for possible solutions. In many groupwork situations the facilitator asks a question in the group's name after having made sure that no one in the group has the answer. You might ask to confirm: "Is your question a group question?"

While the Groups Work

When authority is delegated to groups to manage themselves, students are now doing many of the things you ordinarily do—organizing the materials, answering each other's questions, keeping each other engaged in the task, helping each other to get started, and cleaning up. After teachers discover that they do not appear to be needed because everything is running without them, they often say, "I feel like I've been done out of my job; it all works without me. What am I supposed to be doing?"

Despite the ability of groups to carry on by themselves, your role is not one of *laissez-faire*. Delegating authority does not mean that you are abdicating your role and your responsibilities. You are now free for a more demanding and ambitious teacher role. You now have a chance to observe students carefully and to listen to the discussion from a discreet distance. You can ask key questions to stimulate a group that is operating at too low a level; you can provide formative feedback to individuals and to groups; you can stimulate their thinking; you can look for low status behavior and intervene to treat for status problems; and you can reinforce rules, roles, and norms in those particular groups where the system is not operating at its best.

There is a delicate balance between avoiding hovering and wisely intervening in a group. The price to be paid for intervention is reducing interaction within the group. Ask yourself whether you are willing to pay that price. Although groups should be allowed to make mistakes for themselves, there are times when nothing is to be gained from letting a group struggle onward when

- the group is hopelessly off-task,
- the group does not seem to understand enough to carry out the task,
- the group is experiencing sharp interpersonal conflict, or
- the group is falling apart because they cannot organize themselves.

Don't rush in at the first sign of trouble. Stand close enough to hear but far enough away so that your presence is unobtrusive. Listen intently and diagnose the problem the group is experiencing. Are low-status students being shut out of the group? Is it a problem of group process? Is it some inability to understand the directions? Is it a problem of how to proceed? Is it a lack of background or content knowledge, lack of academic skills, or lack of linguistic proficiency? Perhaps you will decide after watching and listening that the group will solve its own problems and does not need you.

If you decide to move in, what you do or say depends on your hypothesis about what the problem might be. Here are some possible scenarios:

- A group is having trouble getting organized. You remind them of the rules and roles. You ask whether people are playing their roles. You suggest that the facilitator discuss what they have to get done, make a list, and help the group to prioritize what needs to be done first and who can do it. You tell the group that you will be back to hear the results of their discussion. Then you leave.

- A group has "gotten stuck" on a problem and doesn't seem to be getting anywhere. The level of frustration is rising. You ask a few open-ended questions in an attempt to redirect the group discussion. You suggest that the group deal with your questions in their own deliberations—and you walk off.

- A group is not sharing materials cooperatively. You could ask them to stop for a few moments and talk over how they are doing on some of the cooperative norms (ideally, posted somewhere in the room). Then you can ask them to tell you after having had a brief discussion what their conclusions are and what they think they should do about it. Don't linger to supervise the discussion.

- A group is struggling with a difficult text and does not know how to analyze the document. They are in need of some intellectual assistance. You point out some of the key parts. You check for their understanding of what is being asked. You may even fill them in on missing parts of their knowledge. This does not mean you are doing the task for them or directing them how to do it. You are merely moving them to the point where they can cope with the academic and linguistic demands of the task.

- A group of 2nd-graders has plunged into the task without reading instructions. You tell the group that you don't want them to work with the manipulatives until they can tell you just what they are supposed to be doing. You say that you are going to return to the group and ask any member to explain what it is they are supposed to be doing. If that person can explain, then they can get started with the materials. Otherwise, they will have to continue to read and discuss.

In none of these examples are you using direct supervision. Instead, you are using the system of roles and norms to make the groups operate. You are directing the group back upon its own resources—to take more responsibility for its own learning and functioning. In each case, you get in, and then you promptly get out.

In addition to these cases of groups experiencing severe difficulties, you may want to intervene in order to deepen or extend the thinking on the assigned topic. Asking questions and making connections are excellent ways to achieve this end, provided you do not stay around to answer your own questions or to call on various group members to guess what you have in mind. Without giving an answer, you can help students to analyze a phenomenon or a problem in terms of its parts and interrelationships. For example, a group of students in science are having problems making a flashlight. The teacher responds by saying, "Not everyone's flashlight is working. Have you tested each part of it to see if it's working? By sharing with each other the parts that work, you might be able to figure out how to get it working." Questions beginning with "why" or "how come" are good for stimulating analytic thinking. You might ask a group of students examining the *Crusaders' Handbook*, "Why do you think the Crusaders tried to dehumanize the enemy?"

Your attention will also be necessary if one group finishes their work very quickly while the others need more time. You might open up the task once more by asking some questions about analyzing the problem further, or about generalizing the task to another situation. For example, you might ask: What other ways are there of . . . ? How can we use what we learned in . . . ? Do you think this is true of all . . . ? What would happen if you did things another way? You might also ask the group to consult further references to extend their activity and their thinking. Questions such as these can be difficult to articulate on the spot. Often teachers generate a list of conceptual, high-level extension questions ahead of time and keep them on a clipboard, a tablet, or another device to refer to as needed.

Management of Conflict

Disagreement about ideas is a healthy sign as long as intellectual disagreement does not degenerate into sharp interpersonal conflict. Some interpersonal conflict is inevitable and should not be taken as a sign of failure. Nor should it be an opportunity for you to intervene and take over the reins immediately, acting as arbiter, juror, and judge.

What can you do? Ask the group what seems to be the difficulty. Then ask them to think of some alternative strategies for handling the conflict. If you have prepared your class with strategies for conflict resolution, as described in Chapter 4, they will be able to envision alternative ways to behave. If you have really delegated authority, then the group should take responsibility for solving its interpersonal problems. Even younger students are able to develop workable strategies for managing conflict when challenged to do so and when the teacher persists in demanding that they talk things through until they find a solution.

If the problem is due to a volatile combination of students, make a note to avoid putting that group together again in the near future. Changing the composition of groups on a regular basis and rotation of roles will help to defuse interpersonal problems so that the conflict does not become chronic. If, however, you think you are seeing the same problem in a number of groups, there may be a difficulty with the way you have prepared the students and/or the nature of the task. Take the time to have a whole-class discussion and see if you can locate the general problem. Be prepared to make adjustments in your task, to do some retraining and strengthening of rules and roles, or to develop some strategies with the class as a whole that will solve the problem.

Holding Students Accountable

Many teachers would like to grade groupwork and to use systems of points or extrinsic rewards for acceptable behavior because they know that it is important to hold individuals and groups accountable. However, as explained earlier, these strategies are unnecessary and possibly detrimental when the management system just described works. There are multiple alternatives in the system you can use for this purpose. When you intervene while the groups are working and require the group to pull itself together and function, you are holding the groups accountable.

You also hold the group accountable by requiring a presentation of their group product during the wrap-up phase. When a group has failed to work together well and has not addressed the questions raised on the activity card, they need to know that you are aware of what has happened and expect them to do better in the future. You may choose to deliver this feedback to the group while they are still working at learning stations and reserve your more general commentary on what is to be learned from their experience for the rest of the class during wrap-up. For example, you could point out that the next group to do this task should be sure to work with the omitted discussion questions. If, however, you start a round of applause for every group performance no matter how weak, the students will realize that there is no group accountability in the system. Ms. S., a veteran high school chemistry teacher, writes about the problems encountered when a group of students refuses to work productively and is unable to deliver the final presentation to the class. Her feedback was as follows: "It is very disappointing that the group was unable to teach their lesson today. After we wrap up all the other presentations, I would like the class to discuss what can be done when a group is unable to work together. It will be necessary for everyone to learn the material that would have been covered by this group" (Shulman, Lotan, & Whitcomb, 1998, p. 29). Then she asked for the next presentation.

By providing feedback to groups on their group process, you can show that you intend groups to take responsibility for what happens while they are at work. Simultaneously, you can confirm their accomplishments, recommend effective strategies they employed to other groups, or point out the difficulties that will require some attention. Feedback on group process can take place while the group is working or during wrap-up. While helping the groups to learn more effective strategies, your feedback also has the function of letting the students know that you are watching their behavior very carefully and holding them accountable for what happens in their groups.

Individual accountability is maintained by checking the individual reports, the databases that record students' individual work, or the group products. If individuals find that you do not know whether or not they have completed a group report or if they are pretty sure you never read these documents, they may become "free riders" in their groups.

Teacher's Role for Orientation and Wrap-Up

During orientation, you are clearly in direct charge of the students. Their job is to listen and to ask questions if they do not understand. This does not mean that a long lecture is necessary. Students, particularly younger ones, will "tune out" after several minutes. Those teachers who use visuals, models, or demonstrations and who conduct an interactive discussion concerning what they are about to experience are much more successful in holding the class's attention than those who attempt to tell everything that the students will need to know.

During wrap-up, you listen closely to group reports, provide feedback, and further the discussion. Asking higher-order questions at this time will encourage students' thinking. Following student presentations, you would do well to comment on what has been learned from the exercise. It is necessary to make connections between the activities and the central concepts they are supposed to illustrate. Otherwise, students get lost in the interesting and concrete details of their group products and forget the point of the lesson.

Wrap-up is also the time to provide feedback and debrief on what you observed while students were at work in their groups. If you constantly interrupt to provide feedback while they are in groups, you will run the risk of hovering and reducing the interaction. Many teachers find that it is better to circulate among the groups, listening and taking notes. Then, during wrap-up or during the orientation the next day, they provide feedback to groups and individuals. Feedback, under these circumstances, has the double function of holding groups accountable and of helping the students with their understanding of the intellectual tasks at hand. It is a priceless opportunity to offer public acknowledgement to students who have done very well in the context of groupwork—particularly those who are not high achievers in conventional academic tasks.

WORKING AS A TEAM

One of the most gratifying experiences for a teacher is to plan and carry out groupwork designs with trusted colleagues. Just as students use each other as resources in groupwork, teachers can do the same. With the joint wealth of past experience as to what tasks work well with students and as to how instructions can be made clear, teachers can be highly creative as they work together. They can also provide honest and constructive feedback as ideas develop.

When instruction is complex, as is the case with groupwork, having colleagues work together means that they are able to be of great assistance to each other while crafting the groupworthy tasks—a groupworthy task in itself as mentioned earlier. Having the option of working together while the class is operating is one of the best possible scenarios. Perhaps one teacher can stop to work with a group needing intervention while another keeps an eye on the classroom as a whole. One teacher can prepare the orientation while another can do the wrap-up.

Another advantage of a colleague is the benefit that accrues when two or more teachers hold formal, scheduled meetings. In these meetings (even if they are relatively short), one has a chance to consider various problems that have come up, to raise possible alternatives, to choose one, and to talk once more in the next meeting about how good or bad the decision was. This kind of thoughtful and evaluative decision making is very difficult to carry out all by oneself. In research with teachers, Cohen and Intili (1982) have repeatedly found that teachers who hold regular team meetings are better able to implement complex and sophisticated instruction than those who rely on brief huddles just before and during class. Common preparation time during the school day is a highly beneficial opportunity for teachers.

The last major advantage of working with a colleague lies in having someone to make an observation and systematic evaluation of your groupwork in progress. It is almost impossible to run groupwork and evaluate what is happening at the same time. Chapter 11 includes a number of simple techniques for a colleague to use in helping to evaluate your groupwork. Even beginning teachers can provide helpful feedback using these techniques. And you can return the favor by observing in your colleague's classroom.

Finding Ways to Team

There are two kinds of teaming; one requires more organizational change than the other. The first kind is joint teaching, where your colleague actually teaches jointly with you in your classroom. Successful teams can include a resource teacher working with a classroom teacher for one period a day, a teacher and a teacher assistant or student teacher, or a teacher and a well-prepared parent volunteer. If your class is difficult to control and unused to groupwork, you might need the support of another person, especially at the beginning. If your tasks are complex—such as using different science experiments at different learning stations, or working with sophisticated equipment like video cameras—and if you have different groups of young students doing very different tasks, another person becomes a necessity. This is as true for classrooms as it is for any other organization: Complex technology is more effective when staff and professionals collaborate more closely, that is, when complex technology matches complex structures (Perrow, 1961; Scott, 2013).

If you have a colleague on the faculty with whom you would like to try some of these groupwork activities, talk to the principal or to the department chair about finding ways to work together. If a large room such as a multipurpose room is available, it is possible to combine two classes for the actual groupwork. If the classes are from different grades or if you are including a group of students with special educational needs, you will be surprised to see how well students of different ages and levels of academic achievement can work together in this setting. If you are combining age groups, it is especially important to pick a task that older students can extend and develop, but also one that younger students will be able to manage with assistance. It will also be necessary to include special training to show students how to help others without doing the work for them.

If you decide to work with an assistant, a student teacher, or a volunteer, take the time to educate that person as to your expectations of them during the teaching process. If you do not train them, the result will be that they will move in, try to supervise directly, and even hover over the groups. Assistants or volunteers can become valuable resources if you allow them to bring in suggestions and to make evaluations of what is happening. In these circumstances, you are still the decision maker; it is the role of your assistant to observe and gather data about what the problems are during the course of groupwork. You also expect that they will make constructive suggestions during team meetings.

If you cannot arrange for joint teaching, the next best thing is teaming for planning and evaluation purposes. It would be useful to find the time for brief meetings with a colleague, a student teacher, or a mentor for planning purposes. In addition, finding time for that colleague to visit your classroom would be particularly beneficial and you can return the favor. It is during these visits that the evaluation tools can be used. Following the observation and the evaluation, the team can discuss the results of the evaluation and decide what should be done to improve the implementation. Many principals are supportive of this type of collegial effort to improve instruction. Some administrators even volunteer to take over classes for an hour while the visits are going on.

Collegial interaction of this sort is highly rewarding. Evaluations of programs requiring this kind of collegial interaction have consistently revealed that teachers find working with a colleague in planning, observation, and evaluation one of the most satisfying and stimulating of their professional experiences. Despite initial doubts and trepidations about having another teacher watch them at work, they find that constructive and specific feedback from a colleague who is facing the same kind of practical classroom problems is helpful; they realize that they have wanted and needed this kind of feedback for a long time. One of the ways in which schools facilitate collegial interactions among teachers is through forming professional learning communities (McLaughlin & Talbert, 2006). Educators and policymakers also see great promise in professional systems that support peer assistance through mentor teachers or teachers on special assignment (Grossman & Davis, 2012).

Treating Expectations for Competence

It is time now to return to the dilemma of groupwork discussed in Chapter 3. What have we done about the problem of high status students dominating interaction and of low-status students withdrawing from the group? There is an even more fundamental question: Have we done anything to change low expectations for competence, the underlying cause of nonparticipation by low-status students?

Recall that high status students are generally expected to do well on new intellectual tasks and low-status students are generally expected to do poorly on these same tasks. When the teacher assigns a group task, general expectations come into play and produce a self-fulfilling prophecy in which the high status students talk more and become more influential than the low-status students. The net result of the interaction is that the low-status students are once again perceived as incompetent. This occurs even if groups are given a rich, multiple-ability task that does more than stress ordinary academic skills. Groupworthy tasks are a necessary albeit insufficient condition for creating equal-status interactions.

Two strategies will have some impact on this problem: (I) establishing cooperative norms such as "everyone participates" and "everyone helps," and (2) giving every student a part or role to play. Both of these strategies will raise the participation rates of both low and high status students and will prevent high status students from doing all the talking. Furthermore, low-status students, just by talking and working together, will improve their performance.

Doesn't that take care of the status problem? Well, not completely— because not much has happened to change expectations for competence. Imagine a well-prepared group with different students playing different roles; on the average, the low-status students might just be talking as much as the high status students. Nevertheless, members of the group still think of the low-status students as having less power-ful ideas and fewer useful suggestions than the high status students. The low-status students may be active, but they probably are still less influential and less active than the high status students. The low-status students still feel that their contributions to the group are less valuable and less competent than the contributions of the high status students. Furthermore, in moving from the successful group experience to other group tasks, there is no improvement in expectations for competence.

To boost active behavior in low-status students that will be perceived as competent, and to produce expectations for competence that will transfer to other tasks, changing the essence of those expectations for competence is imperative. Without such change, expectations remain uniform, and consistently negative. Creating positive expectations for intellectual competence that will combine with the preexisting set of negative expectations is necessary.

If you resolve the problem of consistently low expectations effec-tively, students who have been unsuccessful in your classroom previously will demonstrate their abilities and their skills and acquire a sense of competence that will be acknowledged by their classmates. As you pro-ceed to other groupworthy tasks, students can expect themselves, and can be expected by classmates, to make useful and relevant contribu-tions to each new assignment. Designing situations where previously low-status students can demonstrate successful performance is key to raising their expectations for themselves and for changing their class-mates' perceptions of them.

FROM LOW STATUS TO INTELLECTUAL RESOURCE

One way to change low expectations for competence is to design a situation where the student who is expected to be incompetent will actually function as an expert. A relatively simple and probably the safest way to do this is to find a task where the student is already an expert. When appropriate and relevant, for example, a Spanish-speaking student could teach classmates a song or a poem in Spanish; a Chinese-speaking student could introduce Chinese characters and explain to his peers some of the Chinese writing system; an immigrant student can share with her classmates important past and present historical events in her native country. However, even this fairly obvious strategy requires careful analysis. Do not assume that because a student has a Spanish or Chinese surname or speaks some Spanish or Chinese, he or she knows how to teach something in Spanish or Chinese. Teaching someone else is a separate skill from reciting a poem, singing a song, or writing in a different language. You need to prepare the student carefully for this teaching role and make sure she or he has the tools to be successful.

Speaking in Spanish is a kind of expertise that everyone, rightly or wrongly, expects Latino students to have. This is a narrow and specific expectation for competence, almost like a stereotype. It is unlikely that the experience of being an expert in Spanish will change expectations for competence on other kinds of tasks because it is a stereotypic expectation associated with ethnicity. A similar situation involving stereotyping would be to expect a female to demonstrate expertise in cooking or an African American to demonstrate expertise in playing basketball. Although people are willing to grant females and African Americans expertise in these two areas, the expectations for competence *do not transfer* to other valued tasks.

Despite these limitations, a narrow brand of expertise has some merit if it gives the low-status child a chance to assume a leadership role like that of teacher. However, unless you point out to the students that the act of teaching the class is a special kind of competence and that it is an important skill, the group will never notice that "teaching the Spanish song" is a different skill from "singing the song."

Every student in your class is an expert in some valued intellectual skill acquired and developed through previous learning experiences inside and outside the classroom. Observe your students and ask them about their interests and experiences outside the classroom. Group-worthy tasks allow you to see skills and talents that ordinary classroom assignments rarely permit. Take note of areas of expertise and find ways to allow different students, particularly those with low academic, social, or peer status, to function as experts in a group. This technique is workable as long as the members actually have evidence that the student is an expert and an intellectual resource; in other words, as long as the student is truly competent. Next, we explore more fully how to change students' expectations for competence for themselves and for their classmates.

EXPECTATION TRAINING:
EVIDENCE FROM RESEARCH

With her graduate students and colleagues, Elizabeth Cohen carried out a number of experiments to demonstrate if and how expectations for competence can be changed. In these experiments, expectations were treated by having the low-status student become a teacher, an expert, and an intellectual resource for a high status student on a new, challenging, and valued task. This method is called "expectation training." Tasks for expectation training are not culturally specific or stereotyped for any group. The researchers used tasks such as constructing a model from straws based on a mathematical principle, building a two-transistor radio, and solving an intricate and ingenious puzzle.

The strength of the intervention lies in the way that it changes expectations for competence held both by the low-status students for themselves as well as those held by others regarding their performance. Theoretically, making low-status students experts on a new task and making them teachers of that task provides two new sources of positive expectations for competence. The students derive positive expectations from displaying competence on the task itself; in addition, they derive expectations for competence from being successful teachers. These new positive expectations combine with the older set of negative expectations and by creating a mixed set they raise the general level of expectations for competence. The welcome result is improved participation and influence on new group tasks.

In laboratory settings, expectation training has consistently produced an increase in the participation and influence of children with low social status; treated groups exhibit a pattern of equal-status behavior. The treatment has worked for African American and white groups (Cohen & Roper, 1972), for Chicano and Anglo groups (Robbins, 1977), for Canadian Indian and Anglo groups (Cook, 1974), and for Western and Eastern Jews in Israel (Cohen & Sharan, 1980).

In a field experiment conducted at a summer school with white and African American 5th- and 6th-grade students, Cohen, Lockheed, and Lohman (1976) were able to show that when expectation training was implemented during the first week, it was possible to maintain equal-status interaction for 6 weeks. African American students taught white students a series of academic and nonacademic tasks. For this purpose, the African American students came to the summer school a week early for advance preparation in their role as teachers. At the end of the program, the African American students were as active and influential, if not more active and influential, than the white students on the standard group task of Shoot the Moon. In this field study, the African American students were from a markedly lower socioeconomic class than the white students. However, in the summer school setting the curriculum did not require conventional school skills as a prerequisite to perform the tasks successfully.

Expectation training is a powerful treatment. The low-status student not only displays impressive competence, but is in a position to direct the behavior of the high status student as does every teacher—a rare opportunity for someone on the bottom of the classroom status order. Even with a nonacademic task such as a complicated puzzle, favorable expectations of those who can visualize the solution and teach others will transfer to a wide variety of group tasks requiring different intellectual abilities.

One of the most difficult things to achieve in this or any other kind of status treatment is to convince the low-status persons of their own competence. It is actually harder to change the expectations these students hold for themselves than it is to change the expectations classmates hold for them. Sadly, low-status students have had too many instances where they were not successful and were thus perceived as incompetent by their peers. You may observe that low-status students can carry out the task and teach it with considerable skill. But you would be surprised to realize that these students still do not see themselves as skillful. Their perception of incompetence is deeply engrained.

This phenomenon is similar to "stereotype threat" first conceptualized and introduced by Claude Steele and his colleagues in the early 1990s (Steele, 2010; Steele & Aronson, 1995). Since then, stereotype threat has been widely recognized as a potential contributing factor to long-standing gaps in the academic performance of members of negatively stereotyped groups such as racial/ethnic minorities and females. Research concerning the social-psychological impact of stereotype threat and interventions designed to mitigate its effects have gained wide recognition recently (Cohen, Garcia, Apfel, & Master, 2006).

Expectation training should never be undertaken without serious thought and planning, and should not be attempted at all if the teacher does not have the resources (classroom assistants, older students, volunteers) to spend time with each low-status student who will play the role of expert. The danger is that if you allow the low-status student to fail as an expert, you will have knowingly exposed that student to another overwhelming negative evaluation. *This must not be allowed to happen.* Individualized coaching is indispensable to assure that the student is highly confident and can demonstrate his or her competence to your satisfaction before going on to act as an expert and teach.

Expectation training is not the most practical of classroom treatments. Most teachers do not have the time or the opportunity to prepare students for their role as teacher or expert so that a successful performance is guaranteed. Even if another adult is assigned this task, she will need to be carefully trained so that each student reaches a specific criterion level of competence before any demonstration of teaching skills takes place. Although this kind of intervention might sometimes not be practical for many busy teachers, the laboratory experiments and the subsequent field experiment demonstrate both the need and the potential value of interventions designed to change expectations for the performance of low-status students.

Over the years, we have worked with many teachers as they take steps to change students' expectations for competence by using two kinds of status treatments: the multiple-ability strategy and assigning competence to low-status students.

THE MULTIPLE-ABILITY STRATEGY

As you see people working together, you see all of the abilities that other students have that you didn't see before. There was this one kid, and he was really shy. He was always, like out of everything. He was never doing something or speaking out until we had an art project we had to do and he, like he just *visualized,* just got a pencil and piece of paper and like acted and draw a lot things that people didn't even see in him until that one time that we saw another part of him. (Maria, a 7th-grade student, Campbell, CA)

Maria is a student in a classroom where the teacher has been using a multiple-ability treatment for status problems. Maria does not think of her fellow students as "smart" or "dumb." She sees her peers as having multiple intellectual abilities, and groupwork as an opportunity to find out about those special abilities.

Furthermore, Maria realizes that the groupwork tasks her teacher assigns require many different intellectual abilities, skills, and competencies. After listing and describing many of these abilities, her teacher has said many times: "None of us has all of these abilities. Each one of us has some of these abilities." Thus, at the beginning of a new task, Maria expects that each student will have something valuable to contribute and that no one student will know or be able to do it all. As a result, she and other group members are prepared to listen to contributions from each group member and are less willing to sit back and let one person do most of the contributing.

The effectiveness of this treatment lies in altering the set of expectations with which students start on a new task. Instead of uniformly high expectations, high status students are expected to show strengths and weaknesses like everyone else. The same is true for low-status students, who are now expected and expect themselves to be competent at some of the important abilities and skills relevant to this task. The teacher has created a *mixed set of expectations* for everyone. Thus, when the students work together, the gap in expectations for competence between high and low-status students is smaller than in classrooms where teachers do not use such a status treatment.

Research Evidence

The multiple-ability treatment was developed by Tammivaara (1982) in a laboratory study. Participating students were selected on the basis of having high and average estimates of their own reading ability. Her treatment consisted of explaining the different abilities necessary for a survival task of Lost on the Moon (see Hall, 1971) before the groups began their discussions. The host experimenter said: "No one person will be good at all these abilities, but each person will be good on at least one" (p. 216). Furthermore, students were told that reading had no relevance to this particular task because all of the objects were pictured on cards. Those groups that had heard the multiple-ability introductions showed equal-status behaviors, whereas those who had not heard such an introduction exhibited a pattern of dominance by the high-ability readers. This study demonstrated that one can effectively interfere with status processes by defining multiple abilities as relevant to a task, thereby preventing students from assuming that academic status will be the only relevant basis for predictions of competence.

Rosenholtz (1985) created a 1-week multiple-ability curriculum for classrooms of 4th-graders who had known each other for some time and who had many opportunities to make evaluations of each other on reading ability. In this classroom experiment, Rosenholtz created a mixed set of expectations, not by telling the students about abilities but by having them experience three new abilities in the context of small groups, each supervised by an adult. The three new abilities were visual thinking, reasoning, and intuitive thinking. Group tasks were carefully engineered so that high-achieving readers could not dominate and struggling readers would gain more favorable evaluations of their competence. This was accomplished by having students take turns at guessing the answers and by using tasks where everyone contributed something different to the final product. Groups were recomposed between tasks, so students worked with a wide variety of their classmates.

On the standard game of Shoot the Moon, the results showed that low-achieving readers who had experienced the curriculum were significantly more active and influential on the new task than comparable readers from an untreated class. Behavior did not fully equalize status in treated groups in that there was still a tendency for strong readers to be more active and influential. But the advantage of the high-achieving readers was greatly reduced by the treatment.

The multiple-abilities curriculum provided low-status students with the opportunity to develop favorable self-evaluations and to be evaluated favorably by peers in the context of tasks defined as requiring new and different abilities—tasks where division of labor and turn-taking prevented status phenomena from operating. Once the favorable evaluations had been formed, they combined with the old set of expectations for competence and modified the status effects on a new and different task.

In multilingual, academically heterogeneous classrooms where small groups were working on discovery tasks in math and science, Cohen (1984) demonstrated strong status effects. When teachers used a multiple-ability status treatment for this same setting, similar to that used by Tammivaara (1982), effects of status on interaction were reduced, although not eliminated (Cohen, Lotan, & Catanzarite, 1990). High status individuals were still more likely to offer assistance than low-status individuals, suggesting that status was associated with expectations for higher levels of competence. An additional strategy became necessary to strengthen the impact of status treatments, as described later in this chapter.

What Are Multiple Abilities?

Use of the multiple-abilities strategy means thinking in a new way about human intelligence. Instead of thinking about how intelligent or unintelligent, smart or dumb, competent or incompetent a student is, consider different kinds of intelligence, intellectual abilities, and "smarts" that are called forth in different kinds of situations and for different aspects of a given task. In this context, the word "abilities" connotes its basic meaning of "being able to (do an activity)." Take, for example, the task of teaching. Among many other intellectual abilities, teaching requires interpersonal intelligence, organizational acumen, conventional academic skills, verbal agility, as well as creativity. Teachers plan interesting lessons, they formulate intriguing questions, they provide valuable feedback to students, they communicate with families—the list is endless. Teachers use their many different intellectual abilities in what they do all day, every day.

When we think about the adult world of work, it might be easier to recognize that many different kinds of abilities are essential for any profession or any job, just as with teaching. Yet often when we think about intelligence among students, we automatically narrow the concept to conventional academic criteria—being good at reading, writing, and computing quickly. That narrowness is, in part, a reflection of the narrowness of school curricula focused merely on basic skills and of accountability systems that rely solely on outcomes of standardized testing of students' performance. Instead of reflecting the way adults use their minds, such school curricula and testing systems reflect a limited and counterproductive conceptualization of what is to be learned and demonstrated as "smarts," and what is required to be seen as smart in school.

The narrowness of conventional academic tasks and assessments is one of the features of classrooms that help to create a unidimensional status order, where students rank each other on one dimension of ability. One is good, average, or "no good" at school tasks. Furthermore, one of the earliest indicators of the child's academic ability is his or her achievement in reading. Reading ability becomes an index of general intelligence in many classrooms for both students and teachers.

The multiple-ability approach is in line with current work on reconceptualizing human intelligence. For a long time, human intelligence has been thought of as unidimensional; it could be characterized by a single number; people (and whole races) could be ranked from gifted to stupid. Stephen Jay Gould, in his important book *The Mismeasure of Man* (1981), has done the field of education a great service by tracing the history of this idea to its roots, deep in Western culture. His analysis of biases present in his research on the concept of intelligence raises fundamental doubts as to whether we can continue to think of intelligence as unidimensional. With the introduction of multiple intelligences in his book *Frames of Mind*, Howard Gardner (1983/2011; 1993) redefined and reconceptualized human intelligence as multiple and rooted in specific areas of the brain. He distinguishes among different kinds of intelligences (e.g., linguistic, musical, logical-mathematical, spatial, bodily-kinesthetic, interpersonal). Sternberg (1985) sees intelligence as a set of processes that individuals bring to bear on situations with which they are faced. For Sternberg, intelligence is both multidimensional and imminently trainable. "Abilities Are Forms of Developing Expertise" is the title of one of his seminal articles (Sternberg, 1998). Sternberg's (2007) explorations of the relationships among culture, intelligence, and education are illuminating. Different cultures have different views of intelligence. Acts that demonstrate intelligent behavior also vary from culture to culture. Carol Dweck (2008) recognized that a person's implicit or explicit theory of intelligence plays an important role in that person's behavior and actions. According to Dweck (2008), a growth mind-set, that is, a person's recognition that intelligence is multidimensional and malleable, leads to potentially more successful performance through increased motivation and extra effort.

The multiple-ability treatment requires you to convince the students that many different intellectual abilities are necessary to successfully complete groupworthy tasks. Before you can convince students, however, you must analyze the tasks in terms of these intellectual abilities required. There is neither an official nor an exhaustive list of multiple abilities. It is a new way of looking at something we have known all along—that we use our intelligence in many different kinds of ways to solve problems and to accomplish important tasks in work and family life. Keep in mind that adults engage in highly complex problem solving as part of their daily lives. Some of these activities are academic, others are technical or political, and many are interpersonal, social tasks. Examples of such adult activities are managing, coordinating, taking the role of the other, teaching, learning, researching, directing, supervising, writing, drawing, building, developing, investigating, negotiating, evaluating, counting, calculating, and acting. These are all activities you can find in rich groupworthy tasks.

If we could think about students in the same way we think about ourselves as adults, each with strengths and weaknesses to do all that is required to live and work successfully, many of the status problems described earlier would fade. Thinking in this way does not require that each person be labeled as having particular and special abilities and therefore not allowed to acquire and develop new abilities. Rather, we recommend thinking about intellectual abilities as *specific and relevant* to particular activities, so that any person can be shown to have many different and useful abilities. Students should have the opportunities to engage in a wide variety of activities, so that they will continue to develop their intellectual abilities.

Steps of the Multiple-Abilities Strategy

There are two steps to a successful multiple-abilities strategy: (1) convincing the students that many different intellectual abilities are required for the task; (2) creating a mixed set of expectations for each student.

The best time to use this treatment is during an orientation to groupwork. You can convince your students that many different abilities are required through your own analysis of the assigned tasks. Suggest some of the *specific* intellectual abilities or skills that you think these tasks require. You can ask students to suggest abilities or skills that they think will be required. Point out how these abilities are useful for adult problem-solving situations. During the wrap-up, point out which of the multiple abilities that were identified during the orientation were used while completing tasks at the learning stations. You could ask students to share additional abilities that turned out to be critical. Many students, just like Maria, whom we met at the beginning of this chapter, learn how to analyze tasks and to think in this new way quite quickly.

Some students may have excellent reasoning ability. You will want to talk about this general ability in very specific ways. For example, logically analyzing or solving a problem experimentally, figuring out how something works mechanically, analyzing an issue from various perspectives, or making connections between ideas and concepts are all specific ways to describe how reasoning is required by particular group tasks. Instead of describing students in general terms as creative, you could talk about writing or performing a dramatic role for a skit, generating multiple alternatives, thinking of new uses for familiar objects, composing a song, conceiving of an idea for an illustration, imagining what it must have been like to live a long time ago, or taking the role of another person very different from oneself. Some of the groupworthy tasks described earlier require spatial and visual ability. Again, to be more specific, you might talk about diagramming mathematical concepts, drawing an idea as a cartoon, creating a model, or seeing how a sophisticated mechanism can be constructed. Note that using verbs to describe and introduce these multiple abilities makes the overall message more concrete and signals to the students that these activities can and should be learned, developed, and demonstrated.

The second step is critical although often omitted. After explaining that these tasks call for many different abilities, include the following statements: *None of us has all of these abilities. Each one of us has some of these abilities.* Help students see why this is likely to be true. If the tasks are truly groupworthy tasks, it is most unlikely that any one person will be outstanding in all the required abilities. And surely each student will be able to make an intellectual contribution in some way. This message is the heart of the multiple-ability treatment because it helps students to see that there is no such thing as being good or bad at groupwork, but that the most sensible position is to hold mixed expectations for competence. Teachers who are highly skilled in using this treatment often state that for the best possible group product, it will be necessary for students to recognize and use everyone's abilities and to serve as intellectual resources for one another.

Do's and Don'ts of Successful Treatments

Focus on abilities that students see as intellectual. Some students (and some adults) value but do not see some social skills as intellectual abilities. Unless you can convince students that there is such a thing as interpersonal intelligence, don't refer to "getting along with others" or "being nice" as one of the multiple abilities.

Avoid talk about abilities that suggests that some students are good with their heads while others are good with their hands. In general, Western culture rarely considers work with the hands or artistic work as intellectual work. When discussing artistic ability, be specific in the way that Maria was; say "visualizing or creating a design," or "using artistic representations."

Be very specific about how these abilities are important for particular tasks. Encourage students to analyze necessary abilities for themselves. Urge your students to develop new abilities. Refrain from implying that people only have inborn abilities.

The Multiple-Ability Curriculum

Obviously, you cannot use the multiple-ability treatment unless the tasks are groupworthy and actually require multiple intellectual abilities. These are the rich groupworthy tasks described in Chapter 6. If the group assignments are routine seatwork, then the students will never believe that many different abilities are required, nor will they have opportunities to use and recognize many different abilities.

Groupworthy tasks are by definition multiple-ability tasks. Students can discuss challenging questions prior to or as part of creating a final group product. Science tasks are readily seen as requiring multiple intellectual abilities: making observations and recording them precisely, manipulating science equipment carefully, hypothesizing causes and effects, and writing up the report clearly and concisely. Current curriculum standards reflect many of these intellectually and academically necessary practices and uses of language.

Reading, Writing, and Calculating

Basic skills are still part of multiple-ability tasks. For example, someone has to read the activity card. Everyone has to complete an individual report, even if it is only a sentence in the case of a young child or a drawing that serves as a prewriting activity for an emergent writer. Arithmetic operations are often part and parcel of an interesting groupworthy task.

However, basic skills are not a prerequisite for successful participation in the task. Struggling readers can receive assistance from group members. They can listen to the group discussion about what is involved in completing the group product. They can interpret pictures and diagrams on activity cards. Developing writers will be motivated to express their own ideas after participating in the creation of group products that employ central concepts. They can receive peer assistance in expressing and recording their own ideas. They may also be motivated to write about ideas they have contributed or heard in the group discussion. Often, creating collaborative drafts or rehearsing group reports will enhance group members' grasp of the central idea or the essential question.

In the multiple-ability orientation, you and the students will undoubtedly list basic skills as required for the task. Because they are only part of the required set, they will be seen as important but will not, as in many traditional classrooms, have the power to make some students who are struggling in these areas feel as if they cannot ever do well in the classroom.

Once you have set the stage with the multiple-ability strategy, assigning competence to low-status students is a second treatment you can use to modify expectations.

ASSIGNING COMPETENCE
TO LOW-STATUS STUDENTS

Miss Del Rio, a 4th-grade teacher of a bilingual classroom and the author of a case about the experiences of Miguel, a low-status student (Shulman, Lotan, & Whitcomb, 1998), describes what happened when she observed, identified, and made public the abilities Miguel used:

> Miguel was a shy and withdrawn child who spoke no English and stuttered when he spoke Spanish. His Spanish reading and writing skills were very low, and although math was his strength, nobody seemed to notice. Recently arrived from a small community in Mexico, Miguel lived with relatives—more than 10 adults and three children in a two-bedroom apartment. He came to school hungry and tired, and wearing dirty clothes. Shunned by his classmates, who said he had the "cooties," Miguel was left out of group activities. Even when he had a specific role, other members of the group would take over and tell him what to do. Miguel was obviously a low-status student.
>
> When I observed Miguel's group I saw that the other members simply wouldn't give him a chance. Cooperative learning was not helping him at all. Miguel grew more isolated by the day. Students increasingly teased him, and he was getting into fights and becoming a behavior problem. I realized the only way to change students' views about Miguel was to show them that he had certain abilities to contribute to his group. My challenge was to identify his strengths and show his peers that he was competent.
>
> One day in May, we were working in cooperative groups building different structures with straws, pins, clay, and wires. I was observing Miguel's group and saw him quietly pick up some straws and pins and start building a structure following the diagram on one of the activity cards. The other members of the group were trying to figure out how to begin their structure, and as usual, were not paying much attention to

Miguel. I observed that Miguel had used double straws to make the base more sturdy. He knew exactly what to do because he had looked at the diagram on the card. In other words, Miguel knew that the task was to build as sturdy a structure as possible, and he understood the principle of making the base stronger by using double straws.

I knew that this was the chance I was waiting for; it was clear that Miguel had the ability to build things by following diagrams. I decided to intervene, speaking both Spanish and English, since not everyone in the group spoke Spanish. I told the group that Miguel understood the task very well and would be an important resource because he had a great ability to construct something looking at a diagram. I also said that Miguel might grow up to be an architect since building sturdy buildings by following diagrams is one of the things architects need to do. I also told the group they had to rely on their translator so Miguel could explain what he was doing.

I continued observing the group from a distance, and sure enough, a few minutes later the translator was asking Miguel for help. Miguel explained to the members of his group what he had done and why. It was obvious he had abilities that could help him succeed in cooperative learning groups, and his group finally realized it. But I wanted everyone in the classroom to know that Miguel was very good at building structures. So when his group reported on their work, I said I had noticed that they had some problems understanding the task, and I asked their reporter what had helped them complete the task successfully.

He told the class that Miguel had understood what to do and had explained it to the group. I then reinforced the reporter's explanation, adding that Miguel had shown competence in building things by looking at a diagram and that his contribution had helped his group solve the problem successfully. By assigning competence to Miguel in front of his group and the whole class, I made sure everyone knew that Miguel had a lot to contribute to his peers. This was a wonderful example for everyone of how important it is to explore the multiple abilities of all group members in completing the task. After this, things changed for Miguel. His group members not only recognized him as an active member but began using him as a resource to help them balance their structures. (pp. 69–70)

Status treatments such as this one take advantage of the power of the teacher as an evaluator. Students tend to believe and value evaluations teachers make of them. Thus, if the teacher publicly evaluates a low-status student as being competent on a particular multiple ability, that student will tend to believe the evaluation. The other students who overhear are also likely to accept the evaluation's validity. Once the evaluation has been accepted, expectations for competence for this task are likely to result in increased activity and influence of the low-status student. Success at this task will translate into success in future groupwork tasks, as it did in the case of Miguel.

Assigning competence is a powerful intervention. It can do much to boost the participation of a low-status student. Ordinarily you may only watch low-status students to see if they are confused or staying out of trouble. You and the other students in the group may not even notice when the low-status student does something really well. To assign competence you must observe and witness when the low-status students actually do make intellectual contributions. These instances might be rare as you start out with groupwork. You need to make sure to create opportunities for the low-status student to demonstrate competence rather than just waiting for it to happen. It is a good idea to take notes while students perform groupwork and record your observations of what the low-status students are doing and how they are demonstrating their competence.

An effective assignment of competence has three critical features:

- Evaluations are public.
- Evaluations are specific and refer to particular intellectual abilities or skills.
- The abilities/skills of the low-status student are made relevant to the successful outcome of the group task.

Public recognition of competence is a key factor. Assigning competence is not simply a treatment for the low-status student—it is a group treatment; the problem lies partly in the expectations that others have for the low-status student. Therefore the group's expectations for this student must also be changed. Public recognition means that you are making it known that you consider this student competent on a particular skill or ability. This helps to change the student's expectations and the expectations held by classmates for this student.

As students move into middle school and high school, there is a danger that too much fuss over any single student will cause embarrassment to the student and possible sanction from peers. Just state in a matter-of-fact way what you are actually observing about his or her skills; don't gush. Be honest; don't make up stories about the student's abilities and performance that you didn't actually see or that are not valued intellectual abilities. Also, you don't have to reserve this treatment only for the lowest-status students in the class. Many students from the middle to the lower ranges of the status structure and most students if not all greatly benefit from this kind of feedback. It contributes to creating a positive classroom culture because students feel recognized and valued.

If you are very specific about the ability or skill the student is exhibiting, the student and the entire group will know exactly what he or she did well. It is not hard to be specific if you, like Miss Del Rio, speak in concrete terms about skills like building a sturdy structure by following a diagram.

Finally, making the ability relevant to the task has the effect of making the improved expectations for competence especially strong for the current activity. To make the ability relevant, teachers often say something similar to "Rosita is an important resource for this group. She can help you with putting together your tangrams" (or whatever skill or ability you are discussing with respect to the task).

Assigning competence is a sophisticated strategy and not easy to carry out. It is not simple praise. It requires you to observe students in terms of performance on multiple abilities. It also requires you to analyze what they are doing so that your intervention is specific and so that you can make the ability relevant to the task. Many teachers find that it is useful to take notes while students are in their groups and present the assignments of competence the next day when they have had a chance to review and study their notes in peace and quiet. Assignments of competence can be combined in an orientation with feedback to the groups on yesterday's cooperation and performance. In any case, assignments of competence are always welcome.

The more frequently teachers use the multiple-ability treatment and assign competence, the higher the participation rate of low-status students in elementary classrooms (Cohen, 1988). In classrooms where teachers used these treatments more frequently, there was less difference between the participation of high and low-status students than in classrooms where teachers used these treatments less often. We found evidence that the combined use of these two status treatments was associated with higher rates of participation of low-status students and had no effect on the participation of high status students. Analysis at the classroom level was associated with more equal-status interaction and thus with narrowing the participation gap among high status and low-status students in classrooms where teachers combined the use of these two strategies (Cohen & Lotan, 1995).

Thus, these combined strategies for treating status problems are critical for equitable groupwork. They will increase the engagement and participation of low-status students. They will improve expectations for competence in a way that will transfer to new and different group tasks. There is no reason, however, to expect newly acquired favorable expectations for competence to transfer to reading and math lessons conducted in a traditional fashion. If you use ability groups and if these lessons use only a narrow range of skills, you can quickly reconstruct a status order. If you stress competitive marking and grading as the major form of feedback for students, you will also aggravate status problems.

With some changes in tasks and assessment practices and with proper treatment of status problems, you can create a more equitable classroom. Such a classroom has many dimensions of intellectual competence. No one student is likely to be rated highly on all these dimensions. Each individual is likely to be rated highly on at least one dimension. Thus, there are no students who are generally expected to be superior regardless of the nature of the task. Students' competence will be evaluated by the abilities they demonstrate rather than based on demographics and background characteristics such as gender, race, native language, socioeconomic status, or cultural heritage.

To create an equitable classroom, use more groupworthy tasks featuring higher-order thinking and integrating basic skills. Students can be temporarily grouped for instruction for specific basic skills with which they are struggling. As long as students see mathematics, reading, and other subject areas as requiring a variety of skills and abilities, you can avoid reconstructing a status order. These changes enable you to teach at a high intellectual level despite a range in traditional academic skills. Furthermore, the gap in various achievement measures will narrow as more students gain access to challenging curricula and equal-status participation, and will have increased opportunities to demonstrate intellectual competence.

Evaluating Groupwork in Your Classroom

Zach Drew and Kevin Wofsey, two English teachers and graduates of the Stanford Teacher Education Program, worked as a team in planning, implementing, and evaluating a groupworthy task. In their write-up (2012) they included the following evaluation of groupwork in Zach's classroom at a diverse, yet tracked comprehensive high school in the San Francisco Bay Area.

> Our goal for this task was to have students apply their knowledge of characterization to a new context and in doing so explore how characterization operates in a dramatic setting. We also wanted to motivate students to think about the performative nature of drama, as they would be reading a play, which is really meant to be seen and not read. By engaging in this act of translation—moving from an image to a script to a performance— we hoped that students would be better prepared to understand "Fences" as drama and not just as words on a page. Furthermore, this process of translation mirrors that of August Wilson himself, who cites the collages of Romare Bearden as profoundly influential on his writing. Thus, in the completion of this task, students are placed in the position of the author they were about to begin reading. (p. 3)

The two colleagues go on to describe their observations.

> As the observer, Kevin took responsibility for tracking levels of engagement with the Collegial Observations form. During the 45 minutes in which students were working on their group projects, Kevin made four sweeps through the classroom at regular intervals. . . . In retrospect, this process seems particularly valuable, because from a qualitative standpoint, it appeared that the levels of engagement were quite high. The room was abuzz with discussion throughout the 45-minute block of work

time, as discussed in greater detail below, and so it would be tempting to guess that overall engagement was as high as 80% or more.

A more granular reading of the data confirms that not all groups expressed the same degree of engagement. Groups 1 and 7, for example, skewed very heavily toward Talk or Talk/Manipulate while Groups 3 and 5 leaned farther toward Look/Listen and Disengaged. . . . All in all, then, comparing the qualitative observations with the quantitative data serves to show why it is so important to include both types of analysis in this work. (pp. 10–11)

An analysis of a videotape documenting the work of one of the groups yielded the following:

Although we were initially disappointed that our camera captured the group experiencing the most difficulty, we ultimately decided it was valuable to observe this group closely and consider what went wrong. . . . It took this group nearly ten minutes to begin commenting on the image, whereas many other groups began this work within a couple minutes. . . . (Drew & Wofsey, 2012, p. 20)

Zach and Kevin reflected on some of the outcomes of their collaboration. First, they recognized their students' many positive experiences:

Because the task did not rely heavily on traditional, text-heavy academic work, all students, regardless of current language/reading mastery, could join in the work of observing the images and coming up with imaginative interpretations. In addition, students with a more dramatic flair could contribute ideas for scripting and staging their skits. From what we have observed, many students who excel in this area often have difficulty demonstrating competence in the formal atmosphere of a classroom where there is less opportunity for movement. At the same time, students who prefer more traditional activities could use the graphic organizer to collect and organize ideas and evidence to contribute to the finished product. Throughout the course of the groupwork, we saw examples of all of these kinds of contributions, from meticulous note-taking to directing and rehearsing to the creation of artistic props.

In terms of cooperation and participation of all students, the explicit expectation that everyone would take part in the skits did lead to 100% participation on stage, though we did not quite achieve the 100% speaking participation that we had hoped for. Nonetheless, in groups of four students who were given a picture with only three characters, several such groups found a way to create a spoken role for the fourth student, either by means of a narrator or by extrapolating another character who could join into the scene.

We are particularly proud of the mixture of creativity and authenticity this task provided for students in Zach's classroom. . . . Adding to (the) academic rigor and relevance was the relationship between the group and individual products in the task. Having worked together to create a brief vignette, students then had the opportunity to consider another picture individually and write a short story about the characters depicted in it. Given that almost every student launched into this individual task immediately and with great focus, it seems very likely that the groupwork helped prepare them to succeed in the more traditional academic tasks of written analysis and interpretation.

Enjoyment and enthusiasm—the buzz in the classroom was mostly positive. We heard many voices, often so many that it was difficult to isolate individual comments amid the general excitement in the room. Also, even the students who took longer to find their rhythm with the group process eventually arrived at a product they were willing to share with the class, and students also watched each other's skits with attention and interest, enthusiastically applauding each other for their efforts. Finally, we kept our task card brief, which allowed students to dive into the work right away without feeling bogged down by complex or daunting instructions. (Drew & Wofsey, 2012, pp. 25–27)

Next, the two teachers reflected on what could have been planned even better.

Although there was much to celebrate in this activity, there is certainly plenty of room for improvement as well. . . . The video we captured of Group 1 points to a variety of concrete steps we could take in the future to alleviate some of the issues that arose. First of all, if we were to try this or a similar groupwork activity again, we would seriously consider whether purely random groups were the most effective and equitable approach. Perhaps "controlled randomness" would be worth exploring. That is, we could make random lists and then scan over them to see if any of the groups were exceptionally lopsided in terms of gender or status, making small adjustments as needed. Such an approach might have spared Group 1 some of the frustrations they encountered making sense of the task and getting traction with their interpretations. . . . Next, we realize that all the groups would probably have benefited from more explicit modeling of roles, strategies for interpretation, and ways to formulate a skit. . . . Finally, in terms of status interventions, we feel that we could have done a better job of watching groups with a particular eye toward resolving subtle status issues before they escalated into larger problems. In Group 1, for example, if we had been paying closer attention, we might have noticed that no one was listening to A as he read through the Task Card. Rather than let this slide, we could have given a quick reminder to listen to each other, perhaps reminding the Facilitator to pay particular attention to this. Again, this is an area where more careful explanation of the roles could have been helpful. (Drew & Wofsey, 2012, pp. 27–28)

In their evaluation, Kevin and Zach used specific tools such as an observation guide and a video camera to collect and analyze data and to make plans about how to enhance the experiences of the students while working in groups. Systematically analyzing and evaluating the implementation of groupwork are worthwhile activities and can have a significant pay-off. As with many complex pedagogical strategies and approaches, you will experience successes and challenges. Here we provide some tools that will help you collect and analyze data and take a critical, yet lucid look at your planning and implementation of the task. Most important, you will be able to gauge the quality of your students' experiences in addition to and beyond measures of academic achievement. If, as recommended, you are able to find a partner to plan and evaluate with you, you can rely on him or her to provide a friendly, yet critical eye.

TOOLS FOR EVALUATION

Some effective and relatively simple tools to use in evaluating your own groupwork are provided in this section and in Appendix B. Experienced and novice teachers have found them practical and useful. Included within this chapter are sample observation guides and a participation scoring sheet. A sample student questionnaire and a guide for analyzing the data it yields are included in Appendix B. The following discussion will describe these classroom observation tools and how to use them. Depending on which aspects concern you the most, they may be used separately or together. Undoubtedly you will have questions and possibly concerns: Will the students be engaged? How well will I be able to delegate authority and address status problems? Will the students be able to cooperate? How well will the low-status students do? Review the various instruments and select parts or specific questions of concern. For starters, focus on a few important aspects of the evaluation. As you gain more experience, you will be able to broaden and deepen your scope.

Guide for an Observer

We are assuming that you have been able to arrange for a colleague, a mentor, or a student teacher to visit your classroom on the day you plan to start the groupwork. You have discussed with the observer what you are trying to do, what the challenges might be, and which students may require special attention. As a result, the plan for evaluation is a joint decision about what to observe and to whom to pay attention.

While the students start to work in their groups, the observer can move around the room watching and listening. If you point out to the observer the students you are most concerned about, she or he can observe their behaviors carefully. These may be low-status students, students who are learning the language of instruction, students who dominate the conversation, or students who struggle with schoolwork. The observer can also watch you in action.

Figure 11.1 presents a sample guide for the observer. Using these guidelines, the observer can take notes. In case you are not able to secure an observer, you can set up a recording device and record the classroom and yourself.

Figure 11.1 lists possible questions for the observer. Consider reviewing this protocol with the observer during the planning session, and choose or add questions you want to include. Part A focuses on the teacher's orientation. It is particularly important for the observer to arrive in time to see and hear you at this stage. So many problems start with confusion in the orientation. On the other hand, in an effort to make all the details clear, the teacher risks losing the attention of the students by trying to get across too much information.

Part B directs the observer's attention to the groups at work. A good procedure is to look over the whole classroom and count how many students are wandering, unattached to any group, and how many students are waiting for the teacher. The observer scans the classroom and tries to determine how many of the groups seem to be at work on their tasks in the way in which they were supposed to work (Questions 1 and 2). Then the observer can move around to stand near enough to

Figure 11.1. Sample Guide for the Observer

A. Orientation

1. How does the instructor introduce the task?

2. How does the instructor use technology, visuals, and manipulatives to present information, give instructions, and get the students' attention?

3. How does the teacher clarify norms, roles, and the assignment to groups?

4. *For Multiple-Ability Tasks:* How does the teacher carry out a multiple-ability orientation?

5. What are students' reactions to the orientation?

B. Students at Work in Groups

Overview

1. How many groups are engaged in their task? Are there any groups where students are working individually rather than as part of the group?

2. How many students are not part of a group? How many students are waiting for the teacher?

Group by Group

3. Do the students seem confused about what they are supposed to do? If so, is the group functioning to solve the problem?

4. Consider the cooperative norms introduced by the teacher. Is there evidence that students follow these norms? Are some students failing to observe these cooperative norms? Describe.

5. Consider the roles and the expected behaviors associated with those roles. For each role, is there someone playing this role in the group? Are there any roles that are not in evidence? Is the facilitator (if there is one) dominating the group?

6. Do you see any evidence of interpersonal conflict? Describe.

7. Is any one student dominating a group? Is there one student who is saying very little?

C. Focus on Selected Students

The teacher has pointed out students she wants more information about. Observe and take notes on what is happening with each one.

1. Do some of the lower-achieving students understand the task? If they are having difficulty, is someone helping them?

2. Are low-status students participating? Are they playing their assigned roles? How are members of the group interacting with them?

D. The Teacher

1. As students are working in groups, how does the teacher provide information and get students back on task?

2. If a problem arises, does the teacher get the group members to solve it for themselves?

3. How does the teacher provide feedback to the groups and to individuals?

4. Was the teacher able to assign competence and if so, what was the group's reaction?

each group to hear and see, but not so near that students become conscious of being observed. Questions 3–7 in Part B should be considered for each group. A seating chart with the group numbers helps in the debriefing between the observer and the teacher later on.

Part C has to do with selected students who might be struggling in group settings. It is important to spend about 5 minutes observing and listening to each of these students, taking notes on the questions for each one.

Part D addresses you, the teacher. The first two questions raise common problems that teachers have when they first start groupwork: hovering over groups in a way that inhibits their interaction, spending too much time trying to keep students on task instead of letting the groups take responsibility, and spending too much time trying to get the students through the task instead of letting them help each other.

Even if you do manage to avoid these problems, your chief concern may be the mechanics of getting everyone through the task. At first, providing effective feedback to the groups and asking them stimulating questions to encourage their thinking might be challenging. This skill comes with time and practice. Be sure that the observer has sufficient time to watch you in action so as to get a fair picture. The last question concerns your use of the status treatment of assigning competence. When you are carrying out this treatment, an observer will record a specific and public recognition of a student's intellectual competence and the relevance of her contribution to the work of the group.

The Student Questionnaire

You can collect important data by asking students to complete a questionnaire. For younger students, you can read the survey items out loud. Multiple-choice questions can be done with clickers or applications on mobile devices. A sample student questionnaire is included in Appendix B. These questions have been successful with children as young as 9 years old. Some of the items allow you to examine the experiences of low-status students. By requesting that students put their names on the questionnaire, you can focus on the responses of students you are particularly interested in at some time or other. You can see if any low-status students were picked as having the best ideas or were chosen as having done the most or least talking in the group. There is usually a reliable relationship between students' reports of such matters and systematic scoring by an observer.

If you have used a multiple-ability strategy, then students should be able to list one or more abilities that they thought they used well during the groupwork. Also, they will probably be able to list some of the multiple abilities you introduced in addition to reading and writing.

The outcome of the training in cooperative norms can be confirmed with this questionnaire. Do students report experiencing problems with not being listened to or with talking much less than they wanted to? Did people have trouble getting along in the group? Would they be willing to work with this group again? You can choose questions according to your major concerns and add others.

A guide to analyzing the student questionnaire is also included in Appendix B. This guide is organized by the kinds of questions many teachers want answered about their groupwork. Data analyses are suggested to provide some answers to each question.

Nanor Balabanian and Diana Dean, history/social science teachers and graduates of the Stanford Teacher Education Program, used a student questionnaire to gauge student interest in the task they had designed and implemented in a diverse charter high school in the San Francisco Bay Area. Nanor was the teacher and Diana the observer.

> When we asked students how interesting they found the work of their group, 22% of them responded very interesting, 48% responded interesting, and 26% responded not very interesting, and only 6% said not interesting at all. We realized that nearly 3/4 of our students found our project to be interesting. I think this was a major strength of our lesson because the students were mostly engaged in the task and were actually interested to participate in it. What was also interesting was that the majority of students who said they found the project "Very Interesting" were generally low-achieving students. We found this to be intriguing because it might have been due to the fact that this project gave them multiple points of entry, ones in which they could achieve and perform well. (Balabanian & Dean, 2012, p. 11)

Systematic Quantitative Observations

In addition to your qualitative observation and the student questionnaire, you or an observer can conduct systematic scoring to gauge student participation. These observations can focus on the overall proportion of students on task or off-task or on the rate of participation or airtime of each student in a group.

Collegial observations (whole class). When you or an observer use the tool of collegial observations, you take a snapshot of the overall level of engagement in the class. By observing group after group closely yet unobtrusively, you can record the number of students in each group who

1. are talking and working together on the task by manipulating the materials and the resources (e.g., calculators, test tubes, algebra tiles, etc.),
2. are manipulating without talking,
3. are reading or writing without talking,
4. are looking or listening but are not actively participating in the conversation,
5. are disengaged, and
6. are waiting for the teacher.

Account for all the students in the classroom by putting a hash mark in the appropriate category as you take a mental snapshot of the group. Be sure to "call them as you see them" in that particular moment.

By adding together the number of students in the first four categories, you estimate the proportion of students on task. The number of students off task is reflected in the category labeled "Disengaged." The sixth category indicates that the students might be confused or waiting for the teacher to resolve their problem.

Figure 11.2 is an example of an observation taken during an engaging groupwork activity in a 6th-grade earth science class. Students were designing an experiment that tests the effects of carbon dioxide on the temperature of the air in a closed container.

The percentage of students in the first category—Talking or Talking and Manipulating, is particularly significant. Researchers at the Program for Complex Instruction at Stanford University found that the higher the proportion of students in that category, the higher the average gain scores on various achievement measures. This finding was replicated across grade levels and subject areas from 2nd grade to high school (Cohen & Lotan, 1997a).

Melissa Meloy, Liz Beans, and Adrian Cheng (2012), whose work we presented previously, used this tool to evaluate the implementation of their project. They wrote:

> Throughout the implementation of this task, students maintained high levels of engagement. [Figure 11.3] shows the percent of students who

Figure 11.2. Collegial Observation Instrument

Collegial Observation - Whole Class

Teacher Name_*E.C.*_____   Date of obs _*Oct. 15*_

Total # of Students_*31*_____   Time of obs_*11:40*___

Grade_*6*_____   Unit _*Climate Change*_

Observer Name _*N.H.*_____   # diff. group tasks_*1*_

Small Groups	Talk or/ Talk/Manip	Manip only	Read/ Write	Look/ Listen	Disengaged	Waiting for teacher	N for rows
1	//			/		/	4
2	///	/			/		5
3	/	//		/			4
4	///		//				5
5		//	/		/		4
6	//	/		/			4
7	////						4
8							
9							
10							
N for columns	15	6	3	3	2	1	30

Total N in Small Groups   _30_

Away from center:
In transition on task   _/_____
Wandering, fooling around, disengaged   _____
In other academic work   _____

Total N, Away from Center   _/_

were engaging in six types of activities while working through the group task. The observers noted student engagement at three different time points throughout each day of the implementation. Each time point was taken approximately ten minutes apart and recorded on an observation data sheet. The number of students engaging in each type of participation was totaled, and the percent of students engaging in each activity

Figure 11.3. (Day 1) Data Showing Overall Student Engagement and Participation at Three Different Times During the Group Task

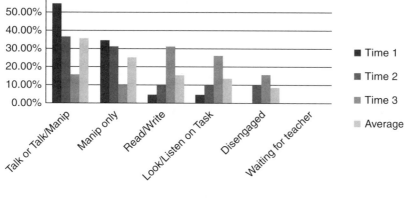

was found by dividing the total number of people doing each type with the number of students in class. Finally, an average of each time point was taken for each type of engagement. (p. 30)

The teachers used the data to look for patterns, identify needed improvements in the task, and consider other changes.

Based on the change in levels and types of engagement throughout the first day it seems as if there were more points of access during the first part of the activity because there was a high percentage of students talking and manipulating the materials, and no student was observed to be disengaged. Around the middle of the period when groups transitioned to making their posters, the engagement level dropped overall. There was a drop in the number of students manipulating materials, probably because groups had begun to solve the problem and had completed or nearly completed the Halloween to Thanksgiving transformation. By the third time point on the first day, students were primarily reading, writing, and listening. At this point all groups were working on their posters, so the points of access were limited. This suggests that while completing the gummi transformation is a groupworthy activity, making a poster is not. It is worth noting that while levels of disengagement increased later in the task, overall engagement levels were still high, with nearly 85% of students on task in one way or another. (Meloy et al., 2012, p. 31)

Observations of Individual Participation

Select the "target students" you are interested in observing. These may be any or all of the following: students with low academic status; students who tend to dominate; students who have little social influence among their classmates; quiet students who usually don't participate; students with limited language proficiency; and/or students who disrupt the classroom. Next, design a scoring sheet, such as that shown in Figure 11.4, in which you draw the location of the various groups around the classroom with a box to represent each student in each group. Point out the location of the target student within the group when the observer is ready to score. Have the observer label the boxes in each group to represent the target students.

The observer should spend at least 5 minutes scoring each group. We are assuming that there will be five or six groups with four or five students each. The observer simply makes a hash mark inside the appropriate box for every task-relevant speech act a student makes. That speech can be as short as "OK," or it can run for several minutes. A speech act ends when the person stops talking, starts talk that is social or unrelated to the task, or is interrupted by another speaker. Off-task talk is not recorded. It is

Figure 11.4. Sample Participation Scoring Sheet

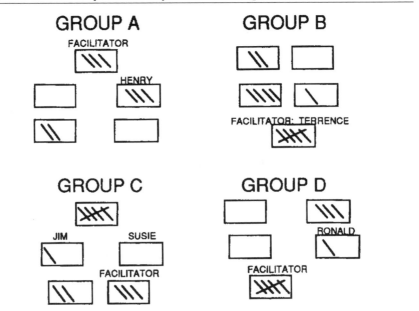

important to record the contribution of the target student. Sometimes errors will be caused by members of the group moving around and in and out of the group. If the target student moves away from the group and ceases participating, it should be so noted. The observer has to stand close enough to the group to hear and see, but not so close as to make the students aware of what he or she is doing.

The tabulation and analysis of these data are quite simple (see Figure 11.5). How many of the low-status target students were never seen participating? How many students in the whole class were never seen participating? If the low-status target students make up half or more of the nonparticipating students, you are observing a status problem. More precise calculations can be made by examining the number of times the target students were scored in comparison to the number of times other people in their groups were scored. The simplest way to do this is to compare the average number of speeches of target students to the average number of speeches for other members of their groups (see the second sample calculation in Figure 11.5).

Then compare the target students' figures to the average figure for the group. Are they below average? Are most of the target students below average in their respective groups? If the groupwork task has

Figure 11.5. Sample Participation Scoring Calculations

How many of the nonparticipants in the class (i.e., students who never talked) were low-status students?

a. Total nonparticipants	6
b. Low status nonparticipants	1
Percentage low status (a ÷ b × 100)	17%

Conclusion: Very few of the nonparticipants were low-status students.

How did the rate of target students' participation compare with the average rate of their groups? (Sample calculation given here is for Group A; calculations for other groups should be made in the same manner.)

	Target Students	**Other Students**
Number of students	1	4
Total number of speeches	3	5
Average speeches per student	3	1.25

Conclusion: Henry talked more than average for his group.

been effective in moderating status effects, some target students should be below average, some close to average, and some above. This method of scoring also allows you to tell at a glance if a group member is dominating the interaction by talking far more than anyone else. If you are concerned that the facilitators are doing too much of the talking, have the observer note the facilitators on the chart so that you can examine their rate of speaking in comparison to the average rate of other members of the group.

The figures for any single target student should be viewed with caution because it may well be that the particular 5 minutes that the group was being scored were not representative of the group's pattern of interaction as a whole. This method of scoring has the advantage of objectivity but the disadvantage of allowing only limited conclusions to be drawn from the numbers, whereas the student questionnaire has the advantage of the richness of the inferences that can be drawn but the disadvantage of the subjectivity of the responses.

Use of Recording Devices

To get a deeper insight into the nature of the interaction and the quality of the discourse in the groups, the use of a recording device is very useful. Listening to and/or watching a recording can illuminate some of the issues you hadn't noticed during the hustle and bustle of any lesson, but particularly of a lesson where six to eight groups are in simultaneous operation.

Chris Alger, a teacher-author, occasionally recorded her students' interactions in groups (Shulman, Lotan, & Whitcomb, 1998). When listening to the recording, she came to a heart-wrenching realization about a particular interaction she had with a group that included Dennis, one of the low-achieving, low-status students in her class. Dennis wasn't participating, nor was he engaged in the task. Yet, when Chris, the teacher, asked the other members of the group whether they made attempts to include Dennis, they said they had. However, Chris realized that it was all a pretense:

> Several months later, I began to reflect as I listened to the tape of that interaction. I had to listen three times before I realized what had really transpired that day and a fourth time before glimpsing the implications of my role.
>
> I had seen with my own eyes that Dennis wasn't engaged with the group. They had all lied to me about his involvement. I knew it was a lie,

but hadn't confronted Dennis because I'd believed that he'd close down even further. (Shulman et al., 1998, p. 63)

Alger's analysis led her to consider the ethical implications of her actions in the classroom:

In a teacher-centered classroom, the withdrawn behavior of a student like Dennis is between him and the teacher. His fellow students are aware of the behavior, form opinions about him because of it, and may in turn reinforce his own low expectations of himself, but they are generally unaffected by his behavior. By contrast, in groupwork situations, a student's silence—Dennis's unhealthy invisible act—impacts his fellow students. They count on each other to help the group get a good grade, and one student's silence becomes a noticeable absence. . . . In the end, it proved difficult to alter people's perceptions of Dennis, both his classmates' and his own—and as I now realize, my own. We all participated in letting him remain aloof, and our collective failure to take responsibility for helping Dennis is itself immoral. What became apparent during my fourth review of the audiotape was my own collaboration in Dennis's silence. I realized I had addressed the other members of the group as if Dennis were truly invisible. Instead of assigning competence, I did the opposite. I disembodied, objectified, and ultimately disempowered Dennis. No wonder the expectations of his peers were lower than I would have liked. In my own way I had unwittingly silenced him. (Shulman et al., 1998, pp. 63–64)

Obviously, most busy teachers won't have the opportunity to listen to or watch a recording multiple times and engage in such deep analysis. However, such reflections can be particularly valuable when thinking about the subtleties and implications of classroom interactions.

Increasingly in professional learning programs, recording devices are used productively to support the development of ambitious teaching strategies. Many teachers are engaged in "video clubs" and are watching and analyzing classroom events together. Brittany Leknes and Lily Xu, teachers of mathematics and graduates of the Stanford Teacher Education Program, summarized their analysis of a short video segment captured in a mixed-grade algebra class. Their attention to issues of unequal status among members of the group is of particular interest.

Students in (this) class do group work as part of their everyday classwork, so this task was not a stretch for their normal behavior. We did not observe any areas of conflict throughout the task. Students got along well, and made sure to include each other. However, we noticed that the status issues that arise each day were perpetuated by this activity.

We chose to analyze a section of the video that exemplifies the status issues of one high-achieving group. . . . This group consists of two freshman girls with high academic status. The other half of the group was comprised of two boys, a junior and a senior, who have high social status and middle academic status.

In the video clip, one of the high status girls, Sarah, dramatically asked her other group members, "Do you guys get it?" Following this question, she proceeded to explain her steps to solving a synthetic division problem to the other group members, as they followed her reasoning and copied down the answers. In analyzing this interaction, we were torn about whether or not this is a positive interaction. This group traditionally gets along well. In this clip, they were collaborative and seemed happy. However, Sarah, the high status student who usually explains how to do the task to the other members of the class, stayed true to her role, and explained how to figure out the problem to her other group members.

After she was done with her explanation, the other three students seemed to understand the problem better. They said, "Oh, I get it," and asked her follow up questions throughout her explanation. Looking back at the data from the collegial observations sheet, this group always had at least two people talking and interacting with each other. Was this a positive interaction? Students appeared to learn the math and improve their understanding. Was maintaining the status quo enough? These are questions that we continue to struggle with as we analyze this clip. (Leknes & Xu, 2012, pp. 16–17)

Meloy et al. (2012), the science teachers noted earlier in the chapter, recorded some moments of successful and productive groupwork:

The video segment focuses on a group of three students. In this class, groups are determined by the seating chart which is assigned randomly. Students in this particular clip had the opportunity to work together as a group on two previous in-class assignments. One member of this group, a high academic status and middle social status student, was absent the day of task implementation, but she was present on the previous occasions this group worked together.

Levels of participation of the students in this clip were impressive even to an outside observer who knows nothing about the academic or social status of the students involved. When taking into consideration the fact that Noah and Johnny, Johnny especially, have very low participation rates in class, this segment is even more impressive. When first viewing this clip, Henrietta seems to dominate the conversation. Indeed, she did about 50% of the talking, while Noah and Johnny participated evenly with each other. That said, Henrietta tended to ask bigger picture, less focused questions whereas Noah and Johnny tended to ask questions that helped direct the group forward. Henrietta responded to the questions of her group mates with statements that summarized the group thinking in response to the question. It is significant that even though Henrietta dominated the talking during the task, she did not dominate the direction the group went. Rather, she summarized their collective thinking.

All three students were able to participate in the conversation because all students were included in the discussion. This is evident from the fact that all questions were posed to the group as a whole rather than to one specific individual, a practice that could enable equitable opportunity for students to demonstrate competence. Supporting their inclusive question asking, the non-verbal behaviors of students also suggest inclusiveness. The focus of Noah and Johnny cannot be determined due to the angle at which the video was taken, however it is clear from the video that Henrietta mostly looked down at the manipulatives. When she did look up, she engaged both of her group mates. Similarly, all students were engaged with the materials and maintained a posture that opened themselves up to all members of the group.

The video clip also shows some important behaviors on the part of the teacher that helped foster positive interdependence of the group. For example, Henrietta stated that she felt confused, a statement which was ignored by the teacher, even though in the video the teacher is clearly standing right there. Instead, Henrietta was forced to work through her confusion with her group mates. Later, when asked a specific question about what they were supposed to do, the teacher simply restated what had been said in the orientation to the task, once again forcing the group to work out their own collective understanding of the assignment. At a later point, the teacher responded to a question from the group by reflecting the question back at the group, empowering the students to rely on their own interpretations of the information available. (pp. 34–37)

REFLECTING ON GROUPWORK

Schedule a conference with your partner, keep a journal, or just write yourself some notes. Recognize and applaud all that went well. Then, ask what some of the issues are that you will have to attend to next time. Construct an agenda for a meeting with your partner and take time to think about possible improvements. If your groupwork is ongoing, some of the solutions can be put into practice immediately. Start with the questions identified in the planning session for the evaluation. For example, if you were concerned with the clarity of your instructions, then check all the data you have on this point. After pulling together all that has been learned from the evaluation, including the systematic data and your own rough observations, plan and decide on how the next session of groupwork could be improved. Do so in a systematic fashion. Your conference or reflection will be more effective if you make decisions in light of what you have learned from the data collected. What has gone well and can be left alone? What needs some adjustment and what do you and your partner think should be done about it? Note these decisions and file them along with your instructional plans for the groupwork task. Otherwise you might forget what you have learned and will rely on a vague overall judgment of how it went.

What can you do if you carry out a status analysis and conclude that you still have a marked status problem, with some students doing most of the work and low-status students offering very little to the group? Go back to Chapter 10 and see if there are some techniques you can introduce. Perhaps you need to spend more time with a multiple-ability introduction. Perhaps you should observe low-status students during groupwork and find a way to assign competence to those students. Perhaps you need to introduce or reinforce the facilitator role to make sure that everyone participates; and perhaps if the low-status students are encouraged to play this role, they will receive a much-needed boost in expectations for competence.

Obviously you will pick a method of evaluation that is practical and works for you. It makes sense to try one of these techniques at a time. As you gain experience, it will take less time to analyze the data. If you are attempting to treat a particular problem you have identified from the first round of evaluation and you want to evaluate the second round to see if things have improved, be sure to use the same instruments the second time. When you have tried out the new solutions and evaluated them, you will have a tested groupwork format that you and your partner and any other colleagues can use. You will be pleased to find that a carefully thought-out and evaluated design will work well with a wide variety of classes; the students will respond with enthusiasm and excitement year after year.

12 Groupwork in the Bilingual Classroom

Elizabeth Cohen

The dedicated classroom teacher of a bilingual or an English as a Second Language (ESL) classroom faces a scene of enormous complexity—linguistic, academic, and cultural. At the same time as the teacher struggles to help the children understand what is to be done in each assignment, he or she is trying to improve language proficiency and often to remediate basic skills. Furthermore, there are such differences in what each child will need to understand instruction and to make reasonable progress that conventional methods of ability grouping do not really simplify the situation. If teachers group children by language proficiency (as has been recommended by the federal government), what do they do with the academic differences? And if they group by academic ability, how can they be sure that everyone understands the language of instruction?

I am not a specialist in bilingual education, but for the past 14 years I have worked with teachers in elementary classrooms where the issue of language is a central one. Early in this work, I discovered that it was not a clear-cut issue of whether the child was Spanish speaking, English speaking, or proficiently bilingual. Very often we find children who do not test as proficient in either English *or* Spanish. The actual linguistic status of such children is not well understood.

Furthermore, the issues of social class and of culture are thoroughly mixed with the issue of language. Some of these children with limited or minimal English and Spanish come from very poor economic conditions; they are arriving at school with the strengths of their own culture but without many of the preschool experiences that prepare children for the typical curriculum. Also from low income homes are some children who have experienced no schooling; it is not uncommon to find new immigrants of 8 or 9 years of age who have never before been in school.

Many 3rd-, 4th-, and 5th-grade bilingual classrooms contain children with minimal skills in reading and writing any language; some of these students started school with limited English proficiency. They had no access to instruction in a language they could understand; as a result they have not made good academic progress. For those students with proficiency in Spanish but with limited English proficiency, it would seem clear that instruction in the mother tongue in these basic skill areas is critical to ensure academic progress. Many of the classrooms that I have been privileged to work with have proficient bilingual teachers and teaching materials in both languages. Children in these settings have the major advantage of having access to the language of instruction.

To make the scene even more complicated, there are other non-English languages in the schools. With Asian immigrants come a variety of languages such as Laotian and various Vietnamese dialects. Often it is not possible to find in the classroom another child, credentialed teacher, or trained aide who knows the language of the newcomer. These children are typically placed in ESL classes where the top priority is to learn English quickly, sometimes to the neglect of the other academic subjects.

Most commonly, the school's major goals for bilingual and ESL classes are to increase linguistic proficiency in English and to move students up to grade level in basic skills. The mistaken assumption is made that English is a prerequisite to instruction in the basic skills (Cummins, 1979). Emphasis on teaching of English is often at the expense of challenging instruction in the basic skills. As a consequence, the students fall further behind in content while learning the new language.

Groupwork offers a powerful tool for the attainment of both English and basic skills. At the same time, it can be used to enable teachers of such classrooms to provide access to higher-order thinking skills. This chapter will start with the issue of oral proficiency and will move to the problem of presenting the grade-level curriculum to a class that is heterogeneous academically and linguistically. The final section will illustrate how groupwork can be used to produce broad-gauge achievement results with a bilingual approach designed to develop thinking skills.

ORAL PROFICIENCY

In a review of the research literature on how children acquire a second language, McLaughlin (1985) finds that second-language learning is accelerated when learners have meaningful interaction with peers who are native speakers of the language. The idea of native speakers as language models is not new in second-language pedagogy. However, common school practices work against peer interaction between English-speaking and limited-English-speaking children. In the first place, limited-English-speaking children are often removed from the regular classroom and placed in special classrooms either for bilingual instruction or for ESL. Certainly in this setting where they are isolated and stigmatized, they are unlikely to have significant peer interactions with English-speaking classmates. Secondly, within classrooms where there are proficient English speakers, even when cooperative learning is employed, one often finds the Spanish speakers segregated in their own small group.

Today there is a growing number of two-way bilingual immersion programs (Lindholm & Aclan, 1991) demonstrating that where children are instructed in both languages and where the teachers make frequent use of mixed-language groups in cooperative learning, all the students become bilingual. In addition, these children perform very well academically when assessed on standardized tests in both English *and* Spanish.

Krashen (1988) argues that the second language learner must experience "comprehensible input," meaning language instruction that is a bit beyond the learner's current level of proficiency. Simple immersion in an English-speaking group does not present comprehensible input if the child is not ready for such an experience. Further, comprehensible input must be provided in a context that does not evoke anxiety in the limited-English-proficient child. Krashen discusses a number of ways in which comprehensible input can be organized in the classroom and in the playground. In groupwork situations that provide nonverbal cues and context from manipulative materials or charades, for example, interaction between peers may be a very effective way of providing comprehensible input while also instructing on content.

According to Faltis and Merino (1992), the learner speaks and listens in interactions in which it is necessary to communicate. If teachers are skilled communicators, they give clear directions for classroom tasks, structure those tasks so as to require participation, and use classroom materials that enhance meaningful student participation. In this way comprehensible input is provided in an interesting and nonthreatening atmosphere which fosters successful second language learning in much the same way as first language develops.

The language of teaching is especially critical when children are limited-English speakers. Academic activities that require interaction to learn content are preferable to direct language instruction (Cazden, 1988).

These recommendations are very similar to what I have called "rich tasks for groupwork." Particularly if training and the organization of the groupwork have ensured that everyone must participate, it would seem that the stage is set for the optimal conditions that the experts recommend.

Groupwork and the Development of Oral Proficiency

A kindergarten teacher who participated in research in her own classroom as part of the Teacher Investigator Project* was surprised at how easy it was to integrate groupwork into her teaching.

> It was so simple, we didn't realize that it was going to be that simple—we were assuming that it was going to be this tremendous, difficult, complicated thing—and it really wasn't that hard at all. You could adapt a lot of tasks to work in those kinds of situations. So you can integrate normal daily things like reading and math. It don't have to be something you get out of an oral language development book. Once you learn how to give them independence, you can adapt things from the text.

This teacher's class presented typical problems of differences in linguistic proficiency. Many of the children at this school enter kindergarten with a limited vocabulary. Furthermore, this limited vocabulary may be divided between two languages. Some children with limited English proficiency are unwilling to speak in the classroom at all. As one of these children was described, "When he first came and you would ask 'What's your name?' he would just smile." Others in the same class have a good level of proficiency in either Spanish or English.

The issue for this teacher was: How do you get these children to talk? Do you try to teach them some more English through whole-group activities such as drill and practice or through reading out loud to them? And what do you do with those who have a good grasp of English while you are working with those who do not?

---

*The Teacher Investigator Project was financed by the Anglo American Education fund and was conducted under the auspices of the Stanford University School of Education.

With the help of the school's reading teacher, the teacher found that kindergartners given a pretraining program in activities such as Broken Circles that are designed to help them work as a group were then able to participate in many additional activities that stimulated lively discussions. Examples of such activities included giving each group a card with a new word on it and asking them to develop a charade portraying this word so that other groups could guess it. Here, those children who knew English acted as a valuable resource and explained the word to those who did not. Furthermore, everyone had ideas about how the charade should be carried out. In still another task, the reading teacher came to the room with paper pig ears and noses for each group. Their task was to enact "The Three Little Pigs." According to the teacher's report, the children developed numerous adaptations of the original story with a good deal of excitement and maximum communication. This classroom teacher even found that simple tasks requiring visual memory could be adapted to group discussion. She gave them a detailed drawing of an elephant followed by an elephant drawing with many details missing. Each child had to fill in the incomplete version, but they helped each other with the details, for example, "Pedro, you're missing the eye." Before the school year was over, this teacher found it relatively easy to have one or two oral proficiency activities a day. Interestingly, when the teacher and the reading specialist compared tape recordings of a group of children discussing a live animal made before and after these experiences, they were pleased and gratified to find that almost all the children had increased dramatically in their willingness and ability to speak.

Group Composition and Linguistic Proficiency

If the task is rich with context, pictographs, and manipulatives, it is possible to place children who share no common language in the same group. Although it is still quite a struggle for the newcomer, if the group is trained to see that everyone gets the help needed, the children will do a remarkable job of communication. If at all possible, mixed language groups are preferable. Otherwise, the students will not have the benefit of hearing peers with English proficiency. When a child is monolingual in Spanish or in another language, he or she should be combined with English speakers and with a proficient bilingual child. The bilingual child needs to be taught that he or she is a valuable bridge in the group, explaining to the monolinguals what the others are saying and offering special help to the non-English-speaking students. It is also important for the English-speaking students to understand the contributions of the non-English speaker. In the classrooms where both languages were utilized by both teachers and children, Neves (1983) found that the bilingual children had, as a whole, the highest social status; they were most often chosen on a sociometric measure as friends and as good in math and science. As the year progresses in a bilingual classroom, one can often find children who can understand an other language even though they cannot speak much of it as yet. My staff has often observed conversations between a Spanish- and an English-speaking child, each speaking in his or her own language, but clearly understanding the other.

In the Spanish–English bilingual classroom, sometimes members of a group will speak in Spanish and sometimes they will speak in English. Our studies have shown that there is no need to enforce an English-only rule. English proficiency will develop in this context. If there are English monolinguals in the group, the rules of cooperation work against excluding the English speaker from understanding what the others are saying. By the same token, the Spanish speaker will not be excluded in a predominantly English-speaking group.

GRADE-LEVEL CURRICULUM IN HETEROGENEOUS SETTINGS

Very often, by the time the limited-English-speaking students reach the 4th or 5th grade, they speak English in the classroom. However, while they were struggling to master the language, they missed instruction in the basic skills and so are functioning several years behind grade level. The most pressing problem experienced by the teacher is the need to remediate basic skills while moving ahead with the grade-level curriculum.

Once the students have been trained to work in groups, curricular tasks that are required for the grade level, tasks with many basic skill components, can be adapted for groupwork. Students who are more advanced can assist those who are less advanced. Students who are bilingual can assist those who do not understand the English text. From the 4th grade up, the new immigrant can receive excellent assistance because there are so many proficient bilingual students. The efficiency of the teacher is multiplied in this way because there are many "assistant teachers" who are making sure that everyone understands the instructions and the text of the assignment.

A 4th-grade teacher and a 5th-grade teacher I worked with in such settings found that they could teach Spanish and English grammar as well as skills of reading comprehension of a very high order by training their students to work in groups and by composing heterogeneous groups. The 5th-grade teacher reported that the students were able to work with 8th- and 9th-grade textbooks in science. She had the groups paraphrase several sentences for every two pages they read. They had to recognize the topic sentence in each paragraph and to underline the key concepts. They used these key concepts to make up their own table of contents for their version of the material. This was a 3-month assignment given to groups. She reported that their work came back showing excellent comprehension. The students would help each other with the reading and would then discuss how to complete the assignment. Students played roles of reader, recorder, and facilitator. This is an excellent example of how groupwork can permit the teacher of the heterogeneous classroom to teach to the highest level and not to the lowest common denominator or even to the average student.

FINDING OUT

Finding Out/Descubrimiento (De Avila & Duncan, 1980) is a set of activity cards and worksheets designed to foster the development of thinking skills in 2nd through 5th grades. All learning materials are presented in Spanish, English, and pictographs. The Program for Complex Instruction at Stanford University has developed a system of classroom management that is used in conjunction with these materials. In earlier chapters I have already described some of the key features of cooperative learning developed at Stanford for this instructional approach. Chapter 4 described the cooperative techniques used to prepare heterogeneous groups to work at learning stations. Each child is responsible for completing the task and worksheet, but the group is responsible for seeing that everyone gets the help he or she needs. Chapter 8 described the specific roles such as facilitator, checker, and reporter that take over some of the work of the teacher and ensure that no one is left behind or becomes disengaged.

In this chapter I would like to show how Finding Out and the strategies of complex instruction contribute to the development of oral proficiency, acquisition and/or remediation of basic skills, and development of grade-level concepts in math. However, the dramatic gains that we have seen with Finding Out occur *only* when teachers and students receive adequate preparation for complex instruction that involves extensive training for cooperation, multiple roles for students at the learning stations, and delegation of authority by the teacher. The curriculum materials are marvelously engineered, but they are not magic. Unless children have proper access to each other as resources, and unless they are taught to solve problems as a group, many children will not understand what to do with the materials.

Materials and Management

Finding Out activities use the concepts of science and math to develop thinking skills. At each learning station are two activity cards, one in English and the other in Spanish. The cards tell the students what the activity is and ask them some key questions. There are many challenging words on these cards, such as "perimeter," "latitude," and "hexagon." Clearly these words are beyond the reading level of most students in 2nd- and 3rd-grade classrooms, where many cannot read or write at all at the beginning of the school year. Cards have pictographs indicating the nature of the activity. There are also worksheets in Spanish and English for each child at the learning station. They often ask the child to describe what happened; they also ask: "Why do you think it happened?" They may require a child to estimate in advance how big something will be. Then they ask him or her to put down the results of actual measurement and how far off this was from the initial guess. In this way the worksheets require a high level of inference and skills such as estimation, while at the same time requiring basic skills such as reading, written expression, and computation.

Measuring, experimenting, constructing, estimating, hypothesizing, analyzing, and many other intellectual activities allow the child to develop strategies for problem solving. The Finding Out activities always involve interesting manipulative materials. They have been developed so that they do not assume that the child has had a rich set of preschool experiences that are relevant to math and science.

Key concepts, such as linear coordinates, are embedded in the activities. The child encounters linear coordinates repeatedly in different forms and at different stations. For example, at one station, students locate their homes on a map, using the coordinates. At another station they work with longitude and latitude on a globe. After repeated experience with these abstract ideas in different media, the child acquires a fundamental grasp of the idea that will transfer so that he or she will recognize it in new settings, including in an achievement test.

The group has many functions in this setting. In the first place it is essential to assure that all children have access to the task. Unless they get help in reading the activity card, many of the children will be unable to get the benefit of the activity. Other children who can read perfectly well may still have difficulty with figuring out how a balance scale works or with winding coils in the unit on electromagnetism. Students are supposed to ask each other for assistance; they have experienced specific cooperative exercises designed to internalize this behavior and the behavior of helping others without doing it for them (see Chapter 4). The facilitator is specifically taught to see to it that everyone gets the help that is needed. Both cooperation and the many assigned roles help to ensure that each person benefits from the activity.

A second function of the group is to provide a forum where differences in ideas about what to do and about what good answers are can be shared and discussed. The instructions on the activity cards leave a good deal of uncertainty in many tasks. The members of the group have to employ trial and error and must share their results, either by showing each other or by discussion. Again, the children have practiced explaining to each other and showing each other how things work in special exercises (Chapter 4).

A third function of the group is to take care of the problems of children who tend to become frustrated or who often become disengaged. Instead of the teacher having to come around the room to the six learning stations to assist children who are slipping off task, the group functions to make sure that everyone is at work. The rule is: No one is done until everyone is done.

A fourth function of the group is to deal with the problem of linguistic differences. The bilingual child explains to the Spanish monolingual what the others are saying. By the same token, the English speakers are receiving input from the Spanish speakers. The child who lacks English proficiency is exposed to a rich language experience as he or she uses the vocabulary of the activity card in a situation with all the context and nonverbal cues needed for "comprehensible input." Instead of the teacher having to explain everything in both Spanish and English, the activity cards, the manipulative materials, and the linguistic resources of the group take care of this problem. Thus, the child receives simultaneous instruction in language and content (Brinton, Snow, & Wesche, 1990).

At the start of each Finding Out session, the teacher gives a brief orientation, perhaps demonstrating the concepts from one of the most difficult stations in that unit. The orientation can be a lively demonstration using visual aids and involving active discussion with the students. The teacher is asked to include a multiple ability treatment with a discussion of different kinds of intellectual abilities that will be called for in this set of learning stations. As prescribed in Chapter 10, the teacher includes the motto that no one has all these abilities, but each one has some of these abilities. He or she may also talk about the classroom management system, emphasizing norms of cooperation or how she or he wants one of the roles played.

While the students are working at the learning stations, the teaching team (sometimes a teacher and an aide and sometimes two credentialed teachers) circulates around the room, taking care not to interfere with the process of talking and working together. Only the facilitator may be sent to a teacher to ask questions; and even then teachers ask the facilitator to make sure that no one in the group can answer the question. The management system functions to free teachers from spending most of their time keeping students on task and making sure that everyone understands the instructions. Instead of having to be everywhere at once as direct supervisors, they are supportive supervisors. This involves asking higher-order questions, stimulating the children's thinking, extending their activities, and giving specific feedback to groups and individuals. Teachers are on the alert for the display of some of the multiple intellectual abilities such as reasoning, visual thinking, and preciseness, especially on the part of low-status children. If a teacher observes a low-status child performing one of the multiple abilities well, he or she takes time to assign competence to that student by saying specifically and publicly what she has observed so that the student and the group know precisely what was done well.

At the end of each session, there is a wrap-up. The reporter from each learning station may share what the group has discovered. A low-status student may provide a special demonstration of what he or she has done at the learning station. The teacher may point out some difficulties that some of the groups are having with particular learning stations. At this point the teacher may undertake an explanation of a scientific concept. Or the teacher may discuss how cooperation and role-playing are proceeding.

The students experience this approach for approximately 1 hour a day, 4 days a week. They are repeatedly reading and writing in a context that is highly relevant and interesting for them. Even though they may have to accept help, they want to put their own words down on their worksheets. For example, when children see what happens to the kernel of corn held over a Bunsen burner in a test tube, they want to write down their own ideas about why it popped. In the course of exposure to the concepts, activities, and materials, they are developing high-level problem-solving strategies that youngsters in bilingual classrooms rarely experience because everyone is so concerned about their limited English proficiency.

Achievement Results

Starting in 1979, the Program for Complex Instruction collected achievement data from children experiencing Finding Out and compared their scores in a fall and spring testing (early and late during the curriculum experience) to the gains expected in a nationally normed population. The children came largely from working-class backgrounds; many of them were at tending predominantly Hispanic schools in different districts in the Bay Area of California.

In 1979, 253 students from nine classrooms in San Jose were given the Language Assessment Scales (De Avila & Duncan, 1977) early and late in the year. This is a measure of oral proficiency in English and Spanish that is widely used in the United States. Results showed highly significant gains in oral English proficiency on the part of those children who had started with limited or minimal proficiency in English. The students who gained in language the most dramatically were those who tested with minimal proficiency in *both* English and Spanish (De Avila, 1981). Neves (1983) observed a special set of these children with varying language proficiency and found that the more frequently the Spanish monolingual children were talking about the task, the larger were their gains in the English language. This was true even though these children were largely talking in Spanish, but one must remember that they were functioning in heterogeneous groups where English was being spoken.

In all 3 years that we have collected data on the Comprehensive Test of Basic Skills (CTBS, 1981), we have found highly significant gains in language arts, reading, and mathematics subtests. In 1983–84, the CTBS science test was employed for the first time, and it too showed significant gains. Comparing these gains to those expected in the normed population revealed that the students were gaining more than the national normed population in every subtest of the battery.

Particularly striking were the big gains that occurred each year in such subtests as math concepts and applications, math computation, and reading comprehension.

Just as important as these broad-gauge achievement gains was the research that showed how these gains were connected to specific experiences in the classroom. For example, when we visited the classrooms and systematically counted the number of children who were engaged in talking or in talking and manipulating the materials, we found that the proportion so engaged was very closely related to the gains on the math concepts and applications subtest (Cohen, Lotan, & Leechor, 1989). In other words, students whose teachers set the stage for more talking and working together had higher average gains on the section of the math test that dealt with concepts and problem solving. Groupwork is the ideal setting for fostering the grasp of abstract concepts.

In order to maximize the amount of talking and working together, it is necessary for the teacher to delegate authority. When the students were at learning stations, we found that those teachers who were trying to help the children get through their tasks, giving direct instruction, asking many questions, and disciplining had fewer students talking and working together (Cohen et al., 1989). Those teachers who had trained the children well and had some children keeping track of others and helping others complete the task had no need to move from group to group to keep the work going. Also, those teachers who used more small groups found that they did not have to run around the classroom trying to help everywhere; the groups were able to manage better on their own. Because the teacher did not have to do direct supervision, there was more interaction and thus more learning in those classrooms.

Cooperative training and the use of roles boosted everyone's interaction; these strategies also helped low-status children gain access to the manipulatives and to understand the written materials. Frequent use of status treatments helped to boost the expectations for competence of low-status students, leading to increased effort, activity, and influence among these children. As a result, low-status children learned more than they would have without these special features of cooperative training, roles, and status treatments.

Where did the gains in language arts come from? A visit to a Finding Out classroom reveals many students who are studying the activity cards and worksheets, arguing about what they say and what they are supposed to be doing. Those classrooms that had a higher proportion of students reading and writing had higher gains in the test of reading comprehension. Students are reading and writing for a purpose and not as part of some seatwork exercise that does not make much sense to them.

In one 2nd-grade classroom the teacher told the students every day, "Don't touch the materials until you discuss what the activity card says and can tell me what you are supposed to be doing. I am going to come around and ask one of you to tell me what you are going to do." She would do exactly that, often asking nonreaders what they were planning to do with the materials. If the child could not explain, she would say, "I think you are going to have to read and discuss some more. I'll be back to see if you figured it out." Navarrete (1985) made videotapes of groups at work in this classroom. She found that much of the discussion among the children centered on figuring out what the activity card said. The more frequently children sought help, received help, and returned to their task (what Navarrete calls a complete problem-solving sequence), the greater were their gains in reading comprehension. Nonreaders were stimulated to find out for themselves what the activity card said because they were anxious to move on to the interesting manipulative materials. In this way the teacher was able to produce gains in basic skills at the same time as her class registered major gains in the understanding of math concepts.

CONCLUSION

Because educators have such an overwhelming concern with language acquisition, the curriculum for students with limited English proficiency is often so narrow that it limits the students' intellectual development. In addition, the overwhelming emphasis on language can make both students and teachers self-conscious about language usage. Groupwork is an alternative approach that puts language in a useful perspective; language serves as communication in order to accomplish various learning objectives. For example, in complex instruction, people talk about challenging concepts because they want to understand, to communicate with peers, and to learn how to solve problems. Language is used in a meaningful context. It is used to describe, analyze, hypothesize, and infer. Moreover, insofar as possible, children have access to a language that they can understand.

In classrooms where children ordinarily score around the 30th percentile in the fall, the achievement results of using Finding Out are impressive. What can we learn from this experience? Mainly I think we should remember that these results came about as a consequence of carefully designed, theoretically sound learning materials, and as a consequence of hard work on the part of the volunteer teaching teams. Starting in 1982 the implementation was much more consistent from classroom to classroom, and the achievement results were correspondingly stronger. This was a consequence of a 2-week workshop for teachers, and of a classroom management system using cooperative groups that was carefully researched and implemented. Finally, these results came about as a result of extensive support for the classroom teachers by school personnel and our staff. Each teacher ideally had three sessions with a staff developer based on as many as nine systematic observations of her classroom. Without all this, the results would not have been as consistent and powerful.

What if you have no access to such a high-power approach? You can still put many of the central principles used in the curriculum of Finding Out and in complex instruction to work. You can put language into its proper perspective as a tool of communication in a group that is trying to learn something worthwhile. You can use talking and working together to teach concepts. You can implement the classroom management system of cooperative norms and roles. You can create classroom learning stations by adapting from recommended activities in texts; you can create activity cards (preferably in two languages) for cooperative activities that have been published or are exchanged by teachers. You can teach students how to help each other across language barriers. You can provide situations that are rich in comprehensible input and opportunities to converse with peers. You can show students how to use each other as resources so that classrooms with students who are behind grade level need not be deprived of grade-level curriculum or of higher-level thinking skills.

In 15 years of work with teachers and with classroom research, I have found nothing so gratifying as the sight of language-minority students working excitedly in groups, learning how to solve difficult intellectual problems for themselves. It is my hope that you who teach such students will decide to design a setting where you too can watch young scholars talking and learning together.

APPENDIX

Cooperative Training Exercises

MAKING STUDENTS SENSITIVE TO NEEDS OF OTHERS IN A GROUP

BROKEN CIRCLES

The following instructions to the participants and suggested discussion are those of the developers of Broken Circles, Nancy and Ted Graves (1985). Broken Circles is based on the Broken Squares game invented by Dr. Alex Bavelas (1973).

The class is divided into groups of three to six persons. Each person is given an envelope with different pieces of the circle. The goal is for each person to put together a complete circle. In order for this goal to be reached, there must be some exchange of pieces. Group members are not allowed to talk or to take pieces from someone else's envelope. They are allowed only to give away their pieces (one at a time).

Instructions to the Participants

Each of you will be given an envelope containing two or three pieces of a puzzle, but don't open it until I say so. The goal of this exercise is to put these pieces together in such a way that each member of your group ends up with a complete circle. There are a few rules to make the exercise more fun.

1. This exercise must be played in complete silence. No talking.
2. You may not point or signal to other players with your hands in any way.
3. Each player must put together his or her own circle. No one else may show a player how to do it or do it for him or her.

4. This is an exercise in giving. You may not take a piece from another player, but you may *give* your pieces, one at a time, to any other members of your group, and other group members may give pieces to you. You may not place a piece in another person's puzzle; players must complete only their own puzzles. Instead, hand the piece to the other player, or place it beside the other pieces in front of him or her.

Now you may take the pieces out of your envelope and place them in front of you, colored side up. This is a group task, and you will have 10 minutes to make your circles.

Remember, the task is not finished until each of you at your table has a completed circle in front of you. When all of you have finished, raise your hands. (If one group finishes before the others, suggest that they try to discover if there are any *other* ways they could put the pieces together to form different circles.)

Discussion

When all groups have completed the task or the allotted time has ended, the teacher should help the participants to identity some of the important things that happened, analyze why they happened, and generalize to other group learning situations. The following questions can serve as a guide to the discussion:

- What do you think this game was all about?
- How do you feel about what happened in your group today?
- What things did you do in your group that helped you to be successful in solving the problem?
- What things did you do that made it harder?
- What could the groups do better in the future?

Help participants to be concrete about what they did and also abstract about the general implications of what they did and the lessons they learned for the future. In Advanced Broken Circles, one player may block the task for the rest of the group by completing his or her circle satisfactorily, but refusing to share some pieces with the others. This is analogous to a member of a cooperative learning group who tries to work alone and does not help other members.

In the discussion, be sure to come back to the two key behaviors that make a group successful: *Pay attention to what other group members need. No one is done until everyone is done.* Point out when groups report these kinds of behaviors or when they decide that these behaviors will help them to do better in the future.

Directions for making and using Broken Circles are provided next.

Directions for three levels of difficulty are presented. You may wish to use the intermediate and advanced versions, going on to the advanced version later in the year if you feel that this particular lesson needs to be reviewed.

Patterns to Use for Students of Different Ages

Simplest Broken Circles. This pattern is suitable for children 5 to 7 years old in groups of three. Sort the pieces into three envelopes (I, II, and III, as marked in Figure A.1) and give one envelope to each player. Figure A.1 indicates one solution; in this solution each player must give up some of his or her pieces to other players. The diagram shows how pieces held by players I, II, and III can be rearranged to form three circles. Two circles composed of a half and two quarters represents an alternative solution.

Simple Broken Circles. This pattern is suitable for children 8 to 10 years old in groups of four. Sort the pieces into four envelopes marked W, X, Y, and Z. Figure A.2 indicates one solution. Ask the groups that finish first, "How many *other* ways of forming four circles can you discover?"

Advanced Broken Circles. This pattern is suitable for children 8 to 10 years old who have had some experience with Simple Broken Circles. It may also be used as a first exercise with older children, high school students, and adults.

Figure A.1. Simplest Broken Circles

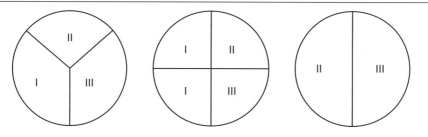

Figure A.2. Simple Broken Circles

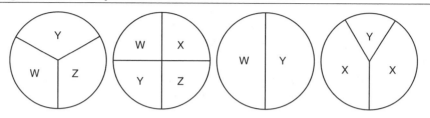

Figure A.3 shows patterns for Advanced Broken Circles. A single set consists of 15 pieces that will make six circles, as shown in the figure. Make one set of six circles for each small group. In Figure A.3, the placement of four pieces varies with the size of the group. For example, if you are playing with six-person groups, the piece marked 6-F goes into the F envelope and the 6-E piece goes into the E envelope, the 6-C piece into the C envelope, and the 6-D piece into the D envelope. Repeat this pattern for each six-person group.

Once you have sorted a group set into the lettered envelopes, put these envelopes into a larger one. You are now ready to hand out the materials to the small groups.

Although it is fairly easy, once you are familiar with the exercise, to modify on the spot a set of six circles for groups of five or less, it is easier

Figure A.3. Advanced Broken Circles

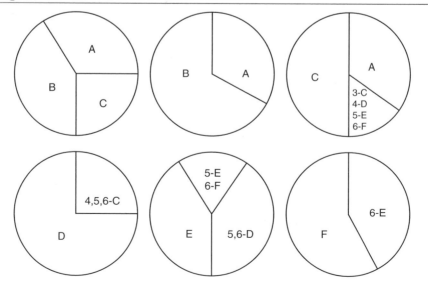

to make up and label sets of varying sizes in advance. Then these can be quickly substituted when required.

Instructions for Making a Set of Broken Circles

The circles can be any size, from that shown to about 20 cm in diameter. However, all the circles within the set should be the same size. Each set of circles should be a different color. This way, each small group will be able to work with pieces that are all of the same color, and different from any other group's color. This will enable you to easily sort the pieces when you are preparing the materials for the exercise.

The easiest way to manufacture the materials for any of the exercises in this appendix is to enlarge the diagrams in the figures with a copy machine to the desired size. Then use the enlargement to reproduce the patterns on sturdy card stock of different colors. You will want to retain the labels in the diagrams of the circles to indicate in which envelope each piece belongs.

Jigsaw Puzzles

Pick out some simple jigsaw puzzles. Each group member has a bag with one-quarter of the pieces (for a four-person group). They have to complete the puzzle without a picture of the product in front of them. They may talk, but the task cannot be completed without each individual contributing his or her share. One child may not take another's piece and do it for him or her. Hints and encouragement may be given, but all the members must do their own part.

Following this exercise, hold a discussion similar to that suggested for Broken Circles. Bring out how this will be useful during groupwork. Students will each have information and ideas that will help complete the tasks given to the group. By sharing this information and these insights with others, everyone will be able to benefit by learning more from the activity.

Preparing Students for Learning Stations with Individual Reports and Manipulative Materials

In order to work in this setting, students will have to learn how to help and explain, to ask questions, and to give good answers. Master Designer and Guess My Rule are two exercises suggested for teaching new behaviors concerning helping and explaining. As the students mature, it is very important to learn how to justify and give reasons for one's arguments as well as how to make one's thoughts clear to others. Rainbow Logic is included for this purpose. You may wish to develop your own activity using these as examples of how to pick out a situation that highlights and gives practice to new behaviors.

MASTER DESIGNER

Materials

This game requires a set of geometric shapes. Each player needs a complete set, but one person in each group takes the role of observer and does not require a set. A total of five persons per group is recommended, but smaller groups are acceptable. The shapes should be made out of some sturdy materials such as oaktag. The exact size of these shapes is given in Figure A.4. In addition, you will need some cardboard or other dividers that can be stood on a table. The idea is that each player can see the other members of the group over the dividers but *cannot* see what the others are doing with their pieces.

Rules and Discussion

One person plays the role of the master designer. This person has to instruct the other players as to how to replicate a design he or she has created with the pieces (all or part of them), but the master designer

Figure A.4. "Master Designer" Shapes

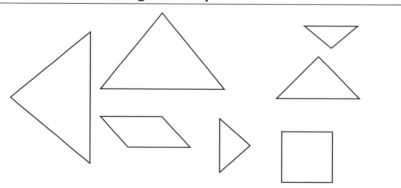

cannot do this task for them. Players cannot see what the others are doing, nor can they see the design of the master. However, group members may ask questions of the master designer. This illustrates an important new behavior:

- Helping students do things for themselves

The group is dependent on the master designer for explaining how it should be done. This is the second new behavior:

- Explain by telling how

In addition to verbal directions, students may use sign language to demonstrate to each other. This will help bridge any language differences you may have in your class.

When any member of the group feels that he or she has figured out the master design, the designer is asked to check the solution. If the master designer says it is correct, then that player too is to help others in the group by explaining how. This rule illustrates another important new behavior:

- Everybody helps

Make up a bright chart with these three behaviors and display it prominently in the classroom.

After everyone in the group has completed the correct design, another student can take the role of the master designer. If you do not have time for everyone to take a turn, pick a variety of students to play this role—not just the natural leaders.

One student plays the role of observer for each round. The observer watches the group and checks off every time he or she sees two of the three new behaviors occur. These are:

- Explain by telling how
- Everybody helps

Also make up a simple scoring sheet so the observer can check off new behaviors every time he or she sees them.

Because this is the first time students have ever been asked to observe, you will need to discuss how a person would know that a student is "telling how" and "helping others." It is not so important that the observer correctly record every time the behavior happens. The fact that someone is watching for and checking off behaviors helps to objectify behavior and will assist the whole group in recognizing such behaviors when they occur.

After the exercise ask each observer to report how many times he or she saw each new behavior. The observer may be able to give some good examples of what was seen. This provides an opportunity for the teacher to reinforce the new behaviors. Follow this with a discussion similar to the one described in detail for Broken Circles. Discuss how these behaviors will be useful for the curriculum. Explain that everyone will have to do his or her own report, so it will be important that everyone comes to understand and do things for themselves.

Guess My Rule

Objective

This is a game that Rosenholtz (1977) developed to illustrate reasoning skills. Students must deduce a central principle that accounts for all of the different-colored sizes and shapes that may be placed in the center of a ring. Someone holds a card, called a Rule Card, on which the central principle, such as "Only red shapes," is written. The rule card holder tells the players whether or not their choice of a playing card fits the rule.

Materials

Each group of five (three players, one rule card holder, and one observer) will need to have a set of rule cards, a large circle of yarn, and a special deck of playing cards. Each playing card displays one of four different shapes (circle, square, triangle, and diamond) in one of three sizes (large, medium, and small) and one of three colors (red, blue, and green); making up one card for each possible combination of shape, size, and color results in a deck of 36 cards. Outline the particular shape in the right size and color on the front of each card, and repeat the color on the border of the card. (It is much easier to draw the shapes on uniform card stock than it is to cut out cards in each shape, and the deck made with uniform cards is also much easier for the students to manipulate.) For each group of players you will also need to make up a set of rule cards. These are the cards with the central principle that the players must deduce. The rules are provided in Figure A.5.

Figure A.5. Rule Cards for "Guess My Rule"

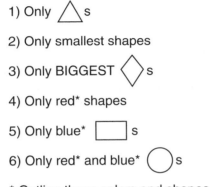

1) Only △s

2) Only smallest shapes

3) Only BIGGEST ◇s

4) Only red* shapes

5) Only blue* ▭ s

6) Only red* and blue* ◯s

* Outline these colors and shapes in the appropriate colors.

Instructions to Students

This reasoning game is called "Guess My Rule" and is played with this special deck of cards. As you can see, there are four different shapes in the deck: a circle, a square, a triangle, and a diamond. Each shape comes in three sizes: big, medium, and small. And each size in each shape comes in three different colors: red, blue, and green. There are many ways to sort these cards into categories. I want you each to think of a way. Here I have some rule cards that have on them different ways to sort the deck into various categories. The object of "Guess My Rule" is for you to try to reason out which rule card I am holding. We will put the playing cards in the center of the table, and you will each take turns picking one card. If the card you've picked fits my rule, I will say "yes," and you can put it in the yarn circle. If the card you've picked doesn't fit my rule, I will say "no," and you can put it outside the yarn circle. Each person can only pick one card at each turn. Once you've found a couple of cards that fit the rule you can try to reason out what my rule is, but you can only try to guess my rule when it is your turn to pick a card.

(The teacher takes one group and plays one simple round with the teacher as a rule card holder. The other students gather around to watch.)

As you can see, this is a game that requires reasoning and some very careful thinking. Many of the things you will be doing at learning stations will require reasoning and thinking. When people have such a difficult problem to solve, one thing they can do is *find out what others think*.

We are going to practice finding out what others think. When it is your turn and you have an idea what the rule is, ask the two other players in your group what they think about your idea. You might say, "I think the rule is all blue shapes. Do you think that's the rule?" If they say yes or no, ask them *to tell why* they think that. After you listen to what they say or if they don't know, ask the other person the same questions. Then *make up your own mind* about what you think is the rule and ask the rule card holder.

Discussion

Have the students practice asking each other what they think and why they think so. Discuss with them why it is important to try to tell why. This is an important new skill.

A third rule is also important preparation for working at learning stations. Because each student is responsible for his or her own report, it is important that all the students feel responsible for making their own decisions about what to do after consulting others.

All of these new behaviors ("Find out what others think," "Tell why," and "Make your own decision") should be printed on a chart and prominently displayed.

As in the previous skillbuilder, there should be an observer. The two behaviors an observer can hear and see are:

- Finding out what others think
- Telling why

The person who is the observer should have a simple check sheet parallel to the one for Master Designer, but with the new behaviors on it.

You are now ready to have each group play the game and take turns with the various roles. One person is the rule card holder, one is the observer, and the other three are players. After each round, other group members get to be rule card holder and observer. The new rule card holder picks up a new card from the deck, which is face down.

After the game, have the observers report how many times they saw the new behaviors on the round they scored. Ask the students to discuss whether or not it was helpful to them to get other people's opinions. See if you can pick up some good examples of students telling "why" if they don't come up with these themselves. Have them comment on what it is like to hear opinions different from one's own and to have to consider those ideas before making up one's own mind. Ask them if they know of any other situation that is like this. Point out that they will have to do this at the learning stations.

RAINBOW LOGIC*

This is an exercise developed by the Family Math program to give students practice in communicating their deductive thinking and spatial reasoning. Students must deduce through a series of questions the pattern of a 3 × 3 color grid. The grid is constructed using rules about the permissible ways in which squares may be placed. Within those rules the group must discuss and decide on the best questions to ask of the grid designer.

Materials

Colored paper squares for each player
4 each of each of 4 colors (more than needed for solution)
3 × 3 grids

Procedure

For the first round, the teacher may be the grid designer. A group can be selected to demonstrate the exercise and the rest of the class can gather around to watch. After the first round, students should take turns being the grid designers in their separate groups. Group sizes can vary from three to five. The person who is the grid designer can also play the role of observer.

The grid designer prepares a secret 3 × 3 color grid, using three squares of each color.

---

*Adapted from Stenmark, Thompson, & Cossey, *Family Math*, Lawrence Hall of Science, Copyright 1987 Regents University of California. All rights reserved.

Rule: All of the squares of the same color must be connected by at least one full side. See Figure A.6 for examples of permissible and impermissible grids.

The goal is for the players to be able to give the location of all colors on the grid after as few questions as possible. Therefore, the group

Figure A.6. Grids for "Rainbow Logic"

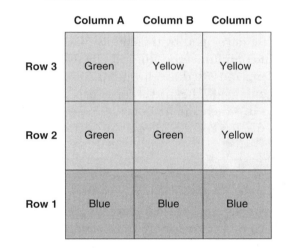

EXAMPLE OF A SECRET GRID

	Column A	Column B	Column C
Row 3	Green	Yellow	Yellow
Row 2	Green	Green	Yellow
Row 1	Blue	Blue	Blue

PATTERNS LIKE THE ONES BELOW ARE NOT ALLOWED

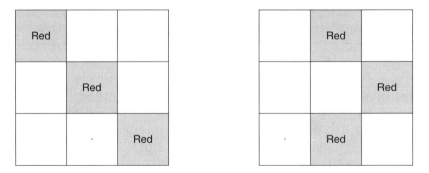

Note: If this seems too easy for the class, try playing with a 4 × 4 grid with the same rules.

should *discuss and decide* before asking the grid master a question. In the course of the discussion, students should share the logic of their thinking: Why will this question get the maximum amount of useful information for solving the problem? During this discussion, there are two new behaviors that the students should learn:

- Discuss and decide.
- Give reasons for your suggestions.

Rules for asking and answering questions:

- Players ask for the colors in a particular row or column (rows are horizontal, columns are vertical).
- The grid designer gives the colors, *but not necessarily in order.*
- Each player should use a grid and colored paper squares to keep track of clues.
- Squares may be put *beside* the row or column until exact places are determined.

Discussion

The observer for a particular round should keep track of how often people give reasons for their suggestions. The observer should also watch the character of the discussion to see if people really discussed before they came to a decision. Perhaps one person jumped in and asked the question of the grid designer before everyone in the group was heard from or before a controversy was actually resolved.

After most groups have had the chance to complete a few rounds of the exercise, the teacher should stop the action and have observers from each group report what they have seen. Then the class may discuss how to improve the process of discussion and the process of giving reasons. Let the class proceed to give everyone else a turn at being grid designer and observer. After they have finished the final round, ask the observers to come up and form a panel to discuss whether what they heard improved discussion and justifications in the second part of the lesson. Alternatively, students could write about what they have learned concerning the three cooperative norms and how they fit into group-work in their subject matter.

PREPARING STUDENTS FOR GROUPWORK
THAT FEATURES GROUP DISCUSSION

Epstein's Four-Stage Rocket

This is the original task designed by Epstein (1972) to improve the discussion skills of any age group. There are some minor adaptations of the original version in the material presented.

Pretest

Explain to the class that in order to prepare for the groupwork they need to learn what it takes to have a good group discussion. Divide the class into five-person groups. Give the groups a highly interesting task to discuss. (Two sample discussion tasks are given at the end of Appendix A.) The teacher circulates, listening, observing, and taking notes on examples of good and bad discussion technique. The groups are allowed to discuss for 5 minutes.

Practicing the Four Stages

After the pretest, hold a group discussion on what makes for good discussion and what the barriers are. Tell the class that they are going to practice four skills that are necessary so that a discussion can take off like a rocket (use an illustration of a rocket with four stages) by following these instructions:

Stage 1, Conciseness—"getting quickly to the point and not beating around the bush."

Select a timekeeper who will watch the clock and keep time for the group. Keep discussing the subject for 5 minutes. The timekeeper makes sure that *each person talks for only 15 seconds.*

Stage 2, Listening—"paying attention to what is being said."

Select a new timekeeper. Keep discussing the same subject for 5 more minutes, again making sure that each person talks for only 15 seconds. This time, however, *each person must wait 3 seconds after the person before has spoken before he or she may speak*

Stage 3, Reflecting—"repeating out loud to the group something of what the person before you has said."

Select a new timekeeper. Keep discussing the same subject, making sure that each person talks for only 15 seconds and that he or she waits 3 seconds after the person before has spoken before he or she speaks. In addition, *everyone who speaks must begin by repeating to the group something that was said by the person who spoke immediately before*. This is called *reflecting*. The person who had spoken before has to nod his or her head to mean yes if he or she thinks this reflection is right. The new speaker may not continue until he or she correctly reflects what the person before has said.

Stage IV, Everyone contributes—"all the people in the group have to speak."

Select a new timekeeper. Keep discussing the same subject for 5 more minutes. All previous rules apply, as well as a new one: *No one may speak a second time until everyone in the group has spoken.*

After each stage ask each timekeeper to report on how well their group did on the skill being practiced. The timekeeper may have other observations to make about how difficult it was and what happened. Remind the class why each skill is important.

Posttest

Select a person as observer who has not yet had a chance to play a role like timekeeper. Hold 5 minutes more of discussion without having to observe the rules but trying to use the skills of *conciseness, listening, reflecting,* and *contributions by everyone*. Observers will note down every time they see good examples of each of these behaviors. You may want to create a scoring sheet.

After the posttest, ask observers to tell what they observed. Also ask the whole class to describe some of the differences between the pretest and the posttest.

Note: Unless the class has had some previous experience with discussion, you will find that they will finish discussion tasks very rapidly. You will need to have alternative questions or tasks prepared. Sample discussion tasks are given at the end of this appendix.

IMPROVING GROUP PROCESS SKILLS

The Four-Stage Rocket may be enough to get the groupwork started. However, there are additional skills, especially for group projects, that become more important as groups attempt longer-term, more ambitious projects. One can develop lists of constructive and destructive behaviors for improving group process skills.

Constructive behaviors are ways that help to get the group's work done. A skillful group member

- Has new ideas
- Requests or provides information
- Explains ideas
- Puts ideas together
- Asks if everyone is ready to decide what to do

Especially *constructive behaviors* are those that assist with the smooth operation of the group. A constructive group member

- Asks quiet group members what they think
- Listens with interest to what other people say
- Praises good ideas and suggestions
- Is willing to compromise

Destructive behaviors are common problems that arise in groups and often result in hurt feelings and a poor group product. A destructive group member

- Talks too much
- Listens very little
- Insists on having his or her ideas accepted
- Fails to do something about the destructive behavior of others
- Criticizes people rather than their ideas
- Lets other people do all the work

Choose a small number of these behaviors that you think are of critical importance based on what you think the group will need or problems that you have observed during discussions. It is always better if the class members can select behaviors that need work on the basis of their own experience. Explain to the class that this exercise will help them with these particular skills.

Divide the class into discussion groups after you have presented to them the set of behaviors they are going to be working on. Always use the same label to refer to the selected behaviors. Select one observer for each group who will write down every time one of these particular behaviors occurs. Draw up a scoring sheet. Take observers aside in advance and make sure they know how to observe these particular behaviors. Give the groups a discussion topic that they can work on for 5 or 10 minutes.

Stop the discussion and ask observers to report what they have seen and scored. Pull out from the discussion some good strategies that have been used or alternative strategies to deal with problems that have arisen. The same basic format can be used for any number of skills that you think require practice.

SAMPLE DISCUSSION TASKS

SPACESHIP

The object of this game is to select seven persons to go into a space ship for a voyage to a new planet. You have just been alerted that a giant meteor is on a collision course with the planet Earth and will smash into the general area of the United States. Therefore, it is very likely the end of human civilization as we know it. The spaceship has the capacity to set up life on a new planet. Twelve persons have been chosen by lot to go on the ship; however, an error was made, and now it turns out that there is only room for seven. Your group must decide which seven persons will go to start life on the new planet. Remember, only seven persons can fit in the ship. You must have the agreement of the entire group before a selection can be made. The original 12 individuals to choose from are as follows:

1. A 30-year-old male symphony orchestra violin player
2. A 67-year-old male minister

3. A 23-year-old engineer and his 21-year-old wife (they refuse to be separated)
4. A 40-year-old policeman who refuses to be separated from his gun
5. A male student of your own age from your school
6. A 35-year-old male high school dropout, recently arrested for armed robbery
7. A 32-year-old female 6th-grade teacher
8. A 40-year-old female doctor (medical)
9. A 50-year-old female artist and sculptor
10. A 25-year-old male poet
11. A 1-year-old female child

ALLIGATOR RIVER

Once there was a girl named Abigail who was in love with a boy named Gregory. Gregory had an unfortunate accident and broke his glasses. Abigail, being a true friend, volunteered to take them to be repaired. But the repair shop was across the river, and during a flash flood the bridge was washed away. Poor Gregory could see nothing without his glasses, so Abigail was desperate to get across the river to the repair shop. While she was standing forlornly on the bank of the river, clutching the broken glasses in her hand, a boy named Sinbad glided by in a rowboat.

She asked Sinbad if he would take her across. He agreed on the condition what while she was having the glasses repaired, she would go to a nearby store and steal a transistor radio that he had been wanting. Abigail refused to do this and went to see a friend named Ivan who had a boat.

When Abigail told Ivan her problem, he said he was too busy to help her out and didn't want to become involved. Abigail, feeling that she had no other choice, returned to Sinbad and told him she would agree to his plan.

When Abigail returned the repaired glasses to Gregory, she told him what she had had to do. Gregory was so mad at what she had done he told her that he never wanted to see her again.

Abigail, upset, turned to Slug with her tale of woe. Slug was so sorry for Abigail that he promised her he would get even with Gregory. They went to the school playground where Gregory was playing ball and Abigail watched happily while Slug beat Gregory up and broke his new glasses.

Rank these characters from "best" to "worst": Abigail, Gregory, Sinbad, Ivan, Slug. *Give reasons for your decisions.* (Simon, Howe, & Kirschenbaum, 1972, pp. 292–293)

Conflict Resolution Strategies for Groupwork*

Students are first introduced to two new tools for conflict resolution: "I feel" statements and positive requests. The teacher introduces the new ways of talking, providing definitions, examples, and opportunities to practice. These statements are contrasted with blaming statements; the students learn that "I feel" statements are substitutes for the more familiar strategy of blaming others. This discussion with the whole class is followed by a communication worksheet on which students practice translating blaming statements into "I feel" statements and positive requests.

TEACHER-LED DISCUSSION AND STUDENT PRACTICE

"I Feel" Statements

Most of the time when students feel hurt and become angry because of something someone else has done, they confront each other with accusations in ways that only escalate conflict. "I feel" statements provide a constructive way of expressing unpleasant feelings to others. They enable us to take responsibility for our feelings and the way we react to what others say and do. At the same time these statements let others know how their behavior affects us—without blame.

Blaming statements usually begin with "You" and focus on the other person in a highly judgmental and negative way. "I feel" statements focus on our own feelings in response to the other person's behavior. They consist of three parts: identifying the behavior, expressing the feelings experienced as a result of the behavior, and explaining the reasons for those feelings. A useful formula for phrasing "I feel" statements is:

When you . . . (State problem behavior)
I feel . . . (Express feeling)
Because . . . (State reasons for your feeling)

---

*The materials in this section were developed by Diane Kepner.

Student practice. Share with the class the following examples of "You" statements and contrast them with "I feel" statements related to the same topic. The examples are all taken from common conflicts in small groups. Have a small group of students come to the front of the class and act out the two alternative responses. Have the class analyze the "I feel" statements in terms of the formula. Can they construct alternative "I feel" statements that fit the formula? You can use buzz groups for this exercise.

> *Situation #1:* A member of your group interrupts you constantly when you are talking.

"You" statement: "You're so rude! You never let me say anything!"
"I feel" statement: "When you interrupt me, I feel really hurt because I think that what I have to say is important too."

> *Situation #2:* Two members of the group are holding the task cards so that you can't see the diagrams.

"You" statement: "You guys are always hogging everything!"
"I feel" statement: "I feel left out when you guys have the cards between you because I can't follow what's going on."

> *Situation #3:* A member of your group is busy shooting paper wads at someone in another group and talking to members of the other group.

"You" statement: "You're such a goof-off. You never help."
"I feel" statement: "When you start doing things with people in other groups I feel really upset because we need everyone's help to get this project done on time."

Positive Requests

Most problems are not solved just because an "I feel" statement has been made. Group members must listen carefully to what has been said. For the group to respond constructively, members need to know what should be done. Positive requests can help the group move from understanding feelings to action. This requires that we focus not on what we don't want the other person to do, but on what specific actions we do want the other person to take. We have to ask ourselves "What do I need to have you do differently and what will that new action look like?"

It requires being specific and positive rather than vague and negative in our requests of others.

   Student practice. Go over the following examples with the class. Ask them to describe why the third statement is specific and how it contrasts with the second statement. Positive requests usually begin with "I want you to," "I would," "I'd like you to," and "I need you to." Students may resist the formality of the language in these and the "I feel" statements. After some initial practice in following the formula, you may want to let them put their responses into their "own language," but be sure that you follow this up with an examination and discussion of whether or not their own terms change the nature of the message and, if so, how.

1. *Negative:* "Stop interrupting me."
   Vague: "I want you to listen to me."
   Positive and specific: "I want you to wait until I'm finished before you start talking."
2. *Negative:* "Stop hogging all the cards!"
   Vague: "I want you to share the cards with me."
   Positive and specific: "I need you to put the cards in the middle of the table so I can see."
3. *Negative:* "I want you to stop messing around."
   Vague: "I want you to help our group."
   Positive and specific: "I would like you to fill in the chart with the information from our notes."

   Putting the "I feel" statement and the positive requests together creates a powerful tool for communication by helping students to express their feelings and request changes in others in a direct and honest way. Go back through the examples under "I feel" statements and have the class create positive action statements for these examples.

COMMUNICATION WORKSHEET

As you work in your groups, problems will occur with other members. Use your new knowledge to let them know how you feel and what you need from them. Practice using "I feel" statements and positive requests to express yourself and avoid using blaming messages that add to the problem.

For each of the following situations, write a blaming message followed by an "I feel" statement and a positive request.

Then try writing some situations of your own based on real group experiences that you've had or observed.

1. One member in your group is doing all the building on the project. Every time you try to make a suggestion you are ignored. When you pick something up to try to help, it is taken away from you.

2. One member of your group has been wandering around visiting friends while the rest of you worked on the poster for your presentation. Now, just as you are about to finish, he/she bumps into your desk, causing you to make an ugly mark all the way across the page.

3. There are only three people in your group. The other two are good friends but you don't know them very well. They are sitting close together and acting as if you don't even exist.

4. All the other members in your group are actively discussing the questions for your activity. You would like to say something, too, but every time they ask you for your opinion, they move on to someone else before you've had a chance to put your thoughts into words.

5. One member of your group always gets good grades on all of his/her regular class work but in the group he/she never contributes. You suspect that he/she knows the way to solve the problem you're all working on.

Tools for Groupwork Evaluation

SAMPLE STUDENT QUESTIONNAIRE

Name: _____

Please mark with an "X" on the line to the left of each answer the choice that is most like how you feel for each question. Remember, this is not a test. There are no right answers. I want to know what you think.

Section A

1. How interesting did you find your work in the group?
   _____ a. Very interesting
   _____ b. Fairly interesting
   _____ c. Somewhat interesting
   _____ d. Not very interesting
   _____ e. I was not interested at all

2. How difficult did you find your work in the group?
   _____ a. Extremely difficult
   _____ b. Fairly difficult
   _____ c. Sometimes difficult
   _____ d. Not too difficult—just about right
   _____ e. Very easy

3. Did you understand exactly what the group was supposed to do?
   _____ a. I knew just what to do.
   _____ b. At first I didn't understand.
   _____ c. It was never clear to me.

4. For Multiple-Ability Tasks
    _____ a. What abilities did you think were important for doing a good job on this task?
    _____ b. Was there one ability on which you thought you did very well?
        _____ Yes _____ No

5. How many times did you have the chance to talk during the group session today?
    _____ a. None
    _____ b. One or two times
    _____ c. Three to four times
    _____ d. Five or more times

6. If you talked less than you wanted to, what were the main reasons?
    _____ a. I felt afraid to give my opinion.
    _____ b. Somebody else interrupted me.
    _____ c. I was not given the chance to give my opinion.
    _____ d. I talked as much as I wanted to.
    _____ e. Nobody paid attention to what I said.
    _____ f. I was not interested in the problem.
    _____ g. I was not feeling well today.

7. Did you get along with everybody in your group?
    _____ a. With a few of them
    _____ b. With half of them
    _____ c. With most of them
    _____ d. With all of them
    _____ e. With none of them

8. How many students listened to each other's ideas?
    _____ a. Only a few of them
    _____ b. Half of them
    _____ c. Most of them
    _____ d. All of them, except one
    _____ e. All of them

Section B

1. Who did the most talking in your group today?
2. Who did the least talking in your group today?
3. Who had the best ideas in your group today?

4. Who did the most to direct the discussion?
5. Would you like to work with this group again?
   _____ Yes _____ No
   If not, why not?
6. How well do you think the facilitator did today in his or her job?

GUIDE TO ANALYZING THE STUDENT QUESTIONNAIRE

I. What percentage of the class found the task uninteresting, too difficult, or confusing? (Questions A, B, and C will show you how to calculate the answer using student responses to Section A, questions 1–3.)

   A. What percentage of the students reported that the work was not very interesting or that they were not interested at all? (Add up the number of students who chose d or e on question 1. Divide this number by total who turned in questionnaires to obtain a percentage.)

   B. What percentage of the students reported that the work was extremely difficult or very easy? (Add up the number of students who chose a or e on question 2. Use the same procedure as above to obtain a percentage.)

   C. What percentage of the students reported that the instructions were never clear to them? (Determine the number of students who chose c for question 3. Follow the same procedure as above to obtain a percentage.)

II. *For multiple-ability tasks:* Did the students see the task as involving multiple abilities? (Use Section A, question 4.)

   A. How many students were able to list more than one ability? (Question 4a)

   B. How many students were able to list one ability on which they thought they did well? (Question 4b)

   C. How many of the abilities listed were like those in ordinary schoolwork? (Question 4b)

III. How was the group process? Are there special problems that need further work?

   A. What kinds of problems are checked off frequently on Section A, question 6?

    B. How many students report getting along with half or fewer members of their group? (Section A, question 7; add up a, b, and e.)

    C. How many students report that half or fewer members of their group listened? (Section A, question 8; add up a and b.)

IV. How did the low-status students feel about their experience? (Pull out their questionnaires and make the following tabulations.)

    A. How many of these students found the task uninteresting, too difficult, or confusing? How does this number compare to the total number of students in the class who felt that way? *If a much higher percentage of low-status students were unhappy with the task than the overall percentage for the class calculated in questions 1–3, then your task was particularly unsuccessful with low-status students.*

    B. *For Multiple-Ability Tasks:* How many of the low-status students reported that there was an ability on which they thought they did well? (Section A, question 4b.) *If the multiple-ability treatment is successful, practically all of these students should answer yes.*

    C. Were these students more likely to report that they rarely participated than the rest of the class? (Count up how many of the low-status students chose a or b for question 5 in Section A. Now do the same for the rest of the class.) *If more than half of the low-status students reported poor participation, whereas only 25% or fewer of the students in the rest of the class said they participated rarely, then you still have a status problem in participation.*

    D. Were there some particular low-status students for whom this experience was not a good one? Take those low-status students who report little participation on question 5 and examine their questionnaires as a whole to see if you can find out what the source of the trouble was.

V. How successful was each group in achieving equal status and good group process? (Rearrange the questionnaires so you have all the ones from each group together.)

    A. Did some groups report more interpersonal problems than others? Or were complaints pretty well spread across groups? (Section A, questions 6, 7, and 8.) If three or more members of the same group make one of these complaints about their experience, one could reasonably infer that this particular group had interpersonal difficulty.

B. Were there any groups in which the low-status student was chosen by at least two others as having had the best ideas? (Section B, question 3.) This would indicate that you have been successful in treating the status problem in at least some of your groups.

C. In how many groups did almost everyone choose one of the low-status students as having done the least talking? (Section B, question 2.) This occurs in groups where you have not achieved equal-status behavior. Check such groups' questionnaires over carefully. You may want to appoint these students as facilitators next time.

D. How were the evaluations of the facilitator in each group? (Section B, question 6.)

E. If a low-status student was the facilitator, was he or she chosen by at least some group members as having done the most to direct the discussion? (Section B, question 4.)

VI. How good were the relations between students of different racial or ethnic or language groups? (Divide the questionnaires by racial, ethnic, or linguistic group membership.)

A. Did most of the minority students report getting along with most or all of the other students in their groups? (Section A, question 7.)

B. What proportion of minority versus majority groups said that they would not like to work with their groups again? (Section B, question 5.) Ideally, the proportion should not be much above 15% in either category, and it is certainly not a good sign if the proportion is much higher among minorities than among majority students.

References

Aaronson, E. (1978). *The jigsaw classroom.* Beverly Hills, CA: SAGE.

Abram, P., Scarloss, B., Holthuis, N., Cohen, E., Lotan, R., & Schultz, S. (2002). The use of evaluation criteria to improve academic discussion in cooperative groups. *Asia Pacific Journal of Education, 22,* 16–27.

Ahmadjian, J. (1980). Academic status and reading achievement: Modifying the effects of the self-fulfilling prophecy. Unpublished doctoral dissertation, Stanford University, Stanford, CA.

Alexander, M. G., Chizhik, A. W., Chizhik, E. W., & Goodman, J. A. (2009). Lower-status participation and influence: Task structure matters. *Journal of Social Issues, 65,* 365–381.

Anderson, L. M. (1982). *Student response to seatwork: Implications for the study of students' cognitive processing.* Research Series No. 102. East Lansing, MI: Michigan State University, Institute for Research on Teaching.

Applebee, A., Langer, J., Nystrand, M., & Gamoran, A. (2003). Discussion-based approaches to developing understanding: Classroom instruction and student performance in middle and high school English. *American Educational Research Journal, 40,* 685–730.

Arellano, A. D. (2003). Bilingual students' acquisition of academic language: A study of the language processes and products in a complex instruction classroom. Unpublished dissertation, Stanford University, Stanford, CA.

Awang Had, B. S. (1972). Effects of status and task upon observable power and prestige order of small task-oriented groups. Unpublished doctoral dissertation, Stanford University, Stanford, CA.

Balabanian, N., & Dean, D. (2012). *Group-worthy task write-up.* Stanford, CA: Stanford University, Graduate School of Education.

Bandura, A. (1969). *Principles of behavior modification.* New York, NY: Holt, Rinehart & Winston.

Barron, B. (2003). When smart groups fail. *Journal of the Learning Sciences, 12,* 307–359.

Bassarear, T., & Davidson, N. (1992). The use of small group learning situations in mathematics instruction as a tool to develop thinking. In N. Davidson & T. Worsham (Eds.), *Enhancing thinking through cooperative learning* (pp. 236–250). New York, NY: Teachers College Press.

Bavelas, A. (1973). The five squares problem—An instructional aid in group cooperation. *Studies in Personnel Psychology, 5,* 29–38.

Berger, J., Conner, T., & McKeown, W. (1974). Evaluations and the formation and maintenance of performance expectations. In J. Berger, T. Conner, & H. Fisek (Eds.), *Expectation states theory: A theoretical research program* (pp. 27–51). Cambridge, MA: Winthrop.

Berger, J., Rosenholtz, S. J., & Zelditch, M., Jr. (1980). Status organizing processes. *Annual Review of Sociology, 6,* 479–508.

Berliner, D., Fisher, C., Filby, N., Marliave, R., Cahen, L., Dishaw, M., & Moore, J. (1978). *Beginning teacher evaluation study—Teaching behaviors, academic learning time and student achievement. Final report of phase II-B.* San Francisco, CA: Far West Laboratory.

Bianchini, J. (1997). Where knowledge construction, equity, and context intersect: Student learning of science in small groups. *Journal of Research in Science Teaching, 34,* 1039–1065.

Black, P., & William, D. (1998). Inside the black box: Raising standards through classroom assessment. *Phi Delta Kappan, 80,* 139–148.

Boaler, J. (2006). "Opening our ideas": How a detracked mathematics approach promoted respect, responsibility, and high achievement. *Theory into Practice, 45*(1) 40–46.

Boaler, J., & Staples, M. (2008). Creating mathematical futures through an equitable teaching approach: The case of Railside School. *Teachers College Record, 110,* 608–645.

Bower, A. (1990). The effect of a multiple ability treatment on status and learning in the cooperative social studies classroom. Unpublished doctoral dissertation, Stanford University, Stanford, CA.

Brinton, D. M., Snow, M. A., & Wesche, M. B. (1990). *Content-based second language instruction.* Boston, MA: Heinle & Heinle.

Bunch, G. C. (2006). "Academic English" in the 7th grade: Broadening the lens, expanding access. *Journal of English for Academic Purposes, 5,* 284–301.

Bunch, G. C. (2009). "Going up there": Challenges and opportunities for language minority students during a mainstream classroom speech event. *Linguistics and Education, 20,* 81–108.

Bunch, G. C. (2013). Pedagogical language knowledge: Preparing mainstream teachers for English learners in the New Standards era. *Review of Research in Education, 37,* 298–341.

Bunch, G. C. (2014). The language of ideas and the language of display: Reconceptualizing "academic language" in linguistically diverse classrooms. *International Multilingual Research Journal, 81,* 70–86.

Bunch, G. C., Lotan, R., Valdés, G., & Cohen, E. (2005). Keeping content at the heart of content-based instruction: Access and support for transitional English learners. In J. Crandall & D. Kaufman (Eds.), *Content-based instruction in primary and secondary school settings* (pp. 11–25). Alexandria, VA: Teachers of English to Speakers of Other Languages.

Bunch, G. C., & Willett, K. (2013). Writing to mean in middle school: Understanding how second language writers negotiate textually-rich content-area instruction. *Journal of Second Language Writing, 22,* 141–160.

Carlson, S., & Dumplis, A. (2012). *Was immigration worth it? Or "For class, it was pretty fun."* Stanford, CA: Stanford University, Graduate School of Education.

Cazden, C. (1988). *Classroom discourse: The language of teaching.* Portsmouth, NH: Heinemann.

Cazden, C. (2001). *Classroom discourse: The language of teaching and learning* (2nd ed.). Portsmouth, NH: Heinemann.

Cohen, E. G. (1972). Interracial interaction disability. *Human Relations, 25,* 9–24.

Cohen, E. G. (1982). Expectations states and interracial interaction in school settings. *Annual Review of Sociology, 8,* 209–235.

Cohen, E. G. (1984). Talking and working together: Status, interaction and learning. In P. Peterson, L. C. Wilkinson, & M. Hallinan (Eds.), *The social context of instruction: Group organization and group processes* (pp. 171–187). New York, NY: Academic Press.

Cohen, E. G. (1988, July). Producing equal status behavior in cooperative learning. Paper presented at the convention of the International Association for the Study of Cooperation in Education, Shefayim, Israel.

Cohen, E. G. (1991). Teaching in multiculturally heterogeneous classrooms: Findings from a model program. *McGill Journal of Education, 26,* 7–23.

Cohen, E. G. (1992). *Restructuring the classroom: Conditions for productive small groups.* Madison, WI: Center on the Organization and Restructuring of Schools, University of Wisconsin–Madison.

Cohen E. G. (1993). From theory to practice: The development of an applied research program. In J. Berger & M. Zelditch (Eds.), *Theoretical research programs: Studies in the growth of theory* (pp. 385–415). Stanford, CA: Stanford University Press.

Cohen, E. G. (1997). Understanding status problems: Sources and consequences. In E. Cohen & R. Lotan (Eds.), *Working for equity in heterogeneous classrooms: Sociological theory in practice* (pp. 61–76). New York, NY: Teachers College Press.

Cohen, E. G., & Intili, J. K. (1982). *Interdependence and management in bilingual classrooms: Final report II.* (NIE Contract #NIE-G-80-0217). Stanford, CA: Stanford University, Center for Educational Research.

Cohen, E. G., Lockheed, M., & Lohman, M. (1976). Center for interracial cooperation: A field experiment. *Sociology of Education, 49,* 47–58.

Cohen E. G., & Lotan, R. (1995). Producing equal status interaction in the heterogeneous classroom. *American Educational Research Journal, 32,* 99–120.

Cohen, E. G., & Lotan, R. (Eds.). (1997a). *Working for equity in heterogeneous classrooms: Sociological theory in practice.* New York, NY: Teachers College Press.

Cohen, E. G., & Lotan, R. (1997b). Operation of status in the middle grades: Recent developments. In J. Szmatka, J. Skvoretz, & J. Berger (Eds.), *Status, network, and structure: Theory development in group processes* (pp. 222–240). Stanford, CA: Stanford University Press.

Cohen, E. G., Lotan, R. A., Abram, P. L., Scarloss, B. A., & Schultz, S. E. (2002). Can groups learn? *Teachers College Record, 104,* 1045–1068.

Cohen, E. G., Lotan, R., & Catanzarite, L. (1988). Can expectations for competence be treated in the classroom? In M. Webster, Jr., & M. Foschi (Eds.), *Status generalization: New theory and research* (pp. 28–54). Stanford, CA: Stanford University Press.

Cohen, E. G., Lotan, R., & Catanzarite, L. (1990). Treating status problems in the cooperative classroom. In S. Sharan (Ed.), *Cooperative learning: Theory and research* (pp. 203–229). New York, NY: Praeger.

Cohen, E. G., Lotan, R., & Holthuis, N. (1997). Organizing the classroom for learning. In E. G. Cohen & R. Lotan (Eds.), *Working for equity in heterogeneous classrooms: Sociological theory in practice* (pp. 31–43). New York, NY: Teachers College Press.

Cohen, E. G., Lotan, R., & Leechor, C. (1989). Can classrooms learn? *Sociology of Education, 62,* 75–94.

Cohen, E. G., & Roper, S. (1972). Modification of interracial interaction disability: An application of status characteristic theory. *American Sociological Review, 37,* 648–655.

Cohen, E. G., & Sharan, S. (1980). Modifying status relations in Israeli youth. *Journal of Cross-Cultural Psychology, 11,* 364–384.

Cohen, G., Garcia, J., Apfel, N., & Master, A. (2006). Reducing the racial achievement gap: A social psychological intervention. *Science, 313,* 1307–1310.

Comprehensive Test of Basic Skills (CTBS). (1981). Monterey, CA: McGraw-Hill.

Cook, T. (1974). Producing equal status interaction between Indian and white boys in British Columbia. Unpublished doctoral dissertation, Stanford University, Stanford, CA.

Correll, S., & Ridgeway, C. (2003). Expectation states theory. In J. Delamater (Ed.), *Handbook of social psychology* (pp. 29–51). New York, NY: Kluwer Academic/Plenum Publishers.

Cossey, R. (1997). Mathematical communication: Issues of access and equity. Unpublished dissertation, Stanford University, Stanford, CA.

Cummins, J. (1979). Linguistic interdependence and the educational development of bilingual children. *Review of Educational Research, 49,* 222–251.

Dar, Y., & Resh, N. (1986). Classroom intellectual composition and academic achievement. *All American Educational Research Journal, 23,* 357–374.

Davidson, N. (1985). Small group learning and teaching in mathematics: A selective review of the research. In R. Slavin, S. Sharan, S. Kagan, R. Hertz-Lazarowitz, G. Webb, & R. Schmuck (Eds.), *Learning to cooperate, cooperating to learn* (pp. 211–230). New York, NY: Plenum.

De Avila, E. A. (1981). *Multicultural improvement of cognitive abilities: Final report to Stoill of California, Department of Education.* Stanford, CA: Stanford University, School of Education.

De Avila, E. A., & Duncan, S. E. (1977). *Language assessment scales, level I* (2nd ed.). Corte Madera, CA: Linguametrics Group.

De Avila, E. A., & Duncan, S. E. (1980). *Finding out! Descubrimiento.* Corte Madera, CA: Linguametrics Group.

Dembo, M., & McAuliffe, T. (1987). Effects of perceived ability and grade status on social interaction and influence in cooperative groups. *Journal of Educational Psychology, 79,* 415–423.

Deutsch, M. (1968). The effects of cooperation and competition upon group process. In D. Cartwright & A. Zander (Eds.), *Group dynamics* (pp. 319–353). New York, NY: Harper & Row.

Deutsch, M. (1992). *The effects of training in cooperative learning and conflict resolution in an alternative high school.* Teachers College International Center for Cooperation and Conflict Resolution. New York, NY: Teachers College, Columbia University.

Drew, Z., & Wofsey, K. (2012). *What in the world are we supposed to do? An analysis of a group-worthy task.* Stanford, CA: Stanford University, Graduate School of Education.

Durling, R., & Shick, C. (1976). Concept attainment by pairs and individuals as a function of vocalization. *Journal of Educational Psychology, 68,* 83–91.

Dweck, C. S. (2008). *Mindset: The new psychology of success.* New York, NY: Ballantine Books.

Ehrlich, D. E. (1991). Moving beyond cooperation: Developing science thinking in independent groups. Unpublished doctoral dissertation, Stanford University, Stanford, CA.

Eisner, E. W. (1994). *The educational imagination: On the design and evaluation of school programs* (3rd ed.). New York: Macmillan.

Epstein, C. (1972). *Affective subjects in the classroom: Exploring race, sex and drugs.* Scranton, PA: Intext Educational Publications.

Faltis, C. J., & Merino, B. J. (1992). Toward a definition of exemplary teachers in bilingual multicultural school settings. In R. V. Padilla & A. H. Benavides (Eds.), *Critical perspectives on bilingual education research* (pp. 276–299). Tempe, AZ: Bilingual Press.

Featherstone, H., Crespo, S., Jilk, L., Oslund, J., Parks, A., & Wood, M. (2011). *Smarter together! Collaboration and equity in the elementary math classroom.* Reston, VA: National Council of Teachers of Mathematics.

Gardner, H. (2011). *Frames of mind: The theory of multiple intelligences.* New York, NY: Basic Books (Original work published 1983).

Gardner, H. (1993). *Multiple intelligences: The theory in practice.* New York, NY: Basic Books.

Gibbons, P. (2002). *Scaffolding language, scaffolding learning: Teaching second language learners in the mainstream classroom.* Portsmouth, NH: Heinemann.

Gillies, R. M. (2002). The residual effects of cooperative-learning experiences: A two-year follow-up. *Journal of Educational Research, 96,* 15–20.

Gould, S. J. (1981). *The mismeasure of man.* New York, NY: Norton.

Graves, T., & Graves, N. (1985). *Broken circles* (game). Santa Cruz, CA.

Greeno, J. G. (1994). Gibson's affordances. *Psychological Review, 101,* 336–342.

Greenwood, C., Horton, B., & Utley, C. (2002). Academic engagement: Current perspectives on research and practice. *School Psychology Review, 31,* 328–349.

Grossman, P., & Davis, E. (2012). Mentoring that fits: Effective induction requires high-quality mentoring and a supportive school environment, tailored to fit new teachers' individual needs. *Educational Leadership, 69,* 54–57.

Hall, J. (1971a). Decisions, decisions, decisions. *Psychology Today, 5,* 51.

Hallinan, M. T., & Kubitschek, W. (1999). Curriculum differentiation and high school achievement. *Social Psychology of Education, 3,* 41–62.

Hoffman, D., & Cohen, E. G. (1972, April). An exploratory study to determine the effects of generalized performance expectations upon activity and influence of students engaged in a group simulation game. Paper presented at the annual meeting of the American Educational Research Association, Chicago, IL.

Holthuis, N. (1998). Scientifically speaking: Identifying, analyzing, and promoting science talk in small groups. Unpublished dissertation, Stanford University, Stanford, CA.

Holthuis, N., Lotan, R., Saltzman, J., Mastrandrea, M., & Wild, A. (in press). Supporting and understanding students' epistemological discourse about climate change. *Journal of Geoscience Education.*

Horn, I. (2012). *Strength in numbers: Collaborative learning in secondary mathematics.* Reston, VA: National Council of Teachers of Mathematics.

Huber, G., & Eppler, R. (1990). Team learning in German classrooms: Processes and outcomes. In S. Sharan (Ed.), *Cooperative learning: Theory and research* (pp. 151–171). New York, NY: Praeger.

Johnson, D., & Johnson, R. (1985). Classroom conflict: Controversy versus debate in learning groups. *American Educational Research Journal, 22,* 237–256.

Johnson, D., & Johnson, R. (1990). Cooperative learning and achievement. In S. Sharan (Ed.), *Cooperative learning: Theory and research* (pp. 23–37). New York, NY: Praeger.

Johnson, D., & Johnson, R. (1992). Encouraging thinking through constructive controversy. In N. Davidson & T. Worsham (Eds.), *Enhancing thinking through cooperative learning* (pp. 120–137). New York, NY: Teachers College Press.

Johnson, D. W., & Johnson, R. T. (2009a). Energizing learning: The instructional power of conflict. *Educational Researcher, 38,* 37–51.

Johnson, D. W., & Johnson, R. T. (2009b). An educational psychology success story: Social interdependence theory and cooperative learning. *Educational Researcher, 38,* 365–379.

Johnson, D., Johnson, R., & Holubec, E. (1998). *Cooperative learning in the classroom.* Edina, MN: Interaction Book Company.

Johnson, D., Johnson, R., & Maruyama, G. (1983). Interdependence and interpersonal attraction among heterogeneous and homogeneous individuals: A theoretical formulation and a meta-analysis of the research. *Review of Educational Research, 53,* 5–54.

Johnson, D., Johnson, R., & Maruyama, G. (1984). Goal interdependence and interpersonal attraction in heterogeneous classrooms: A meta-analysis. In N. Miller & M. Brewer (Eds.), *Groups in contact: The psychology of desegregation* (pp. 187–212). Orlando, FL: Academic Press.

Johnson, D. W., Maruyama, G., Johnson, R., Nelson, D., & Skon, L. (1981). Effects of cooperative, competitive and individualistic goal structure on achievement: A meta-analysis. *Psychological Bulletin, 89,* 47–62.

Kagan, S. (1995). Group grades miss the mark. *Educational Leadership, 52,* 68–72.

Kerckhoff, A. C. (1986). Effects of ability grouping in British secondary schools. *American Sociological Review, 51,* 842–858.

Kinney, K., & Leonard, M. (1984). Group lessons: Geometry. Unpublished manuscript, Stanford University, Stanford, CA.

Krashen, S. D. (1985). *The input hypothesis: Issues and implications.* New York, NY: Longman.

Krashen, S. D. (1988). Bilingual education and second language acquisition theory. In California State Department of Education, *Schooling and language minority students: A theoretical framework* (pp. 51–79). Los Angeles, CA: Evaluation, Dissemination and Assessment Center, California State University.

Kreidler, J. (1984). *Creative conflict resolution.* Glenview, IL: Scott Foresman & Co.

Leal, A. (1985). Sex inequities in classroom interaction: An evaluation of an intervention. Unpublished doctoral dissertation, Stanford University, Stanford, CA.

Lee, O., Quinn, H., & Valdés, G. (2013). Science and language for English language learners in relation to next generation science standards and with implications for Common Core State Standards for English Language Arts and Mathematics. *Educational Researcher, 42*(4), 223–233.

Leechor, C. (1988). How high achieving and low achieving students differentially benefit from working together in cooperative small groups. Unpublished doctoral dissertation, Stanford University, Stanford, CA.

Leknes, B., & Xu, L. (2012). *Group worthy task write-up.* Stanford, CA: Stanford University, Graduate School of Education.

Lindholm, K. J., & Aclan, Z. (1991). Bilingual proficiency as a bridge to academic achievement: Results from bilingual/immersion programs. *Journal of Education, 173,* 99–113.

Lockheed, M. S., Harris, A. M., & Nemceff, W. P. (1983). Sex and social influence: Does sex function as a status characteristic in mixed-sex groups? *Journal of Educational Psychology, 75,* 877–888.

Lotan, R. A. (1997). Principles of a principled curriculum. In E. G. Cohen & R. A. Lotan (Eds.), *Working for equity in heterogeneous classrooms: Sociological theory in practice.* New York, NY: Teachers College Press.

Lotan, R. A. (2006). Managing groupwork. In C. Evertson & C. Weinstein (Eds.), *Handbook of classroom management: Research, practice, and contemporary issues.* (pp. 525–540). Saddle River, NJ: Lawrence Erlbaum Associates.

Lotan, R. A. (2008). Developing language and content knowledge in heterogeneous classrooms. In R. Gillies, A. Ashman, & J. Terwel (Eds.), *The teacher's role in implementing cooperative learning in the classroom* (pp. 187–203). New York, NY: Springer.

Marks, H. (2000). Student engagement in instructional activity: Patterns in elementary, middle and high school years. *American Educational Research Journal, 37,* 153–184.

Marquis, A., & Cooper, C. (1982, July). Peer interaction and learning in cooperative settings. Paper presented at the second international Conference on Cooperation in Education, Provo, UT.

Martella, R., Nelson, J., & Marchand-Martella, N. (2003). *Managing disruptive behaviors in the schools.* Boston, MA: Pearson Education.

McGroarty, M. (1989). The benefits of cooperative learning arrangements in second language instruction. *National Association for Bilingual Association Journal, 13,* 127–143.

McLaughlin, B. (1985). *Second-language acquisition in childhood. Volume 2: Schoolage children.* Hillsdale, NJ: Lawrence Erlbaum.

McLaughlin, M. W., & Talbert, J. E. (2006). *Building school-based teacher learning communities: Professional strategies to improve student achievement.* New York, NY: Teachers College Press.

Meloy, M., Beans, L., & Cheng, A. (2012). *Dr. Sneab's gummi buddies: A groupworthy task for balancing chemical equations.* Stanford, CA: Stanford University, Graduate School of Education.

Michaels, S., O'Connor, C., & Resnick, L. B. (2008). Deliberative discourse idealized and realized: Accountable talk in the classroom and in civic life. *Studies in Philosophy and Education, 27,* 283–297.

Miller, N., Brewer, M., & Edwards, K. (1985). Cooperative interaction in desegregated settings: A laboratory analogue. *Journal of Social Issues, 41,* 63–79.

Miller, N., & Harrington, H. J. (1990). A situational identity perspective on cultural diversity and teamwork in the classroom. In S. Sharan (Ed.), *Cooperative learning: Theory and research* (pp. 39–75). New York, NY: Praeger.

Morris, R. (1977). A normative intervention to equalize participation in task-oriented groups. Unpublished doctoral dissertation, Stanford University, Stanford, CA.

Murray, F. (1972). Acquisition of conservation through social interaction. *Developmental Psychology, 6,* 1–6.

National Governors Association Center for Best Practices & Council of Chief State School Officers. (2010a). *Common Core State Standards.* Washington, DC: Authors.

National Governors Association Center for Best Practices & Council of Chief State School Officers. (2010b). *Common Core State Standards for English Language Arts and Literacy in History/Social Studies, Science, and Technical Subjects.* Washington, DC: Authors.

National Governors Association Center for Best Practices & Council of Chief State School Officers. (2010c). *Common Core State Standards for Mathematics.* Washington, DC: Authors.

Navarrete, C. (1980). Finding out/Descubrimiento: A developmental approach to language and culture in a bilingual elementary classroom. Unpublished manuscript, Stanford University, Stanford, CA.

Navarrete, C. (1985). Problems in small group interaction: A bilingual classroom study. Unpublished doctoral dissertation, Stanford University, Stanford, CA.

Neves, A. (1983). The effect of various input on the second language acquisition of Mexican-American children in nine elementary school classrooms. Unpublished doctoral dissertation, Stanford University, Stanford, CA.

Newmann, F., & Thompson, J. A. (1987). *Effects of cooperative learning on achievement in secondary schools: A summary of research.* Madison, WI: National Center on Effective Secondary Schools, University of Wisconsin–Madison.

NGSS Lead States. (2013). *Next generation science standards: For states, by states.* Washington, DC: The National Academies Press.

Nystrand, M., Gamoran, A., & Heck, M. J. (1991). *Small groups in English: When do they help students and how are they best wed?* Madison, WI: Center on the Organization and Restructuring of Schools, University of Wisconsin–Madison.

Oakes, J. (2005). *Keeping track: How schools structure inequality.* New Haven, CT: Yale University Press.

Palinscar, A., Brown, A., & Campione, J. (1989, April). Structured dialogues among communities of first grade learners. Paper presented at the annual meeting of the American Educational Research Association, San Francisco, CA.

Perrow, C. B. (1961). A framework for the comparative analysis of organizations. *American Sociological Review, 32,* 194–208.

Pfeiffer, J., & Jones, F. E. (1970). *A handbook of structural experiences for human relations training* (Vol. I). Iowa City, IA: University Associated Press.

Qin, Z., Johnson, D. W., & Johnson, R. T. (1995). Cooperative versus competitive efforts and problem solving, *Review of Educational Research, 65,* 129–143.

Robbins, A. (1977). Fostering equal-status interaction through the establishment of consistent staff behaviors and appropriate situational norms. Unpublished doctoral dissertation, Stanford University, Stanford, CA.

Rosebery, A. S. (1992). *Appropriating scientific discourse: Findings from language minority classroom. Research Report: 3.* Santa Cruz, CA: National Center for Research on Cultural Diversity and Second Language Acquisition.

Rosenberg, M. B. (1983). *A model for nonviolent communication*. Baltimore, MD: New Society Publishers.

Rosenholtz, S. J. (1977). The multiple ability curriculum: An intervention against the self-fulfilling prophecy. Unpublished dissertation, Stanford University, Stanford, CA.

Rosenholtz, S. J. (1985). Modifying status expectations in the traditional classroom. In J. Berger & M. Zelditch, Jr. (Eds.), *Status, rewards, and influence* (pp. 445–470). San Francisco, CA: Jossey-Bass.

Rosenholtz, S. J., & Cohen, E. G. (1985). Activating ethnic status. In J. Berger & M. Zelditch, Jr. (Eds.), *Status, rewards, and influence* (pp. 430–444). San Francisco, CA: Jossey-Bass.

Rosenholtz, S. J., & Simpson, C. (1984). Classroom organization and student stratification. *Elementary School Journal, 85,* 21–37.

Rosenholtz, S. J., & Wilson, B. (1980). The effects of classroom structure on shared perceptions of ability. *American Educational Research Journal, 17,* 175–182.

Rubin, B. (2003). Unpacking detracking: When progressive pedagogy meets students' social worlds. *American Educational Research Journal, 40,* 539–573.

Scarloss, B. A. (2001). Sensemaking, interaction, and learning in student groups. Unpublished dissertation, Stanford University, Stanford, CA.

Schultz, S. E. (1999). To group or not to group: Effects of groupwork on students' declarative and procedural knowledge in science. Unpublished dissertation, Stanford University, Stanford, CA.

Schwartz, D. L., Black, J. B., & Strange, J. (1991, April). Dyads have a fourfold advantage over individuals inducing abstract rules. Paper presented at annual meeting of the American Educational Research Association, Chicago.

Scott, W. R. (2013). *Institutions and organizations: Ideas, interests, and identities*. Los Angeles, CA: SAGE.

Sharan, S., & Hertz-Lazarowitz, R. (1980). A group investigation method of cooperative learning in the classroom. In S. Sharan, A. P. Hare, C. Webb, & R. Hertz-Lazarowitz (Eds.), *Contributions to the study of cooperation in education* (pp. 19–46). Provo, UT: Brigham Young University Press.

Sharan, S., Hertz-Lazarowitz, R., & Ackerman, Z. (1980). Academic achievement of elementary school children in small group versus whole-class instruction. *Journal of Experimental Education, 48,* 125–129.

Sharan, S., Kussetl, P., Hertz-Lazarowitz, R., Begarano, Y., Raviv, S., & Sharan, Y. (1984). *Cooperative learning in the classroom: Research in desegregated schools*. Hillsdale, NJ: Lawrence Erlbaum.

Sharan, S., & Shachar, H. (1988). *Language and learning in the cooperative classroom*. New York, NY: Springer-Verlag.

Sharan, S., & Sharan, Y. (1976). *Small-group teaching*. Englewood Cliffs, NJ: Educational Technology Publications.

Sharan, Y., & Sharan, S. (1992). *Cooperative learning through group investigation*. New York, NY: Teachers College Press.

Shulman, J., Lotan, R., & Whitcomb, J. (1998). *Groupwork in diverse classrooms: A casebook for educators*. New York, NY: Teachers College Press.

Simon, S., Howe, L. W., & Kirchenbaum, H. (1972). *Values clarification*. New York, NY: Hart Publishing.

Slavin, R. E. (1983). *Cooperative learning*. New York, NY: Longmann.

Slavin, R. E. (1987). Ability grouping and student achievement in elementary schools: A best-evidence synthesis. *Review of Educational Research, 57,* 293–336.

Slavin, R. E. (2003). *Educational psychology: Theory and practice* (7th ed.). Boston, MA: Allyn & Bacon.

Slavin, R. E. (2010). Co-operative learning: What makes group-work work? In H. Dumont, D. Instance, & F. Benavides (Eds.), *The nature of learning: Using research to inspire practice* (pp. 161–178). Paris, France: OECD Publishing. Available at dx.doi.org/1787/9789264086487-9-en

Smith, K., Johnson, D. W., & Johnson, R. T. (1981). Can conflict be constructive? Controversy versus concurrence seeking in learning groups. *Journal of Educational Psychology, 73,* 651–663.

Solomon, R. D., Davidson, N., & Solomon, E. C. L. (1992). Some thinking skills and social skills that facilitate cooperative learning. In N. Davidson & T. Worsham (Eds.), *Enhancing thinking through cooperative learning* (pp. 101–119). New York, NY: Teachers College Press.

Steele, C. (2010). *Whistling Vivaldi: How stereotypes affect us and what we can do.* New York, NY: W.W. Norton.

Steele, C., & Aronson, J. (1995). Stereotype threat and the intellectual test performance of African-Americans. *Journal of Personality and Social Psychology, 69,* 797–811.

Sternberg, R. J. (1985). *Beyond IQ; A triarchic theory of human intelligence.* Cambridge, England: Cambridge University Press.

Sternberg, R. J. (1998). Abilities are forms of developing expertise. *Educational Research, 27,* 11–20.

Sternberg, R. J. (2007). *Wisdom, intelligence, and creativity synthesized.* New York, NY: Cambridge University Press.

Swanson, P. E. (2010). The intersection of language and mathematics. *Mathematics Teaching in the Middle School, 15*(9), 516–523.

Tammivaara, J. (1982). The effects of task structure on beliefs about competence and participation in small groups. *Sociology of Education, 55,* 212–222.

Tudge, J. (1990). Vygotsky: The zone of proximal development and peer collaboration: Implications for classroom practice. In L. Moll (Ed.), *Vygotsky and education: Instructional implications and applications of socio historical psychology.* (pp. 155–172). New York, NY: Columbia University Press.

Valdés, G. (2011). Realistic expectations: English language learners and the acquisition of "academic" English. In G. Valdés, S. Capitelli, & L. Alvarez (Eds.), *Latino children learning English: Steps in the journey* (pp. 15–41). New York, NY: Teachers College Press.

Valdés, G., Bunch, G. C., Snow, C. E., & Lee, C. (2005). Enhancing the development of students' language(s). In L. Darling-Hammond, J. Bransford, P. LePage, K. Hammerness, & H. Duffy (Eds.), *Preparing teachers for a changing world: What teachers should learn and be able to do* (pp. 126–168). San Francisco, CA: Jossey-Bass.

Van Lier, L. (2000). From input to affordance: Social-interactive learning from an ecological perspective. In J. Lantolf (Ed.), *Sociocultural theory and second language learning* (pp. 155–177). Oxford, England: Oxford University Press.

Vygotsky, L. (1978). *Mind and society* (M. Cole, V. John-Steiner, S. Scribner, & E. Soublerman, Eds.). Cambridge, MA: Harvard University Press.

Webb, N. (1983). Predicting learning from student interaction: Defining the interaction variable. *Educational Psychologist, 18,* 33–41.

Webb, N. (1991). Task-related verbal interaction in mathematics learning in small groups. *Journal for Research in Mathematics Education, 22,* 361–389.

Webb, N., Ender, P., & Lewis, S. (1986). Problem-solving strategies and group processes in small group learning computer programming. *American Educational Research Journal, 23*(2), 243–261.

Webb, N., & Farivar, S. (1999). Developing productive group interaction in middle school mathematics. In A. M. O'Donnell & A. King (Eds.), *Cognitive perspectives on peer learning* (pp. 117–149). Mahwah, NJ: Lawrence Erlbaum Associates.

Westheimer, J., & Kahne, J. (2004). What kind of citizen? The politics of educating for democracy. *American Education Research Journal, 41,* 237–269.

Wiggins, G., & McTighe, J. (2005). *Understanding by design.* New York, NY: Association for Supervision and Curriculum Development.

Wilcox, M. (1972). Comparison of elementary school children's interaction in teacher-led and student-led small groups. Unpublished doctoral dissertation, Stanford University, Stanford, CA.

Yackel, E., & Cobb, P. (1996). Sociomathematical norms, argumentation, and autonomy in mathematics. *Journal for Research in Mathematics Education, 27,* 458–477.

Yackel, E., Cobb, P., & Wood, T. (1991). Small-group interactions as a source of learning opportunities in second-grade mathematics. *Journal for Research in Mathematics Education, 22,* 390–408.

Yager, S., Johnson, D., & Johnson, R. (1985). Oral discussion, group-to-individual transfer and achievement in cooperative learning groups. *Journal of Educational Psychology, 77,* 60–66.

Zack, M. (1988, July). Delegation of authority and the use of the student facilitator role. Paper presented at the triannual meeting of the International Association for the Study of Cooperation in Education, Shefayim, Israel.

Index

About the Authors

Elizabeth G. Cohen (1932–2005) was professor emerita of education and sociology at Stanford University. She carried out research on improving competence expectations of low-status youth. Her work began in the laboratory, but extended to desegregated and multilingual schools. She wrote widely on the subjects of cooperative learning, team teaching, the isolation of the teacher, and collegial evaluation.

From 1982 and until her retirement in 1999, Elizabeth Cohen directed the Program for Complex Instruction. Convinced that sociological theories have meaning for education, she worked successfully with hundreds of elementary and middle school teachers in implementing activity-based classrooms for academically, ethnically, and linguistically heterogeneous populations.

Rachel A. Lotan is professor (Teaching) of education at Stanford University. With Elizabeth Cohen, she co-directed the Program for Complex Instruction beginning in 1986. Since 1999, she has been serving as the director of the Stanford Teacher Education Program. A former secondary school teacher and administrator, she earned advanced degrees in education and sociology at Stanford University.

Working with teachers in the United States and around the world, Rachel A. Lotan shared her knowledge and experiences in building equitable classrooms. She maintains that ensuring that all students in heterogeneous classrooms have access to academically challenging curricula, experience equal-status participation, and can successfully demonstrate their understandings and skills is a fundamental pedagogical and moral objective.